THE BRITISH PRESS

AND

JEWS UNDER NAZI RULE

Dr. Andrew Sharf is head of
he Department of Political His-
ory in the University of Bar-
lan, Israel.

THE BRITISH PRESS
AND
JEWS UNDER NAZI RULE

ANDREW SHARF

*Issued under the auspices of the
Institute of Race Relations, London*

OXFORD UNIVERSITY PRESS

LONDON   NEW YORK   BOMBAY

1964

Oxford University Press, Amen House, London E.C.4

GLASGOW NEW YORK TORONTO MELBOURNE WELLINGTON
BOMBAY CALCUTTA MADRAS KARACHI LAHORE DACCA
CAPE TOWN SALISBURY NAIROBI IBADAN ACCRA
KUALA LUMPUR HONG KONG

© Institute of Race Relations, 1964

Printed in Great Britain by
Hazell Watson & Viney Ltd.
Aylesbury, Bucks

Foreword

WHAT happened to the Jews in Germany is in itself a
horror of such magnitude that the mind shrinks from it.
It is more appalling than other massacres not only
because of the numbers but because it was planned and carried
out as deliberate cold-blooded policy. However unwilling we may
be, we need to be reminded that these are things which human
beings have done and might do again, and there have been a
number of books recounting the actual events.

Dr. Andrew Sharf's book is not one of these. He does not tell
us directly what happened. But he is concerned with a phenomenon of vital importance to us: the habit, deeply ingrained in
these islands, of making the best of every situation, refusing to
believe the worst. From the time the Nazis came into power until
1939, English people tried to persuade themselves that things
could not really be so bad as that, that there must be another side
to the question, and so on. Every form of evasion was eagerly
seized on. It is the psychological machinery of this refusal to
believe the uncomfortable that gives his book its special interest.

In the latter part of his book, Dr. Sharf writes as a partisan and
from the British point of view is open to the charge of lacking a
sense of proportion; the waging of a major war is essentially a
matter of planning what one can do against what one would like
to do. It is not, however, easy to preserve a sense of proportion
when six million of one's fellows are being herded into gas
chambers, and indeed in relation to what then happened there is a
dimension in which the term 'sense of proportion' ceases to have
meaning.

To the Institute of Race Relations the interest of this book lies
not so much in any light it may throw on anti-Semitism as on the
machinery of evasion. The Jews are separated from the European
population by religion, culture, history, and the consciousness
that they are Jews, rather than by biological characteristics; it is
therefore more by analogy than directly that we are concerned

with their problems. But the tendency to evade the unpleasant truth has long been a feature of attitudes towards racial differences both in the United States and in Britain. It is perhaps diminishing slightly but remains a danger.

PHILIP MASON

18th February 1964

Contents

To
Rosa Selmer

Acknowledgements

THIS book would never have been written without the material and moral support of the Institute for Research into the Destruction of European Jewry (a section of the Yad va-Shem Institute, Israel), and in particular of its Principal, Professor Israel Heilprin. It might never have been published but for the Institute of Race Relations, whose Director, Mr. Philip Mason, was willing to risk this departure from previous fields of interest. I would express my sincere appreciation of his sympathetic understanding.

My grateful thanks are due to my friend and colleague Professor Avrom Saltman for his patient correction of inconsistencies, and to Miss K. Sheppard for her onerous task of editing the final typescript. Neither is responsible for the errors that remain.

Last but not least, and in common with many authors, I should like to thank my wife for the great help she gave me by repeatedly going through the material in its early stages, and by encouraging me to persevere.

Abbreviations

HMSO   Her Majesty's Stationery Office

IMT   International Military Tribunal (for bibliographical note, see p. 219)

RGBL   *Reichsgazettenblatt* (the official German 'Gazette')

TWC   Trials of War Criminals (for bibliographical note, see p. 220)

Note: Square brackets within quotations indicate author's insertions.

Introduction

THIS survey of Press opinion was carried out under the auspices of the Hebrew University and the Yad va-Shem Institute for Research into the Destruction of European Jewry. It is based on a collection of cuttings, covering most matters of Jewish interest from 1919 to 1951, which was presented to the Jewish Historical General Archives by the late Mr. Joshua Podro, the well-known Anglo-Jewish literary figure. In addition, Mr. Podro gave a special collection for the year 1933 to the 'Ghetto Fighters' House' (Yitzhak Kaznelson Institute) at the Kibbutz 'Lohamei Hagettaoth', which, naturally, also constituted an important section. Mr. Podro's devotion in assembling these cuttings and the generosity of his gift have provided a first-class primary source for anyone working in the field of contemporary Jewish history, and have earned the particular gratitude of the present writer by reducing his task to manageable proportions.

The survey covers the period of the Nazi régime (i.e. 1933–45) and includes sections on its aftermath—principally the War Crimes Trials. The Podro Collection has rather over 10,000 relevant cuttings for these years, taken from about 800 different newspapers and periodicals, including those published in the Commonwealth and the colonies. This was a substantial amount of material to organize, but it bears no comparison to what would have had to be done if no initial selection of this kind had been available. A number of sample checks against complete Press files showed that in fact there were no serious gaps, and that the material was adequate both in quantity and in variety. The cuttings actually used number above 6,500 drawn from about 150 newspapers and periodicals all published within the United Kingdom—a limitation unfortunately necessary for reasons of space. A complete picture has thus had to be sacrificed, but it would not have differed essentially from the one here presented. The sequence of quotation, and thus of the discussion, is not invariably chronological. It was thought preferable to treat certain aspects separately—for example, reactions to the problem of the refugees—and to follow their development through the whole period. Each quotation is editorial opinion unless otherwise stated, while all excisions and extraneous insertions have been clearly indicated. The distribution of quotations was naturally weighted in favour of representative sources, but, so far as can be judged, no section of the Press has been entirely omitted. There are two exceptions: the Jewish, and the overtly Fascist Press. This exclusion had an explicit purpose—to gather what might properly be termed outside reactions. It was, indeed, originally intended to include some Jewish Press references which might have yielded some illuminating comparisons, but again reasons of space made this impossible. There is one other, more general limitation. In order to reach a conclusion about Press reactions, it has obviously been necessary to mention the events to which they relate, but this has been done in the briefest possible manner since there is no attempt whatever at a fresh assessment of the events themselves. It may be objected that no reactions can be finally assessed without the widest discussion of their background. This is true, and the present survey would merely constitute a small contribution to that end. For example, this limitation is nowhere more obvious than in the treatment of Press reactions to Palestine immigration policies. Plainly, this topic is part of the whole complex and controversial problem of British-Zionist relations, a problem needing its own critical analysis. Accordingly, discussion has been deliberately confined to one specific point which, it is hoped, will be accepted both as having its separate validity and as capable of being fitted into a wider framework.

One other matter deserves consideration. In order to arrive at a more just appreciation of the Press reactions to these events, it is desirable to bear in mind certain factors generally applicable to the British Press of the period. It is obvious that a Press may at once try to mirror public attitude and to mould it. It is probable that both editorial approach and selection of news are the result of a complicated interaction between those two processes. The significance accorded to any given item must depend on how successfully the Press is thought to have achieved those aims: to what extent its relation to its readers is thought of as having a positive value or as being no more than an accidental reflection of some element in the broad climate of opinion. For the British Press in the thirties and forties it is difficult to be sure of a clear-cut answer.

In one sense there can be no doubt that it had acquired a status greater than at any previous time, greater than the Press of many other countries. The gathering and distribution of news had become a major industry. It is computed that, a little after the end of our period, 611 newspapers were sold each day for every 1,000 inhabitants of the British Isles, the highest ratio in the world and nearly twice that in the United States.[1] The importance of the newspaper proprietor had been recognized by every Government between the two wars, a circumstance to which the British peerage bore striking witness. The Press was frequently believed to be a powerful and potentially dangerous political instrument—and this in itself gave it power. But such a belief was becoming less justi-fied. The Press lords had had their great days earlier. In 1924, the *Daily Mail* 'Red Letter' campaign had brought down the Labour Government. In 1929 the *Daily Mail*, together with the *Daily Express*, had done something similar to a Conservative Govern-ment and had elicited Baldwin's passionate denunciation of Press behaviour—'power, power without responsibility—the prero-gative of the harlot throughout the ages'.[2] In 1936, certain news-papers undoubtedly played an effective part in forcing the abdi-cation of Edward VIII.

After that there was a marked decline. The next ten years contain little evidence of the Press directly altering the course of political history. The bitter struggle of liberal and left-wing papers in favour of 'collective security' policies produced not the slightest appreciable result, just as the anti-Labour attitude of the majority of the Press had no effect whatsoever on the 1945 General Elec-tion. The one possible exception was *The Times*, with its editor's personal relationship to Neville Chamberlain and some of his colleagues, in its encouragement of the policies that led to Munich. Nevertheless it is very doubtful whether British diplomacy was seriously affected by this circumstance. If it was, this would be the only incontestable instance of political Press power in the period. Of course, it would be absurd to imply that Governments ceased to pay attention to Press reactions, but any concept of the

---

[1] W. Albig, *Modern Public Opinion*, New York (1956), pp. 66–67, quoting a UNESCO survey for 1952. The next highest was Sweden with 490 per thousand.

[2] C. J. Hambro, *Newspaper Lords in British Politics*, London (1958), p. 49.

relationship between Press and Government must be approached from 1936 onwards with particular caution.

The same caution must be applied to the relationship between the Press and the public. There is evidence to show that the Press neither effectively represented nor was likely to influence a great proportion of its readers. The biggest circulation ever achieved by a British newspaper, and, probably, by any newspaper any-where, was that of the *News of the World*. It was read by every second person of the entire adult population of the British Isles.[3] Views may differ about its political attitude, but it does not greatly matter here, since only 1 per cent of its readers ever troubled to look at its editorials.[4] This state of affairs may be contrasted with *The Times*, whose editorials were normally followed by over half of a readership[5] consisting of 2·5 per cent of the adult population.[6] There is also evidence that a national newspaper would have a substantial proportion of readers whose politics differed explicitly from its own—whether they read its editorial or no. Thus, for example, it is likely that at one point a quarter of the *Daily Mail* readership and a third of that of the *Sunday Dispatch* consisted of Labour Party supporters, while a fifth of those who bought the *News Chronicle* were declared Conservatives.[7] Another estimate had it that more than half of the readers of every national newspaper were likely to oppose its politics.[8] There is evidence of a similar lack of identity on other issues. A survey held on reactions to a Government warning of legal proceedings against the *Daily Mirror*, indicated that, whereas the *Daily Telegraph* supported the warning, more than half of its readers did not—and the situation was almost exactly reversed with *The Times*.[9] Whether these estimates be wholly accepted or not (and it will later be necessary to discuss certain difficulties raised by the technique involved) they do at least suggest the need for reserve in any concept of the Press as either a mirror or a moulder of public opinion. At the same time it is only fair to add that while there was plenty of misleading

[3] J. W. Hobson and H. Henry, *The Hulton Readership Survey*, London (1947), p. 9.
[4] C. Madge and T. Harrisson, *Mass Observation: The Press and its Readers*, London (1949), p. 49.
[5] Ibid.   [6] Hobson and Henry, loc. cit.   [7] Ibid., p. 26.
[8] Madge and Harrisson, op. cit., pp. 91–93.
[9] Ibid., p. 83: for many instances of contradiction between reader and news-paper, see B. Seebohm Rowntree and G. R. Lavers, *English Life and Leisure—A Social Study*, London (1951), Chapter 9.

information, editorial and other, on every sort of political and social topic, there is no evidence of the intention on the part of a newspaper or group of newspapers to mislead from some sinister motive. Such was the view of the 1947 Royal Commission on the Press, whose general conclusion was that the vast bulk of the Press displayed few discernible motives other than to increase circulation by the provision of the maximum amount of entertainment.[10]

There are excellent *a priori* reasons, therefore, why a survey such as this cannot be expected to yield any very startling discoveries of Press influences on Government actions or on public attitudes, why, indeed, it would be unwise to make any sweeping political or social inferences from the material presented, and why any conclusion reached here can only be properly evaluated if related to this background. On the other hand, it would be equally incorrect to minimize the status of the Press as a British institution. If a possible concept of its power should be modified, it would be absurd to deny it any power at all. If it only partially represented the opinions of its readers, it did to that extent represent them, and no Government failed to pay some attention to Press reactions. Many people did think of the Press as expressing the varying voices of British public opinion. And in this, there was, after all, some truth. Much more important, however, was the fact that the rest of the world inevitably tended to equate the British Press with the British people. If only for that reason, British Press reactions to the holocaust have a significance in their own right.

[10] *Royal Commission on the Press: Report*, London, HMSO, Cmd. 7700 (1948–9), pp. 106, 122, 154, 262–7.

I

The New Germany

IN March 1933, the Press of the world began to report a series
of events taking place in Germany to which there was no real
parallel in modern times: violent and systematic anti-Semitism
on a national scale on the part of the Government of a modern
European state. The main sequence can be recounted easily
enough. On 30 January Adolf Hitler had been appointed Chan-
cellor and the National Socialist Party of Germany (the 'Nazi'
party—from an abbreviation of the German title) had begun its
programme of crushing all opposition. In six weeks the revolution
was complete: the entire administration was in the hands of the
Nazis.[1] The Jews had suffered along with the Communists and the
Socialists but the action against them continued after the political
victory had been won, and was clearly exceptional. It began with a
Government-ordered national boycott of all Jewish goods and
services,[2] continued with dismissals from the universities, the civil
service and the Bar, and culminated, in that first stage, with the
threat of a constitutional amendment which would place the non-
Aryan in to the category of *Angehoeriger* (subject) as distinct from
the Aryan *Buerger* (citizen). These official steps were accompanied
by plenty of 'unofficial' incidents.[3]

These events had a particularly strong effect upon the British
Press. They presented it with material to which, in a very fundamental sense, it was entirely a stranger. Not only was open racial
persecution unknown in Britain, but, by the British, it was

[1] One of the best descriptions of this phase is to be found in the dispatch of
the British Ambassador; see *Documents on British Foreign Policy 1919–1939*,
(second series), London (1950) IV, pp. 458–62.

[2] *Voelkische Beobachter*, 10 and 13 Mar. 1933, made clear the part played by
Goering, for example, in preparing the boycott.

[3] Official sources for the more important of these steps are: 'Aryan Paragraph'
as applied to lawyers, RGBL I (1933), 188; to doctors, RGBL I (1933), 222; to
universities, RGBL I (1933), 225. For further reference to the 'subject' and
'citizen' question, see below, pp. 42–46.

scarcely thought of as a European phenomenon at all, at least in the twentieth century; it belonged to the Russia of the Kishinev pogroms or to the Turkey of the Armenian massacres. Thus, the attitude of the British Press was influenced throughout, to a greater or lesser extent, by a lingering sense of disbelief—somewhere, somehow, there had to be a more reasonable explanation than the deliberate decision of a Government to abandon what every British editor, whatever his social or political outlook, had been brought up to believe was civilized behaviour. Indeed some of the earlier explanations in their endeavour to picture something which could be compared to institutions rather better understood in Britain, occasionally achieved somewhat bizarre results. Thus, nearly a year after the establishment of the régime, a special correspondent of the *Spectator*, in the second of a number of articles intended to be a serious contribution towards an understanding of the new Germany, could comment as follows:

Anti-Semitism has been developed into the most essential symbol of this great attempt to unite a scattered people on a racial basis; to give seventy million odd dispirited people a new superiority complex at the expense of those who cannot prove their Aryan blood and thus to make workers and peasants gentlemen . . . the whole Third Reich should really be regarded as a glorified public school system aimed at doing for a whole people what Dr. Arnold did for the upper middle classes.[4]

Before passing to a more detailed survey of early reactions, one particular characteristic of these events ought to be emphasized, which, though perhaps not unique (as in some sense the events themselves were) is striking enough and must be remembered in any judgement of the Press. With certain exceptions, the Nazis made no attempt whatever to conceal what was going on.[5] It may be objected that concealment was hardly practicable. Street violence and the boycott of Jewish shops were not limited to obscure towns and villages in the depths of Germany. Its most vivid incidents took place in the fashionable quarter of Berlin. Similarly, it might well have proved difficult to confine within the national frontiers all knowledge of the miscellaneous anti-Semitic regulations which have been mentioned. Such an objection, how-

---

[4] *Spectator*, 9 Feb. 1934.
[5] The main exceptions were, of course, the concentration camps which, after a short time, could not be seen by the foreign Press. See below, pp. 80–87.

ever, would only be partly valid. Censorship imposed by a modern dictatorship has been shown to be highly effective. Under it rumour and conjecture often fulfil a greater or lesser proportion of the task of normal information. In fact, however, the German Government did not try to impose any such censorship. During the whole six years of peace, every one of those regulations (beginning with that applying to the German Bar, a restriction unprecedented in modern Europe[6]) was published and circulated through perfectly ordinary channels. The world was officially informed and left to draw what conclusions it could, and, while the authorities angrily denied the truth of particular incidents in their street campaign, they did not deny the campaign itself or try to hide the main lines of its development.[7] One or two Press correspondents were expelled, and one saw the inside of a German prison, but in general, freedom of movement for the foreign Press and opportunity to gather news were (with the exception mentioned) almost entirely unrestricted. The boycott, indeed, was as fully reported, not only textually but pictorially, as any national disaster or natural calamity. The *Illustrated London News*, for example, was able to produce several excellent pages of pictures and the main London dailies were not far behind.[8] Occasionally the fact that there were contradictory stories and some exaggeration led to the difficulties inherent in reporting a chaotic situation being confused with the difficulties which a deliberate censorship could bring about if it chose to do so. An example was the following rhetorical query:

Is it going to be as difficult to locate the real truth about what is happening in Germany as it is in Russia?[9]

There was, of course, no parallel whatever. It was, indeed, very hard for the ordinary person to accept that any government would not try to hide what was going on, but the fact is that no censorship of the Russian type was ever applied on the foreign Press. So well

[6] If Czarist Russia be included, Jews were prohibited from many types of legal practice, but baptism removed this disability—since there was no 'Aryan Paragraph'.

[7] To obviate all possible misunderstandings, posters carried by boycott pickets included an English translation clearly to be seen in Press photographs; e.g. in those referred to in the next footnote.

[8] *Illustrated London News*, 8 April 1933; cf. *Daily Telegraph*, 3 April 1933.

[9] *Yorkshire Evening Post*, 25 Mar. 1933.

known was this at the time that certain issues of British papers were banned in Germany now and then because not a few Germans were turning to them for news of their own country. The boycott, the regulations, and the speeches of the Nazi leaders were there for every reporter, while the programme of the Nazi party, published in an English translation the previous year, could be utilized to clarify any point which might still be obscure.[10] Just as there were few or no restriction on the foreign Press, there were very few restrictions on the movements of foreign visitors—even of Jews.[11] Apart from specific periods, such as during the invasion of Austria or at the time of the Munich crisis, there was never any great decline in the number of British tourists, for whom the only obstacle could have been personal distaste. They travelled freely about Germany and, with the exception of the camps, saw what they desired to see; many recorded their impressions in letters to the Press and editors were able to add them to the information gathered by their own reporters.[12]

We are not here concerned with possible reasons for this particular facet of the Nazi régime or with passing some sort of value judgement upon it. These matters are stressed in order to make it very clear at the outset that, whatever else may at this early stage have been obscure about Nazi actions and intentions in other spheres of domestic or of foreign policy, in this particular sphere the ordinary observer could hardly have had any doubts—at least as to the external facts. There was an abundance of easily accessible material, both official and unofficial. If we assume provisionally that the average British reporter and his editor, without being specialists in any sense, wished to give their readers the fullest possible picture of events affecting the Jews in Germany, there was no difficulty whatever in acquiring the desired information day by day and week by week.

Perhaps the best way of illustrating that this situation was somewhat unusual from the point of view of the foreign Press is

[10] G. Feder, *Das Programm der N.S.D.A.P.*, trans. E. T. S. Dugdale, *The Programme of the Party of Hitler*, Munich (1932); reprinted by Allen & Unwin as *Hitler's Official Programme*, London (1934).

[11] Only one or two isolated incidents affecting British Jews are recorded. A Jewish acquaintance of the writer travelled over most of Germany at the beginning of 1938 in perfect freedom.

[12] A selection of those which may throw a light on the relation between the Press and public opinion of the period is discussed in Chapter VII.

to contrast the reporter's position in Germany with that usually obtaining in other non-democratic states then and since; for there attempts to gain and to transmit reliable information about the persecution of a section of the population meet with every sort of official and unofficial hindrance. In those circumstances, Press emphasis cannot but be inference and supposition, while the few available facts tend to be of a contradictory character. Both newspaper and reader can, not unreasonably, dispute the validity of available information, and can feel justified in ignoring it if their opinions warrant it. An inquiry into the Press, such as this, under those conditions, would have a substantial section devoted to a serious inquiry into the events themselves. No such problem can arise in regard to the relation of the British Press towards the Jewish policies of the German National Socialists.

It will be useful, as a basis for subsequent discussion, to say something first about the actual news reports. Three national dailies gained a special reputation and, in a real sense, stood in a class apart. These were *The Times*, the *Manchester Guardian*, and the *Daily Telegraph*. Quite aside from their varying political slants and their equally varying comments and explanations, it is those three which, taking the period as a whole, produced the fullest and the most accurate stories of the persecutions and those stories which perhaps carried the greatest conviction. In the many controversies, public and private, which developed over this, as over other aspects of Hitler's activities, an appeal to one of these three for the actual facts was generally accepted as valid by all participants. More specifically, it was on this reputation that the Board of Deputies of British Jews relied in their initial endeavours to arouse public opinion. Their pamphlets included substantial extracts from these three newspapers as a sufficiently satisfactory confirmation for most intelligent people of what was going on in Germany.[13] At the same time, it is useful to emphasize here something sufficiently obvious, which in a discussion of this kind can only too easily be forgotten. Even this most responsible section of the Press could hardly approach the anti-Semitism of the Nazis as more than one part, however fundamental, of their many other activities. The high level of the reporting does not in itself say

---

[13] *The Persecution of the Jews in Germany*, Joint Foreign Committee of the Board of Deputies of British Jews and the Anglo-Jewish Association (series of three pamphlets), London (1933).

anything about the comparative space reports of anti-Semitism occupied. As might be expected this varied considerably, not only from day to day through pressure from other items editorially considered as more important, but also as among the three newspapers concerned.

During the first two years of Nazi rule, as well as for several months before its inception, the greatest amount of space given to the Jewish question was in the *Manchester Guardian*. At the beginning of 1934, for example, as part of a review of the previous year, it devoted two long articles to an excellent summary of the existing situation after ten months of persecution.[14] The customary annual review of *The Times* did not include much more than a reference.[15] In August 1932, an international conference of Jewish representatives met in Geneva, having as its main objective the formation of a World Jewish Congress, during the course of which many references, not unnaturally, were made to the impending danger in Germany. *The Times*, the *Manchester Guardian*, and the *Daily Telegraph* all printed fair, accurate, and essentially similar kinds of account, but the *Manchester Guardian* allotted rather more space to them than did the other two put together.[16] *The Times* began to give a noticeably greater amount of space to German Jewish matters from 1935[17] while the most copious collection of *Daily Telegraph* references is to be found in 1938, a year in which their sheer bulk outweighs by a considerable extent all that can be discovered on the subject in the rest of the national dailies. It is reasonable to connect these variations with editorial predispositions. The *Manchester Guardian* had a strong traditional interest in the well-being of minorities, reinforced by as traditional a dislike of any kind of right-wing or authoritarian government.

[14] *Manchester Guardian*, 22 Jan. 1934; 23 Jan. 1934. These articles provoked a long explanatory letter from a German District Court Judge which it printed with its correspondent's reply (21 Feb. 1934).

[15] *The Times*, 1 Jan. 1934. It has unfortunately proved impossible to trace the equivalent *Daily Telegraph* review but it is unlikely to have differed greatly.

[16] *Manchester Guardian*, 16 May; 15, 16, 17, 19 Aug. 1932; *The Times*, 15 Aug. 1932; *Daily Telegraph*, 15 Aug. 1932. This selection reasonably indicates the proportion. The *Guardian* stressed by a sub-headline the conference's concern about the Nazi danger.

[17] In that year the Board of Deputies published a fourteen-page pamphlet consisting solely of four articles from *The Times* and did not consider any comments necessary (see Bibliography).

The prominence it gave to Hitler's persecution of the Jews was, in this early period, no greater than that to his persecution of political opposition groups. Quite naturally, the two aspects were often linked by the *Guardian* as by most of the Press, but the specific attitude of the *Guardian* tended in its reporting (though not at all in its comments) to blur distinctions both between different opposition groups, and between such groups on the one hand and the Jews on the other, as objects of persecution. One report on the situation of all these different elements in danger from the Nazis was given the headline 'How Liberals Live in Germany'.[18]

The Times, on the other hand, had as strong a tradition of restraint and a distaste for anything savouring of 'sensationalism' in politics as in journalism. Its main concern was with the consequences, for Britain and for Europe, of this highly unrestrained German upheaval. It has already been implied and it ought to be clearly stated that *The Times* certainly had no illusions about what the consequences were for the German Jews and no desire to minimize them to the British public.[19] It sought, however, to present as balanced a picture as possible with the foreground occupied by the effects of the new régime on the international *status quo*. From 1935 onwards, the problem of the refugees began to give the German Jewish question an inescapably international character and a role of first importance in any dealings of the great powers with Nazi Germany. This development was most responsible for eliciting more and more emphasis from that section of the Press which, in general, had little specific interest in this question—though it would be unjust to deny that ordinary considerations of humanity had their influence as the scope and intensity of the persecution was seen to increase.[20] Considerations of a similar nature apply to the *Telegraph*, though it might well have had, at first, an additional disinclination to print quantities of damaging material about a Government which, in some respects

[18] *Manchester Guardian*, 21 Aug. 1933.

[19] It did, however, give insufficient weight to the *official* character of all anti-Semitic activity; see below, pp. 29–30; 49–50.

[20] However, it can be no accident that even as early as 14 Mar. 1933 *The Times* devoted its first leader to the fiftieth anniversary of the death of Karl Marx who 'was born of Jewish stock whose critical and fermenting genius has always been preoccupied, since the days of the prophets, with the problem of righteousness'.

at least, could claim to be 'conservative' in the more normal sense, and a necessary defence against a Communist or a socialist revolution. Most important of all, perhaps, was the factor that both *The Times* and the *Telegraph* had far stronger inhibitions than had the *Guardian* about giving the appearance of interfering in the internal affairs of a friendly nation. With all these reservations, the most consecutive story is still to be found in their collective pages, which undoubtedly constitute a first-class primary source for all historians of the period.

That section of the Press which, for want of a better term, is usually described as 'popular' approached the whole matter by a rather different and somewhat simpler method. While the newspapers so far discussed were, broadly speaking, concerned with selecting items by a relatively unbiased consideration of their importance, as it then appeared, and with a reasonably full report, their popular contemporaries were chiefly interested in asking two simple questions. The first was, 'are the Jews "news"?' The second, 'how can such news fit in with our political or other line of the moment?' On the answers to those two questions depended the size and the nature of the actual report printed—often without much reference to the adequacy or tone of an accompanying editorial comment.

There was a special circumstance at the time which gave the first question an exceptional importance. In the first years of that decade there was taking place among the leading popular dailies a bitter struggle for new subscribers, which it seemed could not be entirely decided by the provision of progressively more generous gift schemes and competition prizes.[21] It was felt that actual content might have some influence on the outcome and thus the value of a particular item of news tended to be judged more than usually by its potential saleability. A decision to allot more or less space to the troubles of the German Jews was therefore likely to be the result of considerations far removed not only from an evaluation, however biased, of the actual importance of the subject but also to some extent from editorial sentiment.

The *Daily Express* (with which the *Sunday Express* is included for this purpose) is a particularly interesting example of this attitude. It had decided, before the coming to power of the Nazis,

[21] On the circulation war see F. Williams, *Dangerous Estate*, London (1957), pp. 184–213. Once the *Daily Herald* beat its nearest rival 'by a cutlery set'.

that there could be good news value in the Jewish question. Throughout the summer of 1932 it dealt at some length with two matters affecting the Anglo-Jewish community. In the early part of that year a number of incidents were supposed to have occurred indicating that certain of the smaller insurance companies discriminated against Jewish clients, either by refusing them outright, or by varying conditions of acceptance to their disadvantage. As far as can be estimated, the *Express* gave substantially more space than any other newspaper to this alleged discrimination, including a number of special features and considerable correspondence. During the same period, possibly to balance what might be thought a 'negative' approach, it gave almost as much prominence to a series of descriptive illustrated articles on the London *Beth Din*. In the autumn of the same year it provoked a fresh and rather more interesting controversy by printing Joseph Goebbels' own views on the Jewish question, and by giving equal space for reply to one of its correspondents who was himself Jewish.[22] In reporting the world conference to which reference has already been made it stressed by effective use of headlines and layout, more than any other version (including that of the *Manchester Guardian*), the feelings expressed there on the danger which threatened the Jews in Germany.[23]

It is scarcely surprising, therefore, that the *Express* would wish to exploit to the full the news possibilities of the events of the following year. Before the coming of Hitler, references to Jewish topics in the British Press were comparatively infrequent and the series in the *Express* had at least the merit of originality.[24] During 1933 and 1934, they were very frequent indeed. The *Express* enjoyed, as it still does, a highly enterprising editorial direction. It won that circulation war though it was eventually defeated by the *Daily Mirror*. It was thus to be expected that it would seek as original an approach as possible to facts, startling enough in themselves and admitting of little speculation, in order to distinguish itself from its rivals. It had, indeed, a distinct advantage over some of them in owing no explicit loyalty to any particular British political party. The two loyalties which it always has proclaimed

---

[22] *Daily Express*, 29 Nov.; 1 Dec. 1932.   [23] *Daily Express*, 16 Aug. 1932.
[24] The *News Chronicle* printed an almost identical *Beth-Din* article nearly two years later. It was then, too, that the *Daily Herald* referred to discrimination in insurance and, ignoring the *Express*, claimed the matter had been 'more or less secret' till that moment—cf. *Daily Herald*, 4 April 1934.

did, understandably, exercise an appreciable influence. The first was a special kind of insular patriotism which encouraged a curious sense of perspective. For instance, at a meeting of the Minorities Commission of the League of Nations Union the German representative had sought to define the nation as an ethnic entity. Mr. Ormsby-Gore's rejoinder that the British Empire was based on a multi-racial equality of rights, coupled with some laudatory reference to Disraeli, earned the somewhat optimistic headline 'Britain Defends the Jews'.[25] The second was its keen concern for the *Daily Express*. Accounts of the German events were liberally interspersed with references, by name, to its correspondents and the maximum benefit was extracted when one of them had the good fortune to suffer a short term of imprisonment.[26]

These predilections, which certainly did give its columns a definite originality, were, of course, not peculiar to its reports from Germany. A more specific characteristic of these was that, while they included a selection of facts approximately similar to that appearing in other newspapers of similar status, they managed at the same time to convey a recurrent implication that the whole question of a persecution as such, quite aside from possible reasons for it, was some sort of a dispute or debate, the two sides of which the *Express* was determined to present equally to its readers. Nevertheless it had no real doubts, editorially speaking, about the nature or the extent of the persecution. This attitude appears very clearly, with no apparent consciousness of any inconsistency, in a typical paragraph:

The *Daily Express* records the facts [of the persecution] as it recorded the events which led to Hitler's rise to power. Almost alone, this newspaper foretold that happening. The *Daily Express* is neither pro-Jewish nor pro-Nazi, anti-Jewish nor anti-Nazi. It reports the News.

This news from Germany to-day makes feelings of abhorrence and disgust.[27]

[25] *Daily Express*, 5 Oct. 1933.

[26] See, for example, issue of 2 June 1934. It would be unfair to suggest that no contemporary of the *Express* exhibited this engaging pride. A feature article in the *Daily Herald* by Louis Golding ('Hitler—I appeal to you') included the words, 'I write this in one of the greatest organs of opinion in the English-speaking world' (16 Mar. 1933).

[27] *Daily Express*, 25 May 1934. This must be taken as official policy. Compare, however, its comment on 4 Mar. 1933: 'Nothing since the mass persecution of the Jews in Czarist Russia has equalled the anti-Semitic hatred of the Nazis', and the *Sunday Express* leader 20 May 1934 which can hardly be called 'not anti-Nazi'.

This is a comparatively late extract, but the general tone was set very early—not always accompanied by any qualifying comment. In March 1933 the *Evening Standard* printed an article by the German-Jewish writer Leo Feuchtwanger on his experiences at the hands of the Nazi police, but claimed that it was itself 'impartial'.[28] The following day it warned its readers that

the mass campaign of world Jewry against the Nazi government is likely to obscure the real character of the revolution now taking place in Germany. It creates the impression that only Jews and all Jews are being persecuted.[29]

A few days later, the *Sunday Express* printed an exclusive full-length feature by Goering, giving more space to his denials of excesses than did any other British newspaper.[30] The same point was made more succinctly by the *Daily Express*. A full-page picture divided into two sections—a protest meeting by the Board of Deputies and Goering holding a Press conference—bore the captions 'The Accusation' and 'The Denial' respectively with short quotations. There was no comment.[31] Four months later the paper's own account of what was happening was 'balanced' by a feature article about a quarter of which was devoted to the discovery that 'Jews could stroll along the Kurfuerstendam, gay and unmolested, in a country which is at least 60% anti-semitic', and that 'a fat Storm-Trooper resplendent in braid and brass' seemed to be the best of friends with one of them.[32] In a summary of the first year of Hitler's power, a similar approach coloured the only two references to the anti-Semitic aspect. The first read:

Not everybody can belong to the *Volksgemeinschaft* [people's community]. If you happen to be a Communist, a Socialist or a Jew you stand outside. You may even starve while good Nazis take your job.

The second mentioned the 'fate' of German Jewry without being more specific. Apart from the blurring of an important distinction between these groups (political opponents could, in principle, save themselves at the cost of their convictions, a course not open

---

[28] *Evening Standard*, 23 Mar. 1933. *West Africa* 25 Mar. 1933 (see p. 217) called this 'loathsome'. Is this too strong?

[29] *Evening Standard*, 24 Mar. 1933. The reference is to the boycott of German goods. See below, pp. 101–9.

[30] *Sunday Express*, 26 Mar. 1933.   [31] *Daily Express*, 27 Mar. 1933.

[32] *Daily Express*, 25 Aug. 1933.

to the Jew), the question of the existence of a more active persecution than discrimination in employment was in effect left open.[33] It was a question which, according to the same writer a few months later, still 'fascinates the world'.[34] His own contribution, in itself a sufficiently accurate account of the latest developments, 'would help to solve it'. Finally, from 1933 to 1939 less actual space in the *Express* seems to have been allotted to the whole question than might have been expected; less than is to be found in any other national daily. A particularly striking instance is the treatment of the April 1st boycott. Despite the 'sensational' nature of this event, the treatment given it by the *Express* cannot stand comparison with that in the *Daily Telegraph*, where it received very much greater prominence both in space and layout.[35] Perhaps it was felt that the news itself would, in this instance, be more impressive than any conceivable approach to it and that, besides, the *Express* could no longer claim (as it might have done in 1932) something of an exclusive interest in the Jewish question. Its value as a weapon in the circulation war had dwindled.

The news columns of other popular newspapers do not, as a whole, yield so interesting a result. Those which were directly connected with a political party or other group of specific interests displayed every now and then the emphasis expected of them.[36] Some of the more revealing instances are, not surprisingly, provided by the *Daily Worker*. For example, the following news item was printed as an explicit illustration of editorial attitude, after nearly a year of Nazi rule. Its degree of accuracy is not relevant to the present purpose:

BANKERS ARE BANKERS

All the leading Nazi newspapers the other day carried an official notice on the exchange and sale of the new Prussian State Bonds. . . . Jews and guaranteed Aryan stand side by side.

No fewer than twenty Jewish bankers appear. Here are some names:

[33] *Daily Express*, 30 Jan. 1934: 'Hitler's First Birthday'. The same approach to the more general aspect is even more noteworthy—the picture that National Socialism presents to the world on its first birthday 'lacks charm'. But the Nazi movement, less rigidly applied, 'might have set a pattern of great beauty to a grey world'.

[34] *Daily Express*, 25 May 1934.

[35] Cf. *Daily Express* and *Daily Telegraph*, 1 April and 3 April 1933.

[36] If the *Daily Telegraph* be included in this category it was often a surprising exception.

Anton Kohn, A. Levy, Salomon Oppenheim, Jakob S. H. Stern, J. Dreyfus, Mendelsohn, and so on.

Not merely tolerated but endorsed as pillars of the Fascist State, decorated with the glory of the eagle and swastika—bankers are bankers and business is business.[37]

The *Worker* made the same point more succinctly by giving the headline 'Wealthy Jews To Stay' to a somewhat obscure Exchange Telegraph item about a German disclaimer regarding compulsory emigration.[38] It should be remembered that in the eyes of almost everyone outside Germany the implication at that time would have been that this was a class privilege and not a selection of future victims.

Near the other end of the ideological spectrum, the *Catholic Herald* had in 1932 emphatically expressed the opinion that the only effective defence for the Jews in Germany would be a government in which the Catholics had a responsible voice. It thus tended to stress those items of news which mentioned Jews being morally or materially assisted by the Catholics in Germany or abroad.[39] There is no doubt whatever that throughout the Nazi period there were many authentic instances well worth reporting in which the younger religious minority effectively succeeded in shielding and aiding the older. The *Catholic Herald*, however, did not merely confine itself to this not unjustifiable selectiveness, even in the ostensible non-editorial sections. References to anti-Semitic violence or discrimination in Germany were usually accompanied by the reflection that Catholics were experiencing worse sufferings if not in that country then in some other part of the world. This manner of presenting German-Jewish news was an explicit point of policy:

We do not assail Fascist Italy and applaud Soviet Russia, as do some of our loudvoiced and hypocritical contemporaries, to whom wholesale murder and incendiarism in Spain are of no consequence—as they are anti-Catholic—while far lesser wrongs done in Germany are most infamous because done against Jews.[40]

[37] *Daily Worker*, 15 Feb. 1934. The introductory editorial comment is discussed below, p. 25.
[38] *Daily Worker*, 16 Feb. 1934.
[39] Cf. *Catholic Herald*, 14 May 1932; 6 Aug. 1932. Instances of reports of Catholic assistance are, of course, most numerous during the refugee and the war periods.
[40] *Catholic Herald*, 15 July 1933.

In this respect, its attitude did not differ fundamentally from that of other sections of the popular Catholic Press in England and Ireland or of journals peculiar to the Catholic intelligentsia such as the *Tablet*, the *Weekly Review*, *G.K.'s Weekly*, and the *Month*.[41] In another respect, however, the *Catholic Herald* was distinguished by a certain originality. It was one of the very few British papers to accompany its report of German anti-Semitism with the not infrequent comment that Jews had done, and were doing, as much and worse to the Christian population of the Soviet Union. The consequent presupposition that the Soviet Government was for practical purposes Jewish was taken as an obvious and well-established fact, evidence for which needed only to be adduced when someone actually thought of challenging it.[42] At least in one instance the context of the reference to Soviet persecutions of Christians makes it clear that, although the words 'Jew' or 'Jewish' do not appear, this identification is intended, and readers will take it as axiomatic.[43] In this particular comparison of the German and Russian dictatorships (not, it need hardly be said, in its general outlook) the *Catholic Herald* was at one with the organs of the various Fascist groups in England, with one or two of the more obscure Irish papers, and, rather more unexpectedly, with a technical aviation journal of some standing which believed that 'the Russian Bear had been corrupted by "Japhetic" blood'.[44]

Assertions such as these, like those about 'wealthy' Jews in the *Daily Worker*, are of course not of very great significance when they are limited to comments on the news, or even applied to its presentation or selection. However, this kind of approach is an interesting indication of underlying ideologies, and its significance becomes more immediately apparent when similar assertions in-

[41] Cf. 'The Badge of the Catholic Tribe'—'We are more concerned about our own people who in various parts of the world are enduring persecution far more bitter and unjust than that, grave as it is, which at the moment afflicts German Jewry,' *Month*, June, 1933.

[42] *Catholic Herald*, 6 Jan. 1934. Consideration of the evidence advanced is unfortunately not relevant here. It has its own fascination, with a strong family resemblance to *The Protocols of the Elders of Zion*.

[43] *Catholic Herald*, 20 Jan. 1934.

[44] *The Aeroplane*, 31 Jan. 1934. It is a cause for regret that the whole article cannot be reprinted here since it is a truly fascinating example of the more eccentric manifestations of anti-Semitism. The bulk of the Russian population for the past hundred years was identified with 'Japhetic' or 'tartar' Jewry and was held (following Kipling) to constitute a threat to British India; cf. ibid. 24 Jan. 1934.

fluence attempts at explaining events, rather than merely reporting them.

The bulk of the popular Press, however, whether at home or in the Commonwealth, was not concerned with significant approaches. It was simply interested in extracting the maximum value from the situation, and assiduously employed a technique, perfected over some thirty years, of making events which were in themselves extraordinary even more so. This was sometimes no easy task. On 1 May 1934, for example, Julius Streicher, the dedicated leader of German anti-Semitism and the governor of Franconia, published a special issue of his paper *Der Stuermer* in which fourteen generously illustrated pages were devoted to alleged records of ritual murder from 169 B.C. to his own times. It was difficult to find a parallel for such an action by a high official of a modern European state. Of this *The Times*, as usual, gave a simple factual account. Its popular contemporaries, however, were faced with the problem of inventing arresting comments to something which needed none. In some cases they hoped that a comparatively vague description of the contents would stimulate their readers' imagination; in others they made use of every available detail. In general, they were forced to fall back on a miscellaneous collection of phrases, ineffective compared to the actual fact, and not differing fundamentally from one paper to the next.[45]

It was difficult, too, to tell from the ostensibly non-editorial sections of a particular paper where, if anywhere, its customary sympathies or prejudices lay. Its political or other orientation had little or no influence on the presentation of the news. The headlines of the official Labour *Daily Herald* were not easily distinguishable from those of the unofficial Liberal *News Chronicle* or from the, broadly speaking, non-party *Daily Mirror*. In this respect, the *Evening Standard*, the *Star* (the evening version of the *News Chronicle*), and the *Evening News* betrayed no greater differentiation in their news columns. It should be noted that the short-lived but enthusiastic support by the *Daily Mail* of the British Union of Fascists had no discernible effects on its reports from Germany.[46] In fact, it is London's only left-wing Sunday paper *Reynolds News* which can best be remembered for the possibly un-

---

[45] See *The Times*, 2 May 1934; cf. e.g. *Daily Herald*, 12 May 1934; *Observer*, 13 May 1934; *Glasgow Herald*, 16 May 1934.
[46] This lasted from January to July 1934. See below, p. 203.

intended impression produced by its remark, 'Hitler has shown his hand. He has given Germany's industrial future over to twelve dictators endowed with power to crush the Big Jew and the Small German.'[47]

The popular sections of the provincial Press followed the London pattern, since few of them could afford a special German correspondent and had to be satisfied with syndicated articles, apart from the normal news-agency material. It must be emphasized that reference is here being made to news columns only: the peculiar interest of the British provincial Press, particularly of that section of it which does not belong to any of the great combines, lies in its often refreshingly original editorial opinion and in the exceptional amount of space it gives to readers' letters, tourists' stories, and local reactions. Together they form as accurate a picture of the public opinion of the day as any that can be found.[48] Finally, it would be hard to decide, as far as pure news reporting is concerned, who emerged victorious from this contest of making the most of a situation. Even the oldest Conservative London daily, the *Morning Post*, which could not, in any normal sense, be said to have belonged to the popular Press, must be accounted a participant—perhaps motivated by an effort to improve its steadily dropping circulation. It ran a series of articles by Goering and gave one of them the following headline:

HOUNDING OF THE JEWS: GOERING STATES HIS CASE
'Question not Yet Solved'

and introduced it in heavy type thus:

Reasons for the Nazi 'defensive action' against the Jews are given by General Goering in the last but one of his series of exclusive articles.

In fact, less than a third referred to the Jews.[49] As far as the pictorial record of the time goes, one of the most original contributions appeared in the *Daily Herald*. An understandably worried-looking elderly man is seen having his nose measured (with an instrument not unlike the sort used in the better class of shoe shop) in order

---

[47] *Reynolds Illustrated News*, 18 Mar. 1934.

[48] See below, pp. 194; 196–9.

[49] The *Morning Post* was founded in 1772 and was merged with the *Daily Telegraph* in 1937. The reference is to 2 Feb. 1934.

to discover indications of racial origin.[50] But the real victor was the news itself. It was essentially the kind which it was difficult to exaggerate. It defeated all attempts at individual approaches or improvements of its potential saleability. The facts were there—incredible and inescapable. And, in justice, it must be said that the Press as a whole, whether 'popular' or no, distorted or omitted very little, however mixed its intentions may have been.

In one sense it is permissible to claim that there was distortion—of the kind which inevitably occurs in Press accounts of any social or political upheaval. A natural concentration on the particular outstanding incident, coupled with an equally natural disinclination to say very much about the periods and areas in which little was happening, did tend to give the impression that the initial outbursts had had a more widespread and continuous effect on individual lives than they probably had. Until the Nuremberg Decrees of 1935, the anti-Semitic legislation of the Nazis only touched the professions and thus directly injured not more than fifty thousand out of a community of six hundred thousand.[51] Even German thoroughness could not ensure the absolutely instantaneous operation of these regulations everywhere and, at first at any rate, the declarations that exemptions would be granted for war service were occasionally honoured. Open violence was, roughly speaking, restricted to certain carefully staged events and it was possible to pass through much of Germany without meeting its overt manifestation. A sadly high proportion of German Jews was itself not moved sufficiently to make such arrangements for flight as still remained available; though this delay, of course, was also the result of other considerations which are not difficult to understand. In short, in the formal sense it may have been strictly true as the *Financial Times* blandly put it that 'the Nazi regime is an infinitely more exciting affair in the British press than anywhere from the North Sea to the Alps'.[52] Nevertheless, the reality was 'exciting' enough and from a broader point of view not easily capable of exaggeration. Indeed, an apparent over-emphasis of particular incidents was not at all unjustifiable in the long run (al-

[50] *Daily Herald*, 19 May 1933.
[51] Difficulties of replacement slowed down dismissals considerably at first, particularly in law and medicine. The Minister of Trade announced that discrimination was 'impracticable' in business relations (*Berliner Tageblatt*, 27 Sept. 1933). It became progressively less so.
[52] *Financial Times*, 25 Aug. 1933.

though the Press itself was often unaware of this justification) for it was those very incidents which turned out to be, in one way or another, the one permanent feature of the new Germany.

With the distinctions and reservations which have already been made, the Press as a whole agreed, as it could hardly help doing, that the persecution of Jews in Germany was a highly exceptional event, meriting a prominent place in any representative page of news. The situation was of course very different in respect of editorial or quasi-editorial opinion. Occasionally the disparity of approach was so wide that it was hard to believe the same event was being discussed at all—or that the editor had troubled to read his own newspaper. Only on one point was there complete unanimity: this strange business needed more than vivid reporting, more than headlines, pictures, or anything else arresting the attention which a modern newspaper could devise. It needed more than the occasional deprecatory leading article evoked in the past by other unpleasant events abroad which the English, fortunately for them, had always found so difficult to understand. Every organ of the British Press, from the most to the least responsible, all the dailies, the literary and political reviews, the religious weeklies, the publications of miscellaneous eccentrics and even the trade journals were united in one great endeavour of elucidation. The German situation had not only to be reported and described. It had, somehow, to be explained. In a more obvious sense, the Press was also united, or nearly so—that is, in its condemnation of what was going on. But this aspect by itself is not especially important in the immediate context. No British editor could have explicitly condoned the actions of the Nazis against the Jews even had he wanted to do so.[53] It is only when the expected condemnation is placed side by side with a particular explanation or comment that the possibility of a serious review of editorial attitudes is established.

In principle the Press was faced with three questions. What was the real function of anti-Semitism in the policies of the new Government? What did the 'ordinary' German think? How did anti-Semitism, in the first place, become such an issue in this comparatively civilized corner of Western Europe?

In one sense, particularly in regard to the first question, very little explanation was required. Just as what was actually happen-

[53] This statement must be left here as a simple assertion. Its validity and implications are discussed in Chapter 7 below.

ing to the German Jews was neither obscure nor complicated and could, indeed, be related in a few simple sentences, so the explicit intention to bring these events about at the first opportunity and the reason for doing so had long before been publicly and clearly stated both by the Nazi Party and by Hitler himself. The future status of the Jews had been declared at a special meeting of the Party, convened on 25 February 1920, to proclaim its general programme (described as unalterable) to the world:

Only a member of the nation can be a citizen. Only one who is of German blood, irrespective of religion can be a member of the nation. No Jew, therefore, can be a member of the nation.

Whoever is not a citizen may live in Germany only as a guest, and must be subject to alien legislation.

The right of voting on the State's government and laws may be enjoyed only by the citizen. We demand, therefore, that all official appointments of whatever kind, whether in the Reich, the local governments, or the smaller communities may be granted only to the citizen.[54]

The moral aspects of these proposals had been dealt with by Dr. Goebbels in 1929:

Certainly the Jew is also a human being. Never has anyone of us doubted that. But the flea is also an animal—only not a pleasant one. As the flea is not a pleasant animal, we do not feel any duty towards ourselves and our conscience to guard and protect it, and to let it thrive so that it may bite, sting and torture us, but to render it innocuous. So it is with the Jew.[55]

As regards fundamental ideology, of all the numerous references to the Jews in *Mein Kampf* (first published in 1924) which leave no doubt about Hitler's own position, the following is perhaps the most direct and significant:

If the Jew wins, his crown of victory is the death-wreath of Humanity, and this planet will once again, as it did ages ago, float through the ether bereft of men. Eternal Nature inexorably avenges the breaking of her law. And to-day I believe I strive in the way of the Almighty Creator. When I defend myself against the Jews I fight for the work of the Lord.[56]

[54] Feder, *Das Programm*, p. 22.
[55] Joseph Goebbels, *Der Nazi-Sozi*, Munich (1929), p. 8.
[56] Adolf Hitler, *Mein Kampf*, 12th edn., Munich (1932), p. 70.

The plainest and least equivocal statement of all, however, on the value attached by the National Socialists to anti-Semitism is expressed by the editor of the 1920 programme, himself a leading party member: 'Anti-Semitism is, in a way, the fundamental feeling underlying our whole movement. Every National-Socialist is an anti-Semite.'[57]

Despite the fact that evidence such as this was as easily accessible and as little open to misunderstanding as the events themselves, many British editors and leader writers did give the impression that they were either unaware of it, or did not consider it necessary to pay it much attention. In some instances this attitude is not surprising. Marxist or near-Marxist analysis, for example, in this matter as in all others, did not have to look beyond its own first principles. Anti-Semitism was merely one of the many weapons of class rule:

Chosen People

The purpose of anti-Semitic agitation is clear, simple, and amply illustrated by history. The Jew has proved a handy scapegoat for the crimes of every ruling class. Tsarist landlords, priests and capitalists systematically organised pogroms as a regular method of diverting the discontent of the masses.

Hitler's long campaign of blaming the Jews for the workers' misery was exactly similar. What followed the election of March, 1933, was only the harvest of the seed sown.[58]

The Catholic approach had some characteristics in common, the main difference being that anti-Semitism, instead of figuring as 'the inevitable consequence of capitalism', or, in particular, as the expression of a victorious *petit-bourgeoisie*, became the no less 'inevitable consequence' of separation from Catholicism. In the summer of 1933, a certain Pastor Mueller, Hitler's personal representative in church matters, set up a body known as the 'New German Evangelical Church' and was made a bishop for his trouble. Its members, the so-called 'German Christians', apart from according Hitler reverence of the kind more appropriate to the founder of Christianity, were chiefly concerned with applying the provisions of the Aryan Paragraph to the clergy as a whole.

[57] Feder, *Das Programm*, p. 30.
[58] *Daily Worker*, 15 Feb. 1934. This is the passage which continues with 'Bankers are Bankers', etc. See above, p. 17.

They were merely an expression of the same principle which was 'purifying' the Bar and the Universities. However, the British Catholic Press tended to believe that 'German' Christianity was the cause of Nazi ideology rather than one of its results. And it was not only this last theological deviation which was to blame. In one remarkable article anti-Semitism is seen as the end-product of a fine assortment of heresies beginning with the Gnostic Bishop Marcion (died 160 A.D.), not unexpectedly including Luther, and finishing with the view of a semi-comic character from Dostoevsky's *The Possessed* (a work 'reputed to have inspired Lenin') a certain Shigalev, whom the article rather oddly describes as Dostoevsky's concept of a (heretical) master-mind.[59] Whatever may be thought of the relevance of some of this evidence, the chief difficulty here is that, in spite of a long and reasonably accurate summary of miscellaneous German racialist theories which the article also includes, the implicit contradiction in the emphasis given to religious, if heretically religious motivation, is never properly resolved. Neither Catholic nor Marxist was prepared to give sufficient weight to one fundamental factor: The 'Favoured Jew' in Czarist Russia was, almost exclusively, the baptized Jew. Baptism immediately and completely ended all discrimination, except, perhaps, in very exclusive circles, while the unbaptized 'capitalist' was very rarely safe. To that extent, Russian anti-Semitism could be described as 'religious'. In Nazi Germany, the Jew was simply attacked as a Jew with no distinction of class or creed. The path of baptism, even for long-dead generations, was completely closed. A predominantly 'religious' formulation of the problem was thus scarcely adequate.[60] And, as the 'favoured Jewish capitalist', if he ever existed in significant numbers, lasted for a very short time, the 'classic' answer of the Marxist was inadequate too.

[59] *Catholic Herald*, 10 Mar. 1934. Marcion (like most Gnostics) certainly denounced the Pentateuch as the work of the devil. The importance of this in the present context is arguable. Shigalev never said a word about the Jews. He preached a sort of anarcho-dictatorship which was Dostoevsky's concept of the real meaning of all left-wing movements in the Russia of his day. Lenin's *brother* was inspired by the fate of the *original* of another character in the book. In any case, from the Catholic point of view, Dostoevsky was probably the biggest heretic of them all.

[60] Nine years later, in the face of all the evidence, the *Catholic Herald* was still insisting that mass baptism was the only refuge from the holocaust (19 Feb. 1943).

The bulk of Press comment was, of course, rather less doctrinaire. It may be approximately divided into that which tended to classify the German events as mere examples of a recurrent situation not specially peculiar to that country, and that which would link them to something more characteristic of the Nazi or of the German. A typical opinion of the first group was that the Government either deliberately or by a lucky accident had picked on the one acceptable scapegoat both for the country's past sufferings and for its own future errors.[61] It will be noticed that this line of argument is very similar to the Marxist one. In both cases anti-Semitism is a means to an end. In neither is it an essential element of policy.

A crude version of much the same opinion appeared in that remarkable publication the *Saturday Review*:

'Down with the Jews' has not made the real force of Hitlerism, as all who have met its adepts know. Many Jews indeed are to be found among them, for they, like a multitude of other patriotic young Germans, welcomed the movement, first as a weapon against Communism, and then as a means of awakening or exasperating the German sense of nationalism against Poland, France and other 'hereditary' foes.[62]

The comparatively early date of this quotation and its slightly eccentric source do not prevent it from serving as a good illustration of the *reductio ad absurdum* which can result from a persistent believe in any 'nothing but' theory. If Nazi anti-Semitism was so obviously 'nothing but' a means to some quite different end—here one which 'many Jews' are alleged to welcome—there is no reason at all why they too should not join the Nazi Party. All such theories, whether naïve or sophisticated, so long as they made little or no *specific* reference to the history of the Nazi Party and the Jews in Germany, may or may not have been convincing. At any rate their implication was clear enough. If, indeed, parallels to the new persecution could be found to the extent that it appeared as little more than a repetition of what had happened in every age and every country, then there was clearly little more to

---

[61] Cf., e.g., *Nineteenth Century*, December 1933; *Daily Record* (Glasgow), 3 Aug. 1932—certainly, this latter was before the Nazis triumphed but their party's evidence was all available, so the argument is not affected.

[62] *Saturday Review*, 27 Aug. 1932. See below, p. 216.

be said and, it could be argued, little more to be done. The Jews were the pre-destined scapegoats of history.

One approach, of course, settled the whole matter very conveniently: the blank denial, at times of definite incidents, at others of the whole persecution, or more commonly, the assertion that the evidence was too contradictory for any clear evaluation. The whole question of belief and disbelief by Press and public is better discussed as a separate problem on its own, in essence one and the same whether the facts in dispute are the first broken windows in the Kurfuerstendam or the last secrets of the extermination camps.[63] In the present context, however, the following example of such 'judicious' formulation is relevant. It recalls the earnest striving after the truth by the *Daily Express*, but its implications are rather different. It appeared after nearly six years of Nazi rule:

The Effects of Propaganda

The evil done by what is called propaganda—that is falsehood disseminated with a political object—has been amply illustrated this Christmas week. On the two subjects of main interest at the moment to Europe, the Spanish War and the quarrel between the Nazi Government and the Jews, we have been left with a mass of detailed affirmation on no point of which can anyone be certain. The old reliability of news in our Press upon which all reasonable judgements, domestic and foreign, were formed until the Great War, has disappeared.[64]

Clearly, after this, any attempt at critical analysis and explanation is entirely superfluous—'you can't believe what you read in the papers nowadays'. On the other hand, this is perhaps an advance on the view held earlier by a journal of similar tendencies, illustrating the lack of elementary information with which both Press and Government were allegedly afflicted by, *inter alia*, a casual reference to 'the so-called persecution of the Jews in Germany'.[65]

However, there was a second type of approach which did try to grapple with the question in a rather more serious manner. It did begin with the premise that there were exceptional phenomena to be explained if possible. It did admit that these phenomena were taking place in a definite country, at a definite time, and having definite connexions with a specific political movement—in other

[63] See below, Chapter 3.   [64] *Weekly Review*, 29 Dec. 1938.
[65] *G.K.'s Weekly*, 14 Sept. 1933.

words, that generalizations were not enough. There was, however, one reason why this approach, too, often did not produce the quality of results which might have been expected. Surprisingly little direct attention was paid to Nazi policy pronouncements made *before* 1933. Thus the actual evidence of the integral role allotted to anti-Semitism by the movement was inadequately taken into account, and the discussion ranged over a large and miscellaneous collection of facts and suppositions without coming to any particular conclusion. Ignorance of this kind is well illustrated, for instance, by the editor of the *Baptist Times* who thought it was

difficult to discover a motive for this strange return to the policy of the Dark Ages in twentieth century Germany. There does not seem to be anti-Semitic prejudice among German people generally.[66]

Similar if not quite such extreme examples can be found in journals of rather wider influence:

What most astonishes us is the total lack of discrimination. The crime is to be a Jew, and for that no professional eminence, no degree of capacity in business, no public service and no private virtue can atone.[67]

The *Scotsman*, without informing its readers whether it was astonished or not, believed that German anti-Semitism might have 'semi-official backing', a view also held, in almost identical terms, by the *Nottingham Guardian*.[68] The *News Chronicle*, however, had somehow discovered that 'Hitler, to do him justice, has spoken out quite plainly against this disgusting crusade',[69] while the *Sheffield Telegraph* could not think that the Nazi leaders took their own propaganda seriously.[70]

Most marked of all was the comparatively slight attention which *The Times* chose to give to the known sources of Nazi policy, a characteristic in striking contrast to the high standard of its factual reporting. It did refer to the anti-Semitic sections of the Nazi party programme, in a semi-negative manner, saying that they had 'never been formally abandoned'.[71] When the Nazis decided not to

[66] Leader in *Baptist Times*, 6 April 1933.
[67] Leader in *Daily Telegraph*, 18 Mar. 1933.
[68] Leader in *Scotsman*, 11 Mar. 1933; in *Nottingham Guardian*, 9 Mar. 1933.
[69] *News Chronicle* (Manchester), 18 Mar. 1933.
[70] *Sheffield Telegraph*, 27 Mar. 1933.   [71] *The Times*, 3 April 1933.

renew the boycott of April 1st on the day originally announced, it could believe that

the war against the Jews in Germany . . . will at least not be waged with either the irresponsible brutality that disgraced its earlier phase or with the organised thoroughness of an official campaign.[72]

Its comments more than once implied that Hitler himself either did not know, or found it hard to check, the excesses of his followers; an attitude echoed, as has been seen, by other sections of the Press in one form or another, and attributable simply to an insufficient appreciation of what Hitler had often said himself.[73]

This moderation extended by *The Times* towards the head of a friendly foreign state might be classed as 'benefit of the doubt' in 1933, but it becomes truly bizarre when, as late as the end of 1935, *after* the Nuremberg Decrees, the two excellent summaries of the German Jewish scene thought important enough to be reprinted as a pamphlet by the Board of Deputies could conclude with this reflection:

One must either assume that Herr Hitler is unaware of all that is being done since the passage of the laws to bring about a 'tolerable relationship' [the Nuremberg Decrees] or that the fanatics are beyond control.[74]

From *The Times*, at least, some reference to Hitler's official pronouncements might have been expected.

[72] Leader in *The Times*, 5 April 1933. The calling off of the boycott inspired premature optimism in less exalted places too: 'It is a mere misprint on the page of history that may happen once in a way but cannot be repeated,' said the *Daily Sketch*, 1 April 1933. More shortly: 'Nazis Climb Down'—*Edinburgh Evening Dispatch*, 1 April 1933; 'Nazi Raiders Punished by Nazis'—*Daily Mirror*, 15 Mar. 1933—a still earlier outburst of optimism.

[73] See, for example, issue of 13 Mar. 1933 where a conflict over the Jewish question is suggested between Hitler and Goering in which (15 Mar. 1933) Hitler is characterized as the more moderate of the two—with some chance of enforcing his 'more moderate policy'. Such an opinion seems truly incredible. It is only fair to note that on the latter date the *Manchester Guardian* too had one of its very rare moments of hesitation and, in a leading article, thought that more evidence was needed about Hitler's real intentions. Generally, it had no doubts, for example see p. 31 and its comments on the ritual murder number of *Der Stuermer* (*Manchester Guardian Weekly*, 4 May 1934).

[74] *The Times*, 8 Nov. 1935; 27 Nov. 1935. One reason has been suggested above: until the war, to be exact until two days beforehand, *The Times* accorded to Germany and her Government the respect it thought proper in times of peace.

One of the most encouraging exceptions was the *Manchester Guardian*. It rarely had any doubts about the precise connexion of German anti-Semitism with fundamental Nazi policy. As early as April 1932 it printed a collection of extracts from party writings and speeches, similar to those already cited, and introduced them by saying:

The following quotations from the speeches and writings of Hitler and his followers will explain why Jews have been mobbed in Germany, why the windows of Jewish shops have been smashed, why synagogues have been fouled and Jewish cemeteries desecrated.

A year later, on the occasion of the April boycott, it printed a similar summary which should have left no doubt in the mind of the most sceptical as to the significance of what was taking place. It greeted with very restrained optimism the arrest of a few 'unauthorised' looters and called the period immediately after the boycott 'the silent pogrom'. The German Government, it pointed out, 'has changed its policy in detail but not in principle'.[75] Nor was it alone in its understanding of the situation. Its first selection from Nazi documents, for example, was reprinted in full by the *Birmingham Gazette*.[76] The *Yorkshire Observer* quoted some of the points of the party programme.[77] The *Leeds Mercury*, in spite of an article on German anti-Semitism entitled 'The Great German Mystery', stated with commendable plainness in an editorial that 'violent anti-semitism is one of the few clear-cut and unmistakable features of the Nazi outlook'.[78] A long article in *John o' London's Weekly* referred to the programme in some detail, and it ought not to go unnoticed that its entire twenty-five points were reprinted in full by the *News of the World*, a Sunday paper whose normal interest tended to lie in a somewhat different field.[79] The clearest and most consecutive exposition must be placed to the credit of the *Quarterly Review*, which gave space for an important article by Israel Cohen including full use of the sources and a concise and

[75] *Manchester Guardian*, 9 April 1932; 16 Mar. 1933; 1 April 1933; 27 April 1933.
[76] *Birmingham Gazette*, 27 Sept. 1932.
[77] *Yorkshire Observer*, 24 Mar. 1933.
[78] *Leeds Mercury*, 9 Mar. 1933; 27 Mar. 1933.
[79] *John o' London's Weekly*, 1 April 1933; *News of the World*, 26 Mar. 1933. Other odd references are to be found: *Headway* (organ of the League of Nations Union) printed the whole programme, and an abridged version appeared in *Pearsons Weekly*, 13 May 1933.

objective analysis.[80] It should have been required reading for all Berlin correspondents, indeed for all commentators—amateur and professional. For one reason or another, however, the majority ignored or avoided the given facts, preferring to minimize, qualify, or speculate according to their several bents.

One type of serious criticism was often reasonable enough within its limits, in that instead of discussing the Nazis themselves, it tended to concentrate on suggestions of who or what was 'behind' their anti-Semitism. Although in one sense this approach can fairly be likened to the 'nothing but' theories already discussed— i.e. 'behind' Nazi anti-Semitism stands 'nothing but' the capitalist system, loss of faith, 'the eternal scapegoat', &c.—the difference was that here an attempt was being made to bring forward evidence of *specific* phenomena and not more or less general ideological formulae or historical surveys. There was, of course, marked variation in emphasis, but three main lines of explanation can be distinguished. The first type was concerned with immediate causes: the Versailles Treaty, the inflation of the early twenties, and the economic miseries of the Weimar Republic. Within the programme of a party explicitly reacting against all three, 'Anti-semitism fell naturally into place . . . the Jews became identified with "the system".' [81] A broader application of the same idea is to be seen in the comment that 'A wild jealousy of the Jew has always been a mark of trade depression in Europe'.[82]

A second type of equally popular explanation would have classified this new anti-Semitism as simply a *disease* (typical in periods of economic crisis):

The present material decline is gradually revealing the complete set of racial antagonisms which idiot man carries in his subconscious mind, and, in accordance with the true historical pattern, the Jews are the first victims to be selected by desperate nations for punishment.[83]

The third type of explanation used the arguments of the other two as part of the evidence for its identification of all aspects of Nazism, anti-Semitism included, with 'Germanism' or the German character as such, variously defined in racial, cultural, national, or just mystical terms. It is this type of explanation, in the

---

[80] *Quarterly Review*, July 1933. [81] *Round Table*, June 1933.
[82] *Daily Telegraph*, 25 July 1932. [83] *Referee*, 4 Dec. 1932.

multitude of shapes which it took, which can be discerned in the majority of serious attempts at a fundamental analysis:

The key to the enigma, if enigma it is, and the explanation of the apparent contradiction between anti-Semitism and *Kultur*, is to be found in that sinister aberration of thought on racial questions which is known as *Germanism*. It is the creed in which the majority of the German nation moves and lives and has its being. This creed is not only to be found in the teaching of almost all German philosophers, historians and *littérateurs*, but is also shared by the bulk of the nation. Anti-Semitism is one of the constituent parts of Germanism . . . at the back of this doctrine lie the desire and decision of the people to dominate Europe and, if possible, the whole world . . . the race of Hammergod has been deprived of its rightful inheritance by the Treaty of Versailles. . . .[84]

This is an extreme version, cited to show some common implications in their plainest form, one which did not have very wide currency in the British Press. Innumerable milder variations did, however, definitely please editorial taste. The simplest reason was often an ill-defined but continuous undercurrent of hostility to everything German, from which only small sections of the Left and Liberal Press, among them notably the *Manchester Guardian*, were ever wholly exempt.

This is a convenient place for a first mention of this very obvious factor as it worked most directly. Later, however, it will appear in stranger shapes—when, for example, writers clearly found it difficult to strike a balance between their dislike of the Germans and their something less than love of the Jews, or to distinguish adequately between the victims and their executioners. In any event, acceptance of whatever version of the inherent Germanism in Nazi policies involved a further question: How far did the Nazis have the support of the 'ordinary' German?

It should be emphasized here that there is a fundamental distinction between the kind of evaluation which can legitimately be made of Press reactions on this particular point, and those that have been made so far. Nazi policy declarations (whatever their implication) are, in themselves, incontrovertible historical facts and one reasonable criterion of the Press is the extent to which it appears to have been aware of them. The nature of German public opinion, however, like that of British, is not at all a 'fact' of this kind, but is in itself controversial. It would be inappropriate,

[84] *National Review*, July 1933.

therefore, to judge the Press in this instance by comparing its views 'with what was actually happening'.[85] Such views are referred to here for their 'internal' interest—for their connexion with views on other matters, for example on reports of atrocities. Views on German public opinion differed greatly and do not seem to have depended on the intellectual level of the newspaper, or on its political inclination. The following comment from the *Scotsman* should not be taken as the normal Conservative approach:

The general view taken even by cultured Germans in regard to the Jewish problem is that Jews who chose to try to establish themselves there, in an anti-Semitic country, have to take the consequences, now that anti-Semitism has become a cardinal point of the policy of the Government.[86]

A more common estimate was that

there has for many years been a strong anti-Semitic feeling among a certain class of Germans. But nearly all at least agreed that the thing had gone too far. . . . I am definitely of the opinion that there is a strong critical spirit alive in Germany.[87]

Indeed, the most outstanding impression which does emerge is that whereas the majority of serious explanations sought to link the Nazis, together with their anti-Semitism, to German history as a whole, there was little belief that the 'ordinary' German of the time supported (later, perhaps, 'knew about') the anti-Semitism of these same Nazis in practice. This was, without any question, the dominant note struck by the British Press. Actual, active anti-Semitism could not but be the work of a minority—of the ruling group. In this context there was a strongly marked desire to separate the rulers from the ruled.

However, no one denied that the immense majority of the population *acquiesced* in what was going on. It is true that the fact that there were scarcely any open protests could be explained —or excused—by a fear of the inevitable consequences. But it was realized that this point, although obviously relevant, was not quite the one at issue. In the two extracts just quoted, mention is made

[85] An excellent account of 'popular' German anti-Semitism is to be found in M. Lowenthal, *The Jews of Germany*, Philadelphia (1936), pp. 289–346.

[86] *Scotsman*, 10 April 1934.

[87] *Liverpool Post*, 26 Aug. 1933. The *accuracy* of this estimate is not, of course, the point in this or the previous quotation.

of German anti-Semitism not necessarily connected with the new régime. Here is a recognition of what was undoubtedly the fact: hatred of the Jews, whether 'rife' or confined to 'a certain class', considerably antedated the Nazis. What was the cause of this? Did the Nazis, to put it plainly, have any sort of justification for their policy, if not for the way in which it was being applied? Had there been in pre-Nazi Germany something which could seriously be called a 'Jewish problem'?

Most approaches along these lines were simply examples of yet one more sincere attempt to explain phenomena of which the Press had had no previous parallel experience. They were also examples (often to be found when the British face a difficult situation) of 'trying to see the other man's point of view'—in this instance even the Nazi's (or the German's). In fact, the most common type of reference to a 'Jewish problem' in Germany was a passing comment to show that the writer understood that there was a Nazi point of view on the matter which ought not to be left out of the discussion. This sort of comment might be so nearly neutral that it was hard to tell what the writer's own opinion might be:

This, you will say, does not explain the anti-Semitic campaign waged with such ferocity by the Nazis. I have been told by keen observers of the changes of the past few years that the Jews really provided only a convenient step for Hitler on his way to leadership. In the minds of a large proportion of the German population the Jew and big business were synonymous terms.

The Jews, as I mentioned some months ago, held so many of the highest and the best paid positions in Germany. It was felt that their power had become too great and had ousted the Germans born and bred. Hitler merely harnessed that antipathy and whipped it into a thing of fury.[88]

These two paragraphs are given in full because they do provide a good illustration of this type of reference combining the three most usual elements: (1) anti-Semitism is reduced to its 'nothing but' category; (2) an assertion is made about Jewish 'power'—but quite unemphatically; (3) the consciously neutral 'it was felt' sets the tone of the whole.

The same type of reference is to be found in a slightly different form when, in the course of an unambiguous attack on dictator-

[88] *Sheffield Independent*, 28 Aug. 1933.

ship in general and some of the more outstanding Nazi follies (including racialism) in particular, a remark is made about Jews, or German Jews, for which no proof can be required, it is implied, by any reasonable man. Most such remarks tended to be either inaccurate or incapable of a meaningful explanation in any serious sense without an excursus into philosophic or sociological definitions. Here are a few examples:

Some excuse for German Judophobia there may be, for while Germany lay crushed and dismembered in 1919, Jews swept into Germany from Poland and the Baltic States in their tens of thousands. But excuse for inhumanity there can never be.[89]

In fact, the German Jewish population increased from 535,120 in 1910 to 564,379 in 1925, that is by 5·6 per cent. as against the increase of the whole population during the same period by 7–8 per cent.[90]

The undoubted anti-social activities of Jewry, together with their recognised commercial ability, combined to make the Jews the best-hated race on earth.[91]

Oddly enough, the writer of this semi-editorial comment is not in the least a supporter of Hitler and, later in the same article, sharply takes to task another critic whom, he considers, it ill behoves to forget that those activities are the result of centuries of Christian oppression. What in particular those activities may be he does not tell us.

Prominent among such [those who cannot appreciate Hitler's emphasis on labour] is the Jew who only undertakes manual labour until such time as he is in a financial position to reject it.[92]

A glance at the Palestine of his day might have made this particular writer insert a modification.

It is true that the Jewish predominance in the Press and the theatre imported a purely materialistic aspect of life into Germany which had the effect of debasing the high national ideals which formerly united the German race.[93]

[89] *Inquirer & Christian Life* (organ of Unitarianism), 26 Nov. 1932.
[90] H. S. Lindfield, *Statistics of Jews 1931*, New York (1931), p. 45, quoting the census figures of 16 June, 1925.
[91] *Montrose Review*, 13 Oct. 1933.   [92] *Sussex County Herald*, 11 Aug. 1933.
[93] *Saturday Review*, 20 Jan. 1934.

In the very next sentence the concept of a German race is described as 'ignorant ravings', but no elucidation is provided of 'materialistic debasement' which presumably must stand in this meaningless form, leaving merely the impression that, unfortunate as it may be, there was 'something in what Hitler says'—despite those 'ravings'. Those writers for the Press who believed that Hitler—or the Germans—did have some reason for anti-Semitism (however little for committing atrocities) fundamentally believed just this: it was the 'behaviour of German Jewry'. The fact that the above examples are mostly taken from the less important sections of the Press does not invalidate them in this particular context. As will be seen later, they are expressive of a noticeable section of public opinion in Britain.

There are a few examples of an even more explicit attitude. A report in the *Contemporary Review*, while condemning strongly the treatment to which the German Jews were being subjected, spoke of their 'mocking, cynical, destructive kind of outlook, wholly at variance with the robust patriotism and simplicity of life of the ordinary German'.[94] A Church journal quoted this evaluation without the condemnation.[95] The semi-editorial column 'Candidus' in the *Daily Sketch* spoke of the Jews as 'an international force'.[96] The sinister implications here for that paper's usual class of reader could not but have been obvious to the writer. The *Weekly Review* declared that the cause of the persecution was the Zionist Movement, whose intention 'though not definitely avowed, is to secure world domination for the members of its race',[97] while one of the most direct anti-Semitic statements ever printed by a British non-Fascist paper began with the words: 'That which has happened in Germany should serve as a warning to the Jewish people here in our midst.'[98]

It cannot be too strongly emphasized, however, that such comments were very exceptional outside the Fascist Press itself (which, obviously, it would be of little interest to quote in this context). It would never have occurred to the majority to go beyond the casual type of seemingly self-evident comment in their search for 'fair-mindedness'. And yet, unless one *did* go the whole way and fervently believed in a Jewish threat to civilization, and not just in

[94] *Contemporary Review*, Nov. 1933.   [95] *Christian World*, 2 Nov. 1933.
[96] *Daily Sketch*, 17 Mar. 1933.   [97] *Weekly Review*, 1 Dec. 1938.
[98] *West London Observer*, 26 May 1933.

some unfortunate Jewish characteristics, how was it possible to justify any part of what Hitler had done?

We have heard repeatedly in our own columns of 'the other side': of the undue preponderance of Jews in the professions, of the many foreign Jews who flocked in after the war, of the Jews involved in this and that 'scandal'. Were it all true, which it is not, how would it justify the relentless grinding down of the Jewish race, which lives in Germany, so far as it lives, as all private and public reports show, in misery and terror?[99]

We have seen that the major part of the British Press did share these sentiments expressed by the *Manchester Guardian*. It remains to say something of how these sentiments *were* expressed, in the practical sense—how did some of the British Press protest at what was happening?

It would serve little purpose to adduce numerous quotations from the normal type of protest during the first two years of the régime. It can be found in papers of all political complexions, except the official Fascist ones. It was usually based on feelings of humanity and its terms were very similar whatever its source. The passage just quoted is a good example and, indeed, it was the *Manchester Guardian* which was most consistent and most fervent in the stand which it had taken up.[1] All the other important national and provincial organs (even, as had been noted, the *Daily Mail* during its short pro-Fascist period) expressed their detestation of what was happening in Germany.[2] There is, however, another point of interest. It lies in the occasional formulation of a protest which points to that salient characteristic on which much stress has already been laid: a misunderstanding of the situation. One of the most common forms of this was the differentiation between Nazi ideology and Nazi methods:

Nazi views on racialism in general and that aspect of it which relates to Jews in particular, are the Nazis' own affair. People may approve them or criticise them. What scarcely anyone outside the Nazi movement can do, however, is to approve the inhuman treatment which has been meted out to those unfortunate people.[3]

[99] *Manchester Guardian*, 4 Oct. 1933.
[1] Cf. in this context its reactions to the April boycott, especially its leader of 3 April.
[2] Cf., e.g., *The Times* leader, 5 April 1933; *Star*, 28 Aug. 1933; *Staffordshire Sentinel*, 23 Aug. 1933.
[3] *Southampton Daily Echo*, 19 Nov. 1933.

Whether or not the Germans were justified in deciding to eliminate Jews, Pacifists, Communists and others from the privileges of the Reich, there is no justification whatever for premeditated cruelty in the execution of their design.[4]

The fundamental illogicality of this position appears most clearly in the second extract. How could 'elimination' from 'privileges' (i.e. from many types of employment and from the immunity from physical attack normal in a civilized community) be anything but 'cruelty' whether 'premeditated' or not? It is there, too, in the first—somewhat obscured by the implied suggestion, so attractive to the British reader, that people should be allowed to think what they like. However, it is, indeed, an inescapable and unfortunate fact that in practice there is no great gap between the assertion that it does not much matter what people think and the belief, sincerely held or otherwise, that is either not 'fair play' or just pointless to pass judgement on how they put their thoughts into action.

Finally, one other aspect of those early protests ought to be noted: what, if anything, could be done to halt, or mitigate, the attack upon German Jewry? This 'practical' side can be divided into three kinds of approach: (1) appeals to the supposed self-interest of the German Government; (2) more or less long-term plans for setting right the injustices which it was considered Germany had suffered as a result of the Versailles Treaty; (3) various forms of unilateral action, chiefly the boycott of German goods.[5] Of the others, the first was by far the most popular. Over and over again the dominant note was struck: nations which have previously persecuted the Jews have only brought about their own downfall. Lists of prominent German Jews, past and present, and their services to Germany, were quoted and requoted. Hitler was exhorted to pause in his destruction of a vital factor in Germany's prosperity before it was too late.[6] This argument was based on a double fallacy—apart from the material point of whether the German Government would ever pay attention to the British Press.

[4] *Nineteenth Century*, June 1933.
[5] This last will be discussed later in connexion with general Press reactions to Jewish attitudes in Britain, as will also the most practical form of protest— help for the refugees. See below, Chapter IV; Chapter VI.
[6] It is pointless to quote innumerable instances. A good example is the headline 'Hitler Will Be His Own Downfall' (*Daily Sketch*, 17 Mar. 1933); cf. also *Daily Record* (Glasgow), 23 Mar. 1933.

First, it failed to take into account the fundamental character of this new anti-Semitism. If pressed for a reply, the ardent Nazi might well have declared his readiness to perish through the absence of his Jewish fellow-citizens rather than be saved by their aid. Secondly, its very emphasis on Jewish prominence in Germany was itself part of the Nazi case: the Jews had captured all the best posts and it was the duty of a German patriot to end such an intolerable situation. It was hard for British journalists and political commentators to understand that the Jews were *not* being persecuted for alleged crimes or 'anti-social practices' (Streicher's performances were chiefly encouraged to arouse enthusiasm outside the party) but precisely *because of* their positive achievements in commerce, industry, and the professions. Thus, appeals to the national interest were indeed wide of the mark.

Almost as misguided were suggestions of the second type of which the following, appearing on the day of the April boycott, is a fair example: 'Protests and reprisals are superficial reactions. Our job is to reconstruct a world in which the Germany we admire can grow again.'[7] An approach of this kind arose, consciously or unconsciously, from the 'nothing but' type of analysis which has already been criticized. If German anti-Semitism had been 'nothing but' one of the unfortunate results of Versailles, it would have disappeared or at least become less fierce, if its cause had been done away with. It may indeed be true that much of the Nazi success can be explained by the strong sense of grievance at the 1919 Treaties existing in Germany. It may even be true that the particular form taken by German anti-Semitism in the nineteen twenties can be traced to the same cause. But the fact remains that the eventual abrogation of these Treaties, whether by force or by agreement, did not alter by one iota either the fate of German Jewry or that of a single member of the political opposition. And while it would certainly be unfair to expect that anyone should have foreseen in 1933 exactly what would be happening in the international field two years later, it is difficult not to blame the exponents of this approach for inexcusable *naïveté*—inexcusable ignorance of the sources. With sincere and well-meant protests, no less than with other Press comments, there was plenty of room for

---

[7] *Week-End Review*, 1 April 1933. The same day in *Time & Tide* there appeared an article with a very similar argument. There are many other examples; *Daily Mail*, 28 Dec. 1934, is particularly striking.

inaccuracies and inadequacies; for the same reluctance to accept and judge the facts as they actually presented themselves.

Lastly there was a minority which believed that *any* protest, implying, as it did, a right to intervene in Germany's domestic affairs, was fundamentally unjustifiable. On 3 October 1933 a mass protest meeting was held at the Albert Hall which was addressed by Professor Einstein, who had by then left Germany, and other speakers including Sir Austen Chamberlain, Sir William Beveridge, and the Bishop of Exeter. The *Evening News* proclaimed in a leading article:

The lecture is a piece of alien agitation on British soil; its promoters ask nothing better than that it shall make bad blood between this country and Germany. . . . Intelligent and patriotic people will stay carefully away . . . not because they necessarily approve of everything done under the Hitler regime, but because 'fair play' as they see it, means allowing the Germans to run their own country in their own way exactly as we demand the right to run our country in our own way. It will be time for British agitation when British interests are assailed.[8]

This is admittedly an extreme version, conditioned by a peculiar dislike of Professor Einstein. After five years of persecution, the *Spectator*, a journal of more temperate views, thought it right to make precisely the same point: 'except so far as the spirit under-lying the internal regime determines Germany's relationship to other countries, it is quite definitely not our business' and, in the discussion that ensued, it asked:

Could it be argued that we have the right or the power to intervene on their [the Jews] behalf, however strong our indignation or deep our sympathy? The phrase 'not our business' may be surrendered, but the fact that we cannot intervene in Germany's domestic affairs remains a fact.[9]

Political slants, personal prejudices, and even considerations of humanity apart, could either the *Evening News* or the *Spectator* really have brought themselves to comment in this way if they had understood how this 'domestic matter' was a true indication of Nazi character and plans, plans which had inevitably to involve matters not at all 'domestic'—indeed the whole world? This question is neither rhetorical nor unreasonable—some of the Press did succeed in understanding just that.

[8] *Evening News*, 3 Oct. 1933 (leader); cf. leader—27 Sept. 1933.
[9] *Spectator*, 28 Jan. and 4 Feb. 1938.

II

The Nuremberg Decrees

THE main difficulty for the British Press during the first two and a half years of Nazi rule was to appreciate correctly the extent to which anti-Semitism had official sanction in its political manifestations, although the strength of the hatred towards the Jew, from strictly official sources, gradually began to be understood. The fact that the Jew, as such, was still the equal of the Aryan in the eyes of the existing constitution of the Reich gave rise to illusions in the most varied circles. When the *Manchester Guardian*, on one occasion, protested at the dismissal of Jewish employees apparently exempt under existing regulations, it invoked the principle that even such a proceeding as active anti-Semitism on the part of the State should be conducted by the rule of law.[1] Essentially the same thought was expressed more plainly by the *Catholic Times*:

It would be far better, even from the German standpoint, to come to a proper understanding with the Jewish leaders, and to draw up a character of rights and duties, mutually agreed, and binding on both sides. In this way the two races could at least live in peace side by side, without this constant persecution and bad feeling . . .[2]

It was not yet really understood that mentally, so to speak, the Jew had long been outlawed—whatever might be his 'official' position. Nor could it have been clear that, in a very important sense, the Nazis themselves were bound to agree with this argument—a dangerous one, incidentally, for any anti-Nazi case.

The Nazis undoubtedly *preferred* to act within a legalistic framework wherever possible. They felt that this was more acceptable to the ingrained instincts of the majority of their subjects. Some years later, the Commander of an S.A. unit operating in the streets

---

[1] *Manchester Guardian Weekly*, 1 Jan. 1934.
[2] *Catholic Times*, 13 Sept. 1935.

of Vienna was to point out in a report to his headquarters, with commendable perspicuity, that the local population had been displaying a negative attitude to anti-Semitic actions mainly because they did not appear to be included under any law.[3] As soon as the occasion demanded, the Nazis were quick enough to cover themselves with the appropriate formulas. In the early period of their rule there had been, perhaps, room for doubt as to their future intentions, room for the possibility of supposing that their 'full' programme for the Jews might not have been much more than useful election propaganda. In 1935, however, a series of decrees, passed immediately after the Party congress at Nuremberg, removed ambiguities, repaired legal omissions, and made the holding of optimistic views considerably more difficult. Henceforth the population would be divided into two classes—'Reich citizens' and 'State subjects'. Only the first class would enjoy the privileges normally associated with citizenship. Membership of it would be granted only to those who could prove (*a*) Aryan ancestry; (*b*) individual loyalty to the Party State. Members of the second class could not hold any official position or employment, take part in elections, or serve in the armed forces.[4] Regulations defining the term 'Aryan ancestry' were issued on 14 November.[5] The second Nuremberg decree, with its accompanying regulations, prohibited marriages and extra-marital intercourse according to the same principles, the flying of the national flag by non-Aryans, similarly defined, and their employing Aryan female servants of less than forty-five years of age.[6] There followed a mixture of prohibitions and exclusions. One point should not be lost sight of: however small their immediate practical significance might have been, after 15 November the term 'non-Aryan', which they all employed, had acquired a legal and constitutional meaning. Similarly, while the first two decrees did not alter existing practice very greatly, they did give it a legal form which admitted of little individual interpretation within Germany and equally little individual speculation outside her borders. German anti-Semitism was no longer some kind of tactics on the part of her leaders, or an expression of over-

[3] 'An Official Nazi Report on the November Pogroms in Vienna', *Yad va-Shem Bulletin* II (1957), p. 28 (with photostat copy). S.A.—Sturm Abteilung, i.e. 'Storm Detachment'; cf. S.S.—Schutzstaffen, i.e. 'Defence Formations'.

[4] RGBL I (1935), 1146. The two classes were *Reichshoeriger* and *Stadtsangehoeriger* respectively.

[5] RGBL I (1935), 1333.   [6] RGBL I (1935), 1146-7; 1334.

enthusiasm on the part of their followers: it was procedure established by law and embodied in the constitution.

Under these circumstances, it might be thought remarkable that among some of the responsible sections of the Press there was a by no means unambiguous appreciation of this new situation, and some uncertainty as to which aspect merited the greatest emphasis. This uncertainty is well illustrated in the following comment by the *New Statesman*:

The Jews are already pariahs; they are now to be subjected to further penalties. Marriage or intercourse between a Jew and an 'Aryan' are made punishable offences, and any such marriage contracted abroad will be null and void in Germany. No Jew is to be allowed to employ an 'Aryan' under the age of 45 as a domestic servant. These bans, together with the many others already in force *and with the deprivation of citizenship* [our italics] are what the Fuehrer calls 'ways and means by which it is possible for the German people to discover a tolerable relationship with the Jews'.[7]

The putting of the deprivation of citizenship into a final parenthesis is strange indeed. It ought to have been clear enough that, whereas the reference to Aryan servants was merely the last in a long series of insults, and the restrictions on marriage not much more than the legalization of existing practice, it was the deprivation of citizenship which was the one clause of fundamental importance, likely to bring about the most serious consequences.

An even stranger sense of perspective is noticeable at the other end of the intellectual spectrum. The *Tablet*, after mentioning, with a certain *naïveté*, that 'three new bills became Acts without being put to the vote', consecrated its leader to the provision about flying the national flag.[8] But the fact that the Nuremberg legislation merely made some particular types of 'unofficial' persecution 'official' should not have blinded serious observers to the new general development: the reign of anti-Semitism as by law established. The chief feature writer of the *News Chronicle*, for instance, doubted very much if Hitler (whose National Socialism 'as a doctrine'—whatever that meant—'had no chance of survival')

---

[7] *New Statesman*, 27 Sept. 1935. Cf. *Daily Herald*, 17 Sept. 1935, where stress is on Aryan servant prohibition ('60,000 Women lose jobs by new Nazi law') and citizenship exclusion is completely ignored.

[8] *Tablet*, 21 Sept. 1935.

would compel a drastic enforcement of the new laws passed at Nuremberg. Many Germans of the purest Aryan blood are certainly of the same opinion. In any case, apart from the stigma, Jews are not likely to be worse off materially than they were before the Reichstag said ditto to General Goering's promulgation, except under the article which forbids them to employ non-Jewish servants. . . .[9]

The most striking example of confusion among those who ought to have known better is to be found in the statement in the usually well informed *Economist* that there was 'practically no anti-Jewish feeling in Germany other than among the Nazi leaders', that the decrees had aroused 'little public interest', and that their practical importance was 'very slight'.[10]

Odder still, even the *Manchester Guardian* did not realize that the Nazi programme for the Jews had reached an entirely new stage of development. Its leader on the Congress was entitled 'Hitler Marks Time', and that is what it believed he was doing, both in home and in foreign policy. The new legislation only gave legal effect to what was fast becoming a reality. 'The general effect of Hitler's speech [to the special session of the Reichstag which passed the two decrees] has been to start nothing fresh . . . to leave things very much as they are in Germany.'[11] Three weeks later, it made the belated admission that the new laws 'had hardly received the attention outside Germany that they deserved' [because of the Abyssinian crisis] and that the opinion that they only legalized an existing status was no more than 'partly correct'.[12]

In contrast, a more realistic standpoint was adopted by other papers. *The Times* (apart from its idiosyncracy of occasionally calling the anti-Semite extremists 'left wing'[13]) had no doubts at all about the meaning of Nuremberg. In the long run, it pointed out, the new ghetto legislation might 'mean more to Germany than any manifestation by her in foreign affairs. Nothing like the complete disinheritance and segregation of Jewish citizens, now announced, has been heard since mediaeval times.'[14] The *Daily Tele-*

[9] *News Chronicle*, 26 Sept. 1935 (A. J. Cummings).
[10] *Economist*, 21 Sept. 1935; 23 Nov. 1935.
[11] *Manchester Guardian*, 17 Sept. 1935. In its news columns that day it was uncertain whether the new laws would lead to 'a modern form of the ghetto', leave the situation unchanged, or actually improve it.
[12] *Manchester Guardian*, 5 Oct. 1935.
[13] *The Times* ('The Year in Review'), 1 Jan. 1936.
[14] *The Times*, 17 Sept. 1935. Cf. of course the excellent analysis of 8 Nov. 1935 to which reference was made in Chapter I.

graph, in a very similar tone, stressed the contradiction between this legislation and Hitler's complaints about the alleged ill-treatment of the German minority in Memel.[15] Much the same view was expressed by many provincial newspapers of which the *Liverpool Post* leader 'An Affront to Humanity' is a fair example.[16] Finally, it would be wrong to forget the *Daily Worker* which, in its determination ever to be first in the 'fight against fascism', exaggerated somewhat when it claimed that 'throughout history there is no parallel to this cold-blooded measure. . . .'[17] There was a marked and rather curious division of opinion on Nuremberg, which did not by any means follow customary divisions of political, group, or social interests.

But the story of 'constitutional anti-Semitism' is not of course completed by an account of the Nuremberg Decrees. From the period when their publication was being foreshadowed until the autumn of 1938, when affairs reached a new crisis, the German Government was attempting 'to establish legal and settled relations between Jews and Aryan Germans'.[18] The Jewish question was to be 'solved' not by violence but, ostensibly at least, by the due process of law. Thus the streams of new regulations were all in the spirit of the Decrees, whatever might have been their actual date. Furthermore, side by side with these regulations should be placed their interpretation and application, the initiative of this or that local official, decisions of the courts, and special projects of a Governmental or semi-Governmental nature undertaken in that spirit and with the same purpose. Finally, instances of 'spontaneous action' are not wanting even in this 'legal' period. It follows that Press approaches to some of these 'practical' applications should be noted before one comes to a conclusion about divisions of opinion on the fundamental nature or otherwise of the Nuremberg Decrees themselves.

A group of events in the summer of 1935 will serve as an example of 'official', 'semi-official', and 'unofficial' anti-Semitism. At that time a noticeable movement of Jews was taking place from various parts of Germany to Berlin where the laws against them had not been quite so strictly enforced as in the provinces, and where they hoped rather better to escape the notice of the authori-

---

[15] *Daily Telegraph*, 17 Sept. 1935.   [16] *Liverpool Post*, 17 Sept. 1935.
[17] *Daily Worker*, 17 Nov. 1935.
[18] Cf. J. Tenenbaum, *Race & Reich*, New York (1956), pp. 3–4.

ties. In this they were unsuccessful. On 15 July there was an outbreak of street violence reminiscent of the spring of 1933. On 19
July Rear-Admiral Von Levetzow, the head of the Berlin Police
who held the traditional police attitude to all disorders, was replaced by the (in *The Times* sense) 'radical' Count Wolf von Helldorf. On 31 July the Berlin Municipality forbade the further settlement of Jews within its boundaries, and, on 15 August, Julius
Streicher paid his first professional visit to the city and addressed
a large rally on his favourite topic. These events disturbed the
comparative calm of what had come to be taken as 'normality' by
the Press, and they were thus fairly widely reported.

On the factual aspect not much need be said. Correspondents of
the principal national dailies differed only on comparatively unimportant details; their reports, taking first the night of 15
July, gave a more or less identical picture of what had taken place.
Much of the rest of the Press made use of Reuter. But in that ill-
defined territory where news and comment tend to mingle the
situation was rather different. First, the type of heading selected
by the provincial Press of headlines to the Reuter dispatch of
15 July is instructive:

(1) *Yorkshire Post:*
ANTI-JEWISH OUTBURST IN BERLIN'S WEST END
WILD SCENES OUTSIDE CINEMA AND CAFES:
PATRONS BEATEN UP

(2) *Northern Whig*, Belfast:
BERLIN ATTACKS ON JEWS
Sequel to Anti-Semitic Film Scene

(3) *Eastern Evening News:*
ANTI-SEMITIC OUTBREAK IN BERLIN
Press Incident Leads to Disorders
Jews beaten and assaulted

In the first example the obvious intention is to express emotion
at what was happening and to expect it from the reader, while
the second indicates no interest in possible reactions. The third

stands somewhere between the other two.[19] The three papers chosen are part of the staid and solid (one could say stolid) tradition of British provincial journalism. The problem of a different *idiom* did not arise. The variation shown in the three examples quoted could be paralleled from other sources, not only provincial ones. German excesses were reported but a noticeable section had ceased to be very excited by them. The *Evening News* was content to note that 'nobody in this country pretends that Germany today enjoys complete civil and religious liberty'.[20]

Secondly there was the usual interpretation inserted into the story, which although not strictly editorial opinion could hardly be ignored. There is a curious example of this in *The Times*. On 16 July the riots were described as a

deliberate reprisal [for the drift to Berlin], intended to put the Jews forcibly in their place but also fully in keeping with the present wave of fanatical extremism which derived every encouragement from Dr. Goebbels' recent Templehof speech.

On 17 July 'our correspondent' thought that

Last night's anti-Jewish riot seems to have made a rather unpleasant impression in official quarters here, for an outbreak on such a scale was neither expected nor intended. There is certain evidence for the theory that instructions had been issued for a more or less orderly demonstration . . . under discipline. . . . The police at first were present in small numbers and clearly had instructions to look with tolerance on what should have been a more or less harmless parade.

What did *The Times* really think? It is not easy to say. There is a marked tendency to differentiate between leaders and followers —at least between 'extremists' (or 'radicals') and 'moderates'. The same attitude appears in the report on the appointment of Helldorf, described as a 'notoriously radical Nazi':

The *pretext* [our italics] for the admiral's retirement has undoubtedly been found in Tuesday's anti-Jewish riots. Whether he offended by intervening too little or interfering too much is uncertain.

---

[19] The *Northern Whig* printed only about a third of the dispatch. In fairness, it should be noted that it had to deal with troubles nearer home. On the same night there had been five deaths in religious riots in the centre of Belfast. But there the police had not taken sides, a contrast which no newspaper thought of stressing.

[20] *Evening News*, 28 Oct. 1935.

Helldorf's own anti-Semitic record is only mentioned very briefly.[21] However, there were stranger comments than those and in stranger places. The Liberal *Star* described Helldorf (twice) as a 'dashing Storm-Troop leader', expatiated on the 'distinction' of his record in the First World War and referred to his anti-Semitism as follows: 'In 1931 Von Helldorf was arrested in connection with big anti-semitic disorders [*sic*] when police beat Nazi demonstrators with rubber truncheons'.[22] The 'disorders' were a parade led by Helldorf in person on the occasion of the Jewish New Year when worshippers were attacked and beaten on the way to synagogue.[23]

Was active anti-Semitism or 'extremism' as important for Hitler in 1935 as in 1933? This was the real question posed by every event of this kind after the 'revolutionary' period was clearly over—seizure of power and 1934 purge included. Was it necessary, or reasonable, to stress this aspect in reporting or commenting on Jewish events? The *Daily Herald* had no doubts at all. Its issue of 17 July had the unambiguous headline: 'Nazis New Pogrom ordered by Hitler' and it characterized the appointment of Helldorf as a 'Fresh Jew-baiting move',[24] an opinion shared, in effect, by, among others, the *Evening Standard* and the *Daily Telegraph* —though their expression of it was not so forcible.[25] The *Daily Express* comment was similar but very much shorter, perhaps an example of tendencies in space policy previously remarked upon.[26]

After the appointment of Helldorf, violence of varying kind and intensity continued.[27] Its culmination was the municipal ban, and the Streicher meeting. *The Times*, in producing a short but, as is to be expected, excellent summary of Streicher's speech, made use of a phrase which implied that even the Governor of Franconia's official appearance did not perhaps have complete Government sanction: 'Contrary to Nazi practice with well-known leaders, the speech was not broadcast'.[28]

There may have been a thousand and one reasons for this omission—not one is suggested or guessed at. One is left with what

[21] *The Times*, 20 July 1935.   [22] *Star*, 19 July 1935.
[23] *The Times*, 14 Sept. 1931.   [24] *Daily Herald*, 20 July 1935.
[25] *Evening Standard*, 19 July 1935; *Daily Telegraph*, 20 July 1935.
[26] *Daily Express*, 20 July 1935. Cf. p. 17 above.
[27] *The New Statesman*, 3 Aug. 1935, seemed slightly surprised that Helldorf had failed to stop the outrages.
[28] *The Times*, 17 Aug. 1935.

does appear in the paragraph—i.e. the contents of Streicher's speech—with the obvious inference: the Government was hedging on this particular public expression of anti-Semitism. Most of the other leading newspapers reported the occasion in greater or lesser detail. But there was a strange and unexpected comment in the *New Statesman*:

In the *Sportspalast* in Berlin last week, Herr Streicher arranged for some twenty thousand people to be publicly incited against Jews and alien pests and especially foreign newspaper correspondents. Amateur Jew-baiting in the summer resorts of Bavaria continues to be a silly season pastime . . . but, as Dr. Schacht says, for Germany the religious strife is 'of much greater importance than the Jewish question'.[29]

Evaluations are of course matters of personal judgement, but to most intelligent observers this particular evaluation by an intelligent journal must have shown some lack of proportion, not to mention factual accuracy, since the 'amateur Jew-baiting' displayed not a few professional touches.[30]

In regard to the municipal ban there is not a great deal to be said. The foreshadowing of such a measure and the form it actually took was reported without any unexpected comment— except that the *Sunday Times* still managed somehow to place it in the category of 'religious strife'.[31] One gets the impression that, in contrast with all else that was happening, it was felt that this was a comparatively mild and unimportant measure. The Press felt that it was facing a new wave of anti-Semitism, a new wealth of incidents from among which it certainly had the full right to choose those which it judged to be of greater significance. But was this really a new wave? On the fundamental question, the *Manchester Guardian* stood in a class by itself. A few days after the first outburst, it was quoting from German sources: '*Anti-semitism, it is stated, is fundamental to the new Germany*. It is there-fore nonsense to speak of a renewal of this sentiment.'[32] Four days

---

[29] *New Statesman*, 24 Aug. 1935.

[30] See, e.g., report in *Morning Post*, 7 Aug. 1935, of how 350 Jews, including the old and sick, were turned out into the street in the early hours on the order of a burgomeister (surely not an 'amateur' in this context) 'after a week of terror'. 'Left' and 'Right' Press attitudes here present an unusual contrast.

[31] *Sunday Times*, 21 July 1935.

[32] *Manchester Guardian*, 18 July 1935; cf. a similar evaluation (among many) on 11 Mar. 1937.

later it gave the most unequivocal evaluation to be found of the whole situation:

The Nazi spirit

Those who hoped that the Nazis would grow more 'moderate' and therefore more 'reasonable', as time went on will have been disillusioned by the events of the last few days. These events have shown the Nazis to be just as 'extreme' as they were when they came into power . . . the truth all along has been that these excesses are the more obvious manifestations of the Terror and that the Terror is organized and organic: organized by the Nazi leaders and an organic part of the political system they have established. . . .

There have been differences of opinion amongst them as to whether it is advisable to have Jews mobbed in Berlin or only in the country towns. . . . But there is no disagreement as to whether these activities should cease or not; there is simply no question of their ceasing. . . .

At least one other interesting aspect of the Nuremberg period was the attempt to justify the 'legal' solution of the Jewish question which this period symbolized, in the eyes of the German people as a whole. One such attempt took place in 1937: an exhibition entitled *Der ewige Jude* which was opened on the fourteenth anniversary of Hitler's abortive try for power in 1923—the so-called Beer Hall Putsch.[33] Just as in 1935, the clearest report is to be found in the *Manchester Guardian*, which was one of the very few papers to print the declaration of the organizers of the exhibition themselves, that 'the exhibition is educational in purpose and will show particularly why it was necessary to introduce the Nuremberg laws'.[34]

The Times was much less explicit,[35] while from a great deal of Press comment one merely got the impression that this was no more than yet another rather nasty aberration. A stronger and even less justifiable impression could be gained from the comments made about another famous German exhibition held in the same year—that to celebrate the inauguration of the new 'House

[33] The name of the exhibition was translated in some reports as 'The Wandering Jew', in others as 'The Eternal Jew'—the latter is of course correct. It is surprising that *The Times* printed the former version. Can it have been due to the subconscious belief that an adjective so expressive of antiquity as the latter could scarcely have borne a derogatory meaning—even for the Nazis?

[34] *Manchester Guardian*, 27 Oct. 1937. Cf. *Observer*, 7 Nov. 1937, which gives a similar but less clear impression.

[35] *The Times*, 9 Nov. 1937.

of German Art' in Munich. This was a truly extraordinary affair in its own right. It was opened by Hitler himself, in the presence of his chief ministers and of members of the Diplomatic Corps. His address fell into two main sections: the first dealt with the deleterious influence of the Jews upon German art in the pre-Nazi era; the second consisted of some rather original art criticism. There can be no doubt at all that the Nazi leadership considered the occasion as being of the very first importance.[36] The emphasis of Press reports was, not surprisingly, on the second section: Hitler's best-known attack on his particular concept of 'modern art', such as his opinion that 'artists who paint purple seas and green skies suffer from eye disease'.[37] One writer, while disclaiming any support for Hitler's general standpoint, could not help mentioning his own conviction that 'Surrealism' was 'a gross attempt to commercialise the nightmare'.[38] But there is little sign of any suggestion that these remarks of Hitler were anything more than the outpouring of idiosyncrasies by one in the happy position of being able to compel others to listen to them. Even the *Manchester Guardian* leader on the subject limited itself to a slight lifting of the eyebrow.[39] There was no plain understanding that the whole affair was an integral stage in a campaign which fitted into the general framework of Nazi Jewish policy. In fact, of course, it proved to be an example of that miscellany of discrimination against Jews in lesser or greater spheres of cultural activity which had varied from exclusion from amateur choirs in 1933 to exclusion from the film industry in 1935.

A fortnight later the position became rather clearer, and theory was turned into practice. By order of General Goering, the Minister of Education was empowered to 'clean up' all the public art collections in Prussia in accordance with the guiding lines laid down by Hitler in his speech at Munich.[40] In spite of an official act of this kind, there were some then who did not see the con-

---

[36] Among those present were: F.M. von Blomberg (Defence Minister), Gen. Goering (Air Minister), Baron von Neurath (Foreign Minister), Dr. Goebbels (Propaganda Minister), the French and Italian Ambassadors, and members of the Government of Belgium and of the Irish Free State. (*The Times* and *Daily Telegraph*, 19 July 1937.)

[37] This is all there is to be found even in the *Daily Worker*, 27 July 1937.

[38] *Morning Post*, 20 July 1937.   [39] *Manchester Guardian*, 20 July 1937.

[40] The legal basis for all acts of this kind had been the establishment of a Reich Chamber of Culture (RGBL I (1933), 661) from which all Jews were of course excluded, i.e. actually or potentially from the practice of all the arts.

nexion. One leader writer thought that the speech had 'presumably inspired General Goering to his purge of the galleries', while another, in the course of his comments on 'The New Art Purge', did not mention the speech.[41] They did not see that the Munich speech was as much in the spirit of the Nuremberg Decrees as the *Ewige Jude* exhibition. The intention was not only to attack the Jew, but also to explain why his complete exclusion (in this case from all cultural activities) was both justifiable and essential. At that time the British Press found it hard to understand such singleness of purpose—unhappily easy though it became at a later date.

Finally, it is useful to take a glance at some Press comments on a variety of miscellaneous rules and regulations during this period of 'constitutional anti-Semitism', and on the situation as a whole before, and after, the Nuremberg Decrees. With the obvious exception of the citizenship decree itself, nothing strikingly new had arisen. It is not, therefore, surprising that the Press tended to report fresh examples in a more or less matter-of-fact manner. Perhaps the one striking exception was when the sphere of the Press itself was invaded and Jews were excluded from the whole field of newspaper publishing.[42] This did earn headlines in a number of British papers, though the main point of the order was not always at once apparent.[43]

Some special attention was also paid to the various financial restrictions being placed on the Jews and to the beginnings of their exclusion from commercial or industrial fields. Sometimes this development was not properly understood. When Dr. Schacht told the German Government that serious economic consequences would follow any application of the Nuremberg Decrees to the industrial field, the *Manchester Guardian* was well advised to stress that his warning could at best bring about only a futile and hollow reprieve.[44] Even when the facts were known comment was often scarcely appropriate. It was here that *The Times* produced the strangest instance of its occasional inclination

[41] *Glasgow Herald*, 6 Aug. 1937; *Western Mail*, 5 Aug. 1937.
[42] The first regulation in the series was RGBL I (1933), 713.
[43] Cf. *Daily Express* and *Daily Herald* for 26 Apr. 1935, where the emphasis is on the 'strangling of rival newspapers' and on the 'banning of Church influence' respectively. The order certainly had those results too but there can hardly be any doubt that its main purpose was against Jewish participation.
[44] *Manchester Guardian*, 6 Nov. 1935.

to equate active anti-Semitism with some sort of radicalism. When the Nazi Party (not, be it said, strictly speaking, the Government) seized a Jewish-owned light engineering firm in Thuringia, the following headlines appeared:

NAZI EXPERIMENT IN SOCIALISM
JEWISH BUSINESS TAKEN OVER

and there was nothing in the ensuing paragraph to indicate that any irony was intended.[45] To show that there is no discrimination here against a 'right-wing' example, it should be compared to a passage from the *Star*, equally inept in its own way, which appeared not so very long after its morning colleague, the *News Chronicle*, had given a headline to the forcible retirement of seventy-five judges through the operation of the Aryan Paragraph. The title of the feature article from which this passage is taken was 'Berlin is Dull'. Had there been a cross-heading to the relevant paragraph it could well have been 'Not So Badly Treated':

What of the Jews? I met one who for years was a judge and who served through the war. He is not so badly treated, compulsorily retired, but on full pension: though he is a writer, he can no longer publish a book. He's only half a Jew, but even so he is now a 'second class citizen'.

And why was Berlin 'dull'? Because the *Star* writer found 'the appearance of its West End deceptive'. 'Berlin', he said, summing up his impressions, 'was as a holiday place, damned dull'.[46]

More than the news of any regulation, the greatest impact on the Press, before the appearance of the Nuremberg Decrees themselves, was of course made by the announcement that some steps of this kind were about to be taken. It is interesting to compare some headlines and sub-headlines printed that day. These do not include those which have been, and will be, frequently discussed, i.e. *The Times*, the *Daily Telegraph*, and the *Manchester Guardian*. Here are eight in alphabetical order:[47]

Daily Herald
JEWS CANNOT BE GERMAN
VILLAGE BAN 'NOT WANTED HERE'

---

[45] *The Times*, 24 Dec. 1935.　　[46] *Star*, 3 Jan. 1936.
[47] Daily papers all of Monday 29 April, Sunday papers of 28 April. The announcement was on the Saturday, enabling the Sunday papers, as rather strangely on many other occasions in the thirties, to scoop the dailies.

Daily Mail
GERMANY AND JEWS
MAY NOT VOTE OR SERVE IN ARMED FORCES

Daily Mirror
UNHEALTHY BARRED FROM GERMAN CITIZENSHIP
NEW CASTE WILL BE SET UP

Observer
NO JEWS IN THE GERMAN ARMY
NEW CITIZENSHIP LAW

People
NEW GERMAN BLOW AT JEWS
DENIED CITIZENSHIP

Referee
NAZIS' NEW WAR ON RELIGION
JEWS TO BE DEPRIVED OF ALL CIVIC RIGHTS
MANY NUNS ARRESTED

Sunday Pictorial
NO JEW CAN BE A GERMAN
NOT ALLOWED TO HOIST REICH FLAG

Sunday Times
JEWS BANNED FROM CITIZENSHIP
HITLER TO DEPRIVE THEM OF VOTES

On six out of these eight specimens of the popular and Sunday Press, the announcement made an impression broadly consonant with the facts. The *Referee* and the *Daily Mirror*, however, preferred, on this occasion, the somewhat unusual to the strictly accurate. The *Referee*'s headline was simply incorrect: whatever the new definition of citizenship touched, it would not be 'religion'—the editor of the only Jewish-owned non-communal paper in Britain must surely have heard of the Aryan Paragraph?—while its second sub-headline was quite irrelevant. The *Daily Mirror* did not emphasize the basic aspect, and its sub-headline states an interesting possible social consequence but scarcely the immediate

major implication. The reasons for those two individualist devia-
tions are not, in themselves, important. The important thing is
that it was precisely these two papers which gave a real prominence
to their particular interpretation. Put in the way that they put it,
the item was judged to have news value and to be worth extra
space. In its plainer form it was well enough reported, indeed, but
the layout employed was no more striking than that for a more or
less ordinary item of home or foreign news. (This opinion can
claim no *statistical* support whatever. It is not 'scientific'—in the
sense of a modern Press or public opinion survey. Nevertheless,
within its limitations, it is perfectly valid. It merely confines itself
to stressing the fact that the editors of several leading national
newspapers did not consider the importance of this new step foreshadowed by the German Government, when measured relatively,
say, to the 'sanctions' crisis, to be particularly great.)

Aside from the Decrees themselves, there was a marked tendency over these two years or so for the whole German Jewish
question to drop into the background, and for its full meaning to
become rather blurred. Irritation at the publicity given by the
B.B.C. to a protest meeting in Hyde Park, for example, produced
the following comment:

Nobody in this country pretends that Germany today enjoys complete
civil and religious liberty. There are few who do not deplore much that
the Nazi regime has done, and especially its treatment of Jews and certain religious bodies. But do not deplorable things happen in other
countries?

The Nazi regime came into power in Germany through one of the
most bloodless revolutions in history. No regime anywhere commands
such enthusiasm from the nation it rules.

But what of Russia . . .?[48]

Another bizarre (but 'respectable') opinion was that

In certain respects the psychology of the new Germany—curious as the
contrast may be with certain other aspects—has grown more humane.
How Jew-baiting and Red-baiting are to be reconciled with growing
humaneness only Time can show. But the humaneness may win. . . . At
first sight Queen Victoria may seem to have nothing in common with
Hitler. But she rehabilitated the throne, and, more than that, she
seemed to multitudes a living guarantee of fundamental decencies in

[48] *Evening News*, 28 Oct. 1935.

government that they prized and needed. Hitler's role in Germany, odd as the comparison may sound, is not very dissimilar.[49]

Much the same (though less oddly put) was said in the *Spectator* (not editorially),[50] and elsewhere,[51] and was being constantly rebutted by the *Manchester Guardian*.[52]

In one respect, however, the inadequacies of the serious commentators did have a kind of justification. For in a sense the problems of this period were themselves unreal. Reality began on 7 November 1938 when the legalities of Nuremberg were abandoned, and the final phase was initiated for the Jews under Nazi rule. On that day, a young Polish Jew named Hershel Grynzpan living in Paris and brooding on the fate of his parents in Germany, attempted to assassinate the German Ambassador and in fact shot the Third Secretary, Ernst vom Rath.[53] On 9 November, vom Rath died of his wounds. That night, the so-called 'Crystal Night',[54] and the following day, scenes of anti-Semitic violence, surpassing in extent and organization everything that had gone before, broke out all over Germany and Austria. Between 12 and 28 November a number of decrees were issued intending to 'punish' German Jewry for the murder, and complete their economic and social destruction. The best-known and most important were an 'Atonement Fine' of one billion Rm. (£83 million),[55] a prohibition on Jews to engage in any kind of trade as owners, managers, or in executive positions,[56] an order that the Jews themselves must repair their damaged premises foregoing all insurance claims,[57] and an authorization to designated officials to 'exclude Jews from certain localities and to ban them from appearing in public at certain hours'.[58] These regulations, together with all the legislation that had gone before, meant the virtual outlawry of the Jew in Germany and Austria (and, soon after, in Czechoslovakia); that is, in the centre of what was thought of as the civilized world. They

[49] John Murray, Principal of University College, Exeter, in the *Hibbert Journal*, July 1937.
[50] *Spectator*, 16 July 1937.   [51] E.g. in *Daily Telegraph*, 27 Apr. 1937.
[52] E.g. on 11 Mar. 1937.
[53] Incidentally, there were some extraordinary variations in the spelling of the young man's name. Furthest from the truth was the *Daily Mail*, 9 Nov. 1938.
[54] This was the poetical German name for a night of broken glass.
[55] RGBL I (1938), 1579.   [56] RGBL I (1938), 1580.
[57] RGBL I (1938), 1581.
[58] RGBL I (1938), 1676. A good account of these events is given by L. Kochan, *Pogrom 10 November 1938*, London (1957).

meant 'the factual and final end of Jewry in Germany, its absolute annihilation'.[59]

Another event, though in itself unconnected with any Jewish question, must not be forgotten. Less than two months previously, Europe had been on the brink of war over German claims to certain areas of Czechoslovakia. After a conference of the powers at Munich had substantially agreed to those claims, the British Prime Minister, Neville Chamberlain, saw fit to have a further, private talk with Hitler and, as a result, to participate in a separate joint statement expressing a common readiness to solve 'other questions' affecting the two countries 'by the method of consultation' and to strive to 'assure the peace of Europe'.[60] In other words, the Prime Minister thought it right to make a special public declaration of his belief in Hitler's subsequent good behaviour, thus proclaiming that Britain would in some sense be responsible for it. Press reactions, therefore, to the events connected with the Crystal Night could not but be closely related to the general international situation, and to the broad division between those who supported the Government's policy of appeasement and those who did not.

Initial reactions to the Crystal Night were not unexpected. It can never be emphasized too often that the dominant note struck by the British Press in the presence of Nazi anti-Semitism was one of genuine moral outrage.[61] So on this particular occasion too, both the presentation of the news itself and the accompanying comments left no doubt whatever about the fundamental attitude of the Press: murder was a crime which could not be condoned; nor could mass revenge on an innocent community. This point was made with equal force in numerous leading articles by writers with varying political and social interests.[62] Perhaps the *Manchester Guardian* put it most succinctly: certainly vom Rath had had no personal responsibility for the persecutions,

[59] *Das Schwarze Korps*, 22 Nov. 1938. For the full passage and comments, see below, p. 97.

[60] *Documents on German Foreign Policy 1918–1945* (Series D), London (HMSO) II (1950), p. 1017. For an account of the talk, and of some reactions to it, see *Survey of International Affairs 1938*, London (1951), II, pp. 447–50.

[61] An outstanding example was a special fifteen-page supplement in *Time & Tide* including contributions from Bernard Shaw, Norman Angell, and Harold Nicolson (26 Nov.).

[62] See, e.g., leaders in the *Daily Telegraph*, the *Daily Herald*, and the *News Chronicle* on 11 Nov. 1938.

but, since all will agree that a great wrong was committed in thus holding one man answerable for something he had never done, so also the Jewish people can have no responsibility for the crime of a despairing youth of seventeen.[63]

Unfortunately, however, it is equally true that a fair proportion of the explanations of the *causes* of the Crystal Night were as familiar as was the reaction to those events. Even though the majority were by then sufficiently convinced that little of this nature could be 'spontaneous' or 'unofficial' in Nazi Germany,[64] there were still very many who did not understand, any more than they had in 1933, that it was not enough to point with disgust or surprise at the obvious responsibility of the Government. Any explanation which ignored the repeated declarations of the Nazi leaders was bound to be grossly inadequate. Such an explanation, for example, was that of so responsible a provincial organ as the *Leeds Mercury* which considered these events to be evidence of 'wild hysteria' and a 'complete lack of control' on the part of the Nazis.[65] And it was more than inadequate that a weekly of the standing of the *Economist* should describe these same events as 'incomprehensible'.[66] Oddest of all perhaps was the following *Daily Express* comment:

Pray for Tolerance

Sad and wretched is the plight of the Jews in Germany. Everywhere the sympathy of the public will go out to them. They are now the victims of this unfortunate and probably demented boy, seventeen years of age, who killed a German diplomat in Paris.

He has furnished to the enemies of his people an occasion and a motive, but certainly not a justification, for persecution and spoliation of the race everywhere.

At such a moment as this, we in Britain have got to reiterate the virtue of tolerance. We must dedicate ourselves anew to worship at that shrine.[67]

---

[63] *Manchester Guardian*, 10 Nov. 1938.

[64] Occasionally this conviction could have been more forcibly expressed, indeed:

'It is impossible', one leader writer remarked, 'to acquit the Nazi *regime* of all complicity in the criminal acts of terrorism against the Jews which have succeeded the murder of Herr vom Rath in the Paris Embassy'. (*North Eastern Daily Gazette*, 11 Nov. 1938.)

[65] *Leeds Mercury*, 19 Nov. 1938; cf. *Midland Daily Telegraph*, 11 Nov. 1938, which called it the action of 'madmen'.

[66] *Economist*, 12 Nov. 1938.   [67] *Daily Express*, 11 Nov. 1938.

Of whom were the Jews of Germany and Austria the victims? Surely, according to the simplest estimate, of the mobs who, however directed or inspired, gave the Crystal Night its name. If the phrase 'spoliation of the race everywhere' was anything more than a piece of singularly unhappy rhetoric, it could only imply that this particular outburst of persecution would spread beyond the confines of German rule. In other words, the murder was 'an occasion and a motive' (though 'not a justification') for the looting of Jewish shops not only in Berlin and Vienna but also in London and Manchester. Indeed this does seem to be the implication, since the one conceivable meaning of the final paragraph is that only by 'dedication at the shrine of tolerance' could the British people, too, restrain themselves from such actions. This inference is supported by the headline in the Sunday version of the *Express*: 'A Word of Warning to British Jews'.[68] What heavy consequences are here ascribed to the deed of a 'probably demented boy'! Certainly, the details of the careful planning which went into the organization of the Crystal Night and its aftermath were not to be known in their entirety until the Nuremberg Trials revealed certain police instructions, and the remarkable discussions held under Goering's chairmanship at the Air Ministry on 12 November.[69] Nevertheless a great deal *was* known, not least the Nazi record of the previous five years, and the majority of commentators saw clearly enough that the Paris crime had merely served as a convenient pretext; while to speak of the Jews as *Grynzpan's* victims was to make use of barren metaphor.[70]

One of the fullest expositions of this point is to be found in a long and detailed evaluation of Nazi policy and performance from its inception, in the *Yorkshire Post*, which began its leader thus:

The events of the past week in Germany have occasioned an indignant outcry in all countries where free speech and a free press render possible the expression of public opinion. But those events should not have caused surprise since they are in keeping with the whole character and history

[68] *Sunday Express*, 13 Nov. 1938.
[69] The instructions appear in document No. P.S. 3051, IMT XXXI (1948), pp. 515–20, and a report of the discussions in document No. P.S. 1816, IMT XXVIII (1947), pp. 499–540; cf. G. Reitlinger, *The Final Solution*, London (1953), pp. 13–14.
[70] Some of the actual evidence for prior planning was known at the time to the diplomatic correspondent of the *Manchester Guardian* (16 Nov. 1938), who reported that certain Berlin Jews had been privately warned of what was in store for them.

of the Nazi regime from its birth. Even a cursory glance over Hitlerite history from the days of the Munich 'Putsch' suffices to show that the methods have not varied in kind but only in degree, in accordance with increasing power and opportunity.[71]

There were even a number of suggestions that the murder of vom Rath was all *too* convenient, i.e. that it was, directly or indirectly, the work of an *agent provocateur*.[72] But to believe this is to introduce an unnecessary complication. The Nazis would have found some other pretext once this particular stage in their plan for the Jews had been determined upon.

As for the billion-mark fine and other economic sanctions amounting to confiscation of a high proportion of Jewish property, one reason for this form of punishment was the very simple one, that the German Government wanted the money, especially foreign shares. And confiscation of businesses would be an easy way of rewarding Party members. The *Tablet* put this point with more than ordinary elegance: 'it is convenient to have a community of people naturally devoted to acquiring wealth, as bees collect honey, and to be able from time to time on this pretext or that to raid their hives.'[73] Another reason was the equally simple one of retaliation. The Nazi leaders were furious. They were exacting vengeance and some of them half believed their own propaganda that the murder was part of an international Jewish conspiracy. Thirdly, all this was but the culmination of Nazi hatred, which was here able to find a particularly suitable vent.

All these three aspects were adequately covered by the Press. In one form or another the three aspects were there.[74] But very little was said about another aspect. On Saturday 12 November Dr. Goebbels gave an exclusive interview to Reuter's correspondent in which he answered questions on the new decrees. He stated that the events of the previous few days had been nothing but 'symptoms of an infection which has sought to creep into the body

[71] *Yorkshire Post*, 14 Nov. 1938; cf. shorter but similar comments by *The Scotsman*, 12 Nov. 1938; *Glasgow Herald*, 12 Nov. 1938.

[72] See, e.g., *Edinburgh Evening News*, 18 Nov. 1938, which devoted a full-page feature article to this theory. However, Grynzpan's answers to the French police admit of no doubt that his act was what it seemed to be, see, e.g., report in *News Chronicle*, 9 Nov. 1938.

[73] *Tablet*, 19 Nov. 1938.

[74] Calculation of the fine varied from £80 million (*Financial Times*, 14 Nov. 1938) to 'nearly £90 million' (*Evening Standard*, 12 Nov. 1938).

of the German people'. They had dealt and would continue to deal with this infection. The importance of his placing the decrees in a wider framework than merely that of the murder does not seem to have been properly appreciated. His remarks remained modestly hidden in a column of small type. The shortest summary, in fact, appeared in *The Times*.[75]

In the same interview Goebbels spoke of further decrees which would also be in accordance with his aim of removing the Jews from the economic life of the country. A high proportion of the national Press never printed this section at all, while no one, as far as I know, noticed that Walter Funk, the Minister of Economics, made a public statement on 15 November which should have put the matter beyond all doubt, assigning the financial side of the vom Rath affair its proper place in the whole picture of Nazi Jewish policy:

It is impossible to exclude the Jews from public life and to leave them alone in economic life. The final explosion of popular rage . . . occurred at the very moment when we had almost completed the economic exclusion of the Jew. Our preparations enable us now to exclude the Jew entirely from German business economy . . . and to transfer what is left of Jewish property into German hands.[76]

It is not an unfair judgement of the Press to say that there were insufficient signs of understanding anything beyond the purely punitive aspect of these financial measures. In fact, although the contempt and disgust expressed were sufficiently emphatic and sincere, the Press as a whole showed less interest in the German Jewish situation as such than in its implications outside Germany, that is to say in its results, the chief of which was likely to be an infinitely more serious refugee problem. This problem was central to the whole question of Press attitudes and will be separately discussed.[77]

There was, however, another international aspect of the vom Rath affair in which the Press was naturally very interested: the future of Anglo-German relations. As it happened, an immediate and practical example of this aspect was provided by one of those bizarre incidents which the Germany of those days seems to have

[75] *The Times*, 14 Nov. 1938.
[76] Reported by the *Frankfurter Zeitung*, 17 Nov. 1938; cf. IMT I (1947), p. 305, where these remarks formed one of the main counts in his indictment.
[77] See Chapter VI, below.

had the secret of manipulating. On Tuesday 8 November *Der Angriff* ('The Attack'), the official party paper, published a feature article containing a strong suggestion that the Paris crime had been inspired, if not directed, by Winston Churchill, Anthony Eden, Duff Cooper, and others. 'There is a straight line', it said, 'from Churchill to Grynzpan.' British reaction to this truly original piece of detection was understandably sharp. The strongest comment came from *The Times*, which, after expressing its horror at the pogroms of the day after the murder—stressed its belief that denunciation was 'an empty indulgence'. It went on to say:

It is quite another matter when foreign countries and their citizens are wantonly involved against their will in the concerns of another country. They stand then on the basis of positive right, and it is due to self-respect and to the maintenance of correct relations to assert them. . . . This attempt to implicate British politicians . . . is much worse than merely ludicrous. It is wholly intolerable.[78]

One must not be too hard on *The Times*. It could not really have meant that an insult, however flagrant, to Mr. Churchill (which, after all, left him much as he was before) was as bad as, or worse than, the deliberate destruction of the property and livelihood of thousands of harmless individuals. But it was reacting to a new phenomenon. The Nazis had not been content with their usual targets. They had attacked the British. Of course, *The Times* was not alone in this reaction. It expressed that of the Press as a whole with its usual happy clarity.

The *Angriff* article pointed to what was a more fundamental issue of diplomacy. The politicians who had been attacked were chiefly the 'opposition' within the Conservative Party who had attacked the Munich settlement. We are not competent to suggest why the *Angriff* re-opened the question in that way and at that time. The result, however, is very clear indeed. The article helped to establish in the British mind a direct connexion between German internal and German foreign policy—a connexion which had not always been sufficiently noticed. The Jewish issue became linked with the 'appeasement' issue.[79] Even without the *Angriff*

[78] *The Times*, 11 Nov. 1938.
[79] The word 'appeasement' which, until the Munich crisis, had had a blameless, indeed a laudatory, meaning, turned into something very different. It became as someone put it at the time, 'almost a dirty word'. It is here used in what might be called its technical sense: as a description of the policy, or the individuals, supporting the Munich settlement.

article and all that followed, sincere moral reprobation of what had taken place would have implanted serious doubts in pro-Munich circles as to whether Hitler had been quite the right person to receive a personal declaration of friendship from the Prime Minister. The *Angriff*, however, had put the matter in a rather stronger light. If Hitler could do all this to his Jews and then be dishonest enough to blame the British for it, how could his Munich profession of faith be trusted? Was it unreasonable that the majority of leading articles on the Crystal Night should have some re-evaluation of appeasement as an important theme? The newspapers which had supported appeasement were disconcerted; but the others were not exactly delighted that their predictions were being fulfilled. The general atmosphere was unhappy. The feelings of the appeasers were accurately (if somewhat epigrammatically) rendered by a Protestant weekly:

Our hearts were tuned to sing. 'Munich' seemed to strike the note. We filled our lungs to an unwonted depth. But the hour passed and a day passed, and now we should certainly need the blessed stroke of some new note to unite our hearts and voices.[80]

The same point of view was put more prosaically in many papers. Of course apart from the basic difference between appeasers and anti-appeasers, there were also variations of opinion as to how far a 'new note' was necessary, and how much the pogroms had damaged the chances of successful appeasement. Here is a striking affirmation of belief in the appeasement policy, come what may:

There is evidence that the strength of world reaction to the pogrom has astonished Germany, and has shocked it not a little, thus emphasising the marked psychological difficulties with which Mr. Chamberlain is contending in a crusade which must earn the approval in principle of every sound British citizen. Nothing that has happened in Germany can effect that major purpose even though it may postpone its ultimate realisation.[81]

Why was Germany supposed to have been 'shocked' by world reaction—unless 'shocked' was thought of as a synonym for 'infuriated'—and what precisely were Chamberlain's 'psychological difficulties'? One thing is clear. No stronger defence of

[80] *British Weekly*, 24 Nov. 1938.
[81] *Midland Daily Telegraph*, 17 Nov. 1938.

Munich in the face of heavy odds can be imagined. A somewhat less reverent approach was to be found in a *Daily Express* cartoon. Chamberlain is a cork toy—indestructible and irrepressible. He bobs up after every blow—although the Nazi pogrom is the biggest of them all and, for a moment, succeeds in laying him flat on the ground.[82] A *Daily Mail* leader was less explicit, but probably referred to Mr. Chamberlain's effort; it was entirely devoted to praising a pronouncement by Lord Nuffield that prosperity 'can be achieved if . . . we put our trust in Mr. Chamberlain, follow him, and stop meddling in foreign affairs'.[83]

However, most reactions from supporters of official Conservative policy were not so enthusiastic. Both the *Daily Telegraph* and the *Daily Mail* more often spoke of 'the relentless anti-Jewish drive and the profound ill-feeling it engendered between Germany and the rest of the world', or expressed fears that

prospects of an early rapprochement between Germany and the Western Powers have been heavily clouded by the ruthless pogroms and the violent anti-British press campaign in which the German government has thought fit to indulge.[84]

Similar estimates of the situation appeared in the Conservative sections of the provincial Press with a prevailing note of pained disappointment:

Everything is done with the mailed fist. We had all hoped that Munich would mark a new departure from this menacing mentality, but it is already plain that if the pogrom continues hostility to Nazi policy will grow in intensity, making appeasement more difficult than ever.[85]

And the *Bournemouth Daily Echo* as sadly remarked:

Those who support the Government and Mr. Chamberlain's efforts on behalf of appeasement will feel especial poignant regret that the German Government should choose this very critical and otherwise hopeful moment to do something which has shocked the conscience of the world.[86]

---

[82] *Daily Express*, 15 Dec. 1938.   [83] *Daily Mail*, 29 Dec. 1938.
[84] *Daily Telegraph*, 23 Nov. 1938; *Daily Mail*, 1 Nov. 1938. It is probably significant that *The Times* said as little as possible about this particular aspect of the question although it never failed to denounce each instance of cruelty or violence.
[85] *Western Mail*, 21 Nov. 1938.   [86] *Bournemouth Daily Echo*, 22 Nov. 1938.

The clearest statement of the hopes and fears of the appeasers appeared in two successive articles by 'Scrutator' of the *Sunday Times*—a statement which is at least semi-editorial: British sentiment was hardening, perhaps dangerously, over the Jewish question. The conflict of interests was not nearly so serious a barrier as the persecutions. However, this sentiment was 'unpractical' and 'distorted the issues of policy'.[87] This is the position of the unrepentant Munich man in a nutshell. Its implications become clearer when contrasted with that of his opponents.

Meanwhile we must note that not all supporters of Munich expressed their disappointment in terms as responsible as these, or those which have been cited so far. Some bewailed the fact that the pogroms were making it difficult for the Government to win by-elections.[88] Others concentrated their attack on the way the situation was being exploited by 'disruptive elements'. Then came the final highly logical conclusion. Could it be an accident that the situation *was* so convenient for these elements (who in the eyes of people of this kind included everybody from Mr. Churchill to the Trotskyist groups)? The impression left by a careful reading of a leader and a feature article in the *Catholic Times* was that it was *not* an accident. It was a plot by the 'Money Power' to destroy the value of sterling by destroying the influence of Chamberlain, the creator of the 'Miracle of Munich'.[89] This kind of stuff was obviously not representative, but opinions of this kind were printed and cannot be omitted. On the other hand there were more respectable formulations of much the same idea which simply showed bewilderment; why was Hitler prepared to antagonize world opinion and endanger his Munich gains for the sake of an outburst of anti-Semitic violence?

The opponents of Munich did not have the same problem. For them the November pogroms were only part of a series of actions, all examples of behaviour below the minimum level demanded by civilized society. The Crystal Night, like the murder of Dolfuss or the seizure of the Sudeten areas of Czechoslovakia, was the work of men towards whom concessions were both dangerous and useless. The most extreme version of this approach was of course

[87] *Sunday Times*, 11 Dec. 1938; 18 Dec. 1938.
[88] See, e.g., *Time & Tide*, 19 Nov. 1938; to be fair this was not its typical approach usually, or its main point then. But it was a 'practical' point which it did make.
[89] *Catholic Times*, 18 Nov. 1938.

to be found in the *Daily Worker*. The pogroms were not only examples of Nazi behaviour, they were themselves the inevitable results of appeasement. Chamberlain's Government had helped to save the Hitler régime at Munich, and was now preparing to acquiesce in Hitler's latest piece of brutality. The only way to help German Jews—and defend Britain, as well as the peace of the whole world—was to turn out Chamberlain's Government and replace it by a 'democratic' one pledged to make a stand against all dictators. A particularly savage cartoon showed Chamberlain promising Hitler more appeasement. The feet of a crucified Jew can be seen in the background.[90]

Other papers were just as outspoken about the necessary implications of political friendship with Germany. The Conservative *Yorkshire Post* and the Liberal *News Chronicle* differed little in their comments on the meaning of the pogroms in this context. The *Post* said:

It is impossible to understand how anyone who is not himself needlessly duped or is seeking to dupe others can talk seriously of producing European appeasement in confident collaboration with the convinced exponents of Nazi methods.[91]

The *News Chronicle* gave exceptional prominence to two ministerial speeches emphasizing the damage the pogroms had done to future Anglo-German co-operation and asked: 'How can British electors be expected to wax enthusiastic for friendship with a regime that seems to rejoice in cruelty for its own sake?'[92] And the pogroms proved, if proof was still required, that there was an immediate practical danger:

After the Jews, the Roman Catholics, after the Roman Catholics, the nobility and the conservatives, and then the Protestants. Abroad, after

[90] *Daily Worker*, 16 Nov. 1938; cf. especially issues for 29 Nov. and 14 Nov. 1938. We are not here concerned with motives. The *Worker* would scarcely have denied that the pogroms were just one among many questions over which mass opinion could be mobilized both against the dictatorship and against the home Government as part of a general campaign.

[91] *Yorkshire Post*, 11 Nov. 1938.

[92] *News Chronicle*, 14 Nov. 1938. The two speeches (Mr. Geoffrey Shakespeare, Parliamentary Secretary to the Admiralty, and the Earl de la Warr, President of the Board of Education) were, of course, generally reported; an interesting contrast is the lack of emphasis given to them by, for example, the *Evening Standard*, 14 Nov. 1938. The *News Chronicle* view can be paralleled in many other places, see, e.g., *South Wales Argus*, 30 Nov. 1938, for a provincial example.

Czechoslovakia, Poland. Then Rumania and Memel. And then? The intensity with which anti-British feeling is being worked up in Germany now leaves little doubt that if the extremists remain in power, then Great Britain will be the supreme objective in the imperialist and revolutionary campaign which is being conducted under the leadership of Adolf Hitler.[93]

The anti-Munich Press, then, irrespective of political affiliations, was united in its understanding of the pogroms as a proof of the uselessness of the Munich agreement, and a warning of future dangers. Even the opponents of Munich, however, were not as lucid as they might have been. The extract from *Time & Tide* just quoted suggests that there was still an issue in Germany between 'extremists' and 'moderates' even over the Jews. Was Hitler, then, really a 'revolutionary' (as *The Times*, too, had more than once implied)? And to quote another instance of confusion, did the pogroms point to a side of the German character which was 'almost incredible'?[94] Why—and this was essentially the same bewilderment which possessed the appeasers—had Germany chosen to upset the international applecart in this way? Writing in the very same *Time & Tide* a month earlier, in the excellent special supplement to which reference has already been made, the American political commentator Edgar Mowrer had already cleared up this and many other similar misunderstandings:

Americans and particularly Britishers here, since the war, under the influence of an unbroken and subtle propaganda from several sources, tried to persuade themselves that the contemporary Germans are really fine people, that they were much mistreated at Versailles, that they only rushed into Hitlerism because exasperated by the wicked Allies beyond human endurance, etc. Therefore each time the Nazis take another forward step along their deliberately chosen and plotted path of horror, the Anglo-Saxons are astonished and shocked.[95]

The pogroms were one of these steps. They were the open abandonment of legality in Jewish matters, precisely as the crisis which ended with Munich had seen its abandonment in the sphere of international relations.

The pogroms illustrate something which cannot be too strongly

---

[93] *Time & Tide*, 24 Dec. 1938.   [94] *Observer*, 13 Nov. 1938.
[95] *Time & Tide* (supplement), 26 Nov. 1938. Mowrer was the author of one of the best popular expositions of the Nazi régime: *Germany Puts the Clock Back*, London (1933), reprinted twice in a 'Penguin' edition (1938 and 1939).

stressed: Nazi readiness to abandon a legal cover when it was no longer considered necessary. The moment when a criminal decides that he can be openly criminal is highly important for the society in which he lives. As the invasion of the Sudeten areas was important for the European community, so was the Crystal Night important for the German Jews. Both showed the Nazis feeling strong enough to use force without a legal covering—and who is to say, on a short-term view, that they were wrong? Hence the attacks on Churchill and his friends, the epithet of 'guttersnipe' applied to Lord Baldwin,[96] the utter contempt for world opinion, and the unrestrained character of the speeches of the Nazi leaders. And although everything was fully and faithfully reported by the British Press, one is left feeling that the open abandonment of legality was not properly appreciated. The immense majority of commentators believed that, if anything, the pogroms were a sign of Nazi weakness, a sign of internal troubles for the stilling of which the customary scapegoat was required. They believed that the régime was drifting into bankruptcy and that the billion marks were intended to save it—or help in the re-armament programme. Perhaps. Yet the main reason for the imposition of that fine was surely precisely that the Nazis felt that they were strong. They could snap their fingers at the world. At last they could treat the Jews as they had wanted to do, as they had planned to do for so long.

[96] It should never be forgotten that the attack on Churchill occurred *before* any British reaction to events, in fact, before the Crystal Night itself. It was provocative, not retaliatory. The attack on Lord Baldwin was a reply to his appeal for refugees.

III

Belief and Atrocities

THE Nazis began by discriminating against the Jews. They ended by murdering about six million of them—perhaps two-thirds of those who eventually came under their rule. This is a fact of history—irrespective of any controversy about the actual statistics of extermination.[1] It has been described many times before, and with considerable success, since the documentary evidence is available in an abundance of detail relatively rare for events of history on this scale. We are concerned with a subsidiary question: to what extent, and at what periods was this evidence available to the British Press and what impression did it make?

There are two good reasons why part of an inquiry into Press reactions ought to be devoted to this question. The first is the obvious one, that physical maltreatment was the logical conclusion of Nazi behaviour at each stage of their policy; eventually it became the 'final solution'. The second reason is that stories of physical maltreatment start off with a certain disadvantage. It usually seems easier to believe that someone has been unjustly dismissed from his post than that he has been brutally assaulted, that he has been unjustly imprisoned rather than tortured. To what extent, and from what causes, did the British Press believe reports of physical maltreatment?

At the beginning of 1944 there appeared an article by Arthur Koestler entitled 'On Disbelieving Atrocities'.[2] At that time he was

[1] The actual figure in the indictment at the War Crimes Trial was 5,721,000 (IMT II, 36). Reitlinger, op. cit., pp. 489–501, discusses the statistics in separate German-occupied territories and suggests that it may have been as low as 4,194,200. However, even a reduction of two million does not, as he points out, alter the fact that this was the greatest act of extermination yet known.

[2] A. Koestler, 'On Disbelieving Atrocities', *New York Times Magazine*, Jan. 1944; reprinted in *Time & Tide*, 5 Feb. 1944, and in his book *The Yogi and the Commissar*, London (1945), pp. 94–99.

of course primarily concerned with the end-product of Nazi policy—with the death camps and the crematoria—but he advanced a general theory applicable to the explanation of disbelief in any act of physical cruelty. He called it 'The limitation of awareness':

A dog run over by a car upsets our emotional balance and digestion; three million Jews killed in Poland cause but a moderate uneasiness. Statistics don't bleed; it is the detail which counts. We are unable to embrace the total process with our awareness; we can only focus on little lumps of reality. . . . Those limitations of awareness account for the limitations of enlightenment by propaganda. People go to the cinemas, they see films of Nazi tortures . . . but they do not connect it with the realities of their normal plane of existence.

This argument had considerable force; it *was* hard to imagine suffering one did not see, and it became steadily harder as the scale grew greater.

There was also another obstacle. A particular word was usually applied to physical maltreatment—the word 'atrocity', a word which had unfortunate associations for the Press. Its usage began in the year 1876 when Gladstone wrote his famous pamphlet denouncing Turkish methods of crushing a Bulgarian revolt. It was then, too, that the controversy which arose about the credence which Gladstone's allegations deserved left British journalists with the impression that the word 'atrocity' applied to a story was an imputation on its authenticity. We are indebted to Sir Harold Nicolson for an extremely clear expression of this attitude in the course of a review, in the *Daily Telegraph*, of a reprint in pamphlet form of Israel Cohen's classic exposure of the Nazi case:[3]

Many and varied have been the propaganda leaflets which I have read during the last twenty years. I can recall Italian publications accusing Arabs of atrocities in Cyrenaica, and Arab brochures placing upon the Italians the blame for any incidents which may have occurred. The Macedonian and Albanian questions produced a whole library of propaganda literature, illustrated by gruesome photographs, which were frequently identical. The two Balkan wars elicited many reprints of previous pamphlets [an allusion to Gladstone]. During the Great War we had Belgian atrocities and Armenian atrocities, and we shall

[3] Israel Cohen, *The Jews in Germany* (London, 1933); reprinted from the *Quarterly Review*, July 1933; see above, pp. 31–2.

shortly be receiving bright little books upon the Chaldeans and
Assyrians. Such publications, however divergent may be their purposes,
have a common failing. Instead of concentrating upon a few typical outrages they overload their pages with exhibits which are too numerous
to be effective. Lassitude, rather than indignation, is the result.

It was from this point of view that Sir Harold went on to criticize
the early pamphlets of the Board of Deputies to which reference
has already been made, and to praise by contrast Israel Cohen's
pamphlet, together with another short work of the same kind,
because, in his opinion, 'instead of adducing evidence against the
brutality of the Nazis they have, with calm logic, exposed their
stupidity'.[4] Sir Harold, like many others equally experienced in
international affairs, was tired of atrocities.[5] Inertia and suspicion
of the atrocity story are the two factors which must be borne in
mind when Press attitudes to reports of actual violence are being
discussed.

In contrast to these general factors, it must never be forgotten
that a substantial proportion of Nazi anti-Semitic activity during
this first period was performed publicly and officially. It could not
be denied, however tortuously the facts might be explained. This
firstly applies to one category of physical maltreatment—the
attacks on individual Jews in the street, in their shops, offices,
consulting-rooms, and places of residence. Sporadic actions of this
kind had considerably ante-dated the coming to power of the Nazis,
and there had never been any concealment about them.[6] The first
great outburst of organized anti-Semitism had culminated, as we
have seen, in the April boycott; its preliminaries and accompani-
ments of violence had also been perfectly open. Very little attempt
was made to prevent reports and pictures of these or subsequent
incidents from going abroad.[7]

[4] *Daily Telegraph*, 25 Aug. 1933. The implication that atrocities were committed by or could with justice be imputed to 'both sides', however grotesque
its application to the German Jewish situation, did have a certain currency and
is discussed above, pp. 18–19.
[5] It is only fair to say that ten years later he expressed precisely the opposite
point of view in the *Spectator* (17 Dec. 1943).
[6] A long report of plunder and violence in Berlin and Nuremberg, for example, appeared in the *Berliner Tageblatt*, 7 Nov. 1923.
[7] Two pictures achieved wide circulation. One is of a Jew with his head
shaven and his clothes torn paraded through the streets with a placard round his
neck, the other is of a Jew being dragged in a dustcart. Cf., e.g., *Daily Herald*,
27 Mar. 1933, and *News Chronicle*, 3 April 1933.

The plainest and most consecutive accounts of these incidents, particularly during the early period, are to be found in the *Manchester Guardian*. It seems that neither its special correspondents nor its editorial staff were afraid of inducing 'lassitude' amongst its readers by 'overloading their pages with numerous exhibits'. The *Guardian* believed that it was following the best traditions of objective journalism and rendering a necessary service to those who wished to know what the German-Jewish situation really was, by printing *all* reliable details of incidents as they occurred, rather than 'concentrating upon a few typical outrages'. It began by publishing, a few days before and again a few days after the April boycott, impressive surveys of the physical indignities and terrors (quite apart from the 'legal' and 'semi-legal' discriminations already discussed) to which German Jews were being subjected. The list was a very long one, consisting of miscellaneous assaults, 'each of which could henceforth be described with perfect justice as typical', including beatings, robbery, and murder.

The anti-Semitic outrages of the last few weeks are far more horrible than could reasonably have been imagined at first. Nothing like them has been known in Germany for generations.

It was precisely of these and similar extracts included in the Board of Deputies pamphlets that Sir Harold Nicolson had complained.[8]

During the same period, similar reports appeared in most of the British Press. The reports of the *Daily Telegraph*, though closest in character to those in the *Guardian*, were not nearly so complete. *The Times* reports were much more general altogether. Their emphasis was on a wider question: to what extent had Hitler's seizure of power actually resulted in violence? Could what violence there was be justified in any way, for instance towards the Communists? Jewish victims, as distinct from the many others who suffered in the terror, were not often mentioned.[9] The popular Press concentrated on one or other startling incident and had no great interest in methodical compilation. On the day of the first of the *Manchester Guardian* articles cited, for example, the *Daily Herald* contented itself with one of the incidents described there,

---

[8] *Manchester Guardian*, 27 Mar. 1933; 8 April 1933. Reprinted in the Board of Deputies Pamphlet No. 1 (1933), pp. 18–23. An extract appeared in *The Yellow Spot*, London (1936), p. 34; see below, pp. 76–77; 81.

[9] See, e.g., *The Times*, 15 Mar. 1933.

but gave it headlines in heavy type with a three-column spread.[10] But the Press well understood how important physical violence was within the general picture of the Nazi régime, and that it ought to be given special attention. It may well be that for some editors this emphasis was motivated by the more immediate consideration that violence, and particularly murder—whether ideological or private—generally has news value. The objective result, however, was much the same: readers of any British newspaper were left in no doubt that violence directed against certain groups of people was an integral part of the new Germany.

This is well illustrated by the reports of the actual boycott. The day seems to have passed off comparatively quietly. That is, the emphasis was on propagandist rather than on physical attacks. The major exception was Kiel, where a Jewish lawyer was lynched in prison, after he had been arrested for alleged complicity in the death of a Storm Trooper. The vast majority of the national Press emphasized this incident by giving it some sort of headline in their boycott reports, or at least by a bold cross-head to the relevant paragraph. Here is a random selection of headlines from the national Press of 2 April 1933 (Sunday) and 3 April 1933 (daily papers):

BOYCOTT OF JEWS, LYNCHING CASE AT KIEL (*The Times*)

BOYCOTT OF THE JEWS IN GERMANY, JEWISH PRISONER MURDERED (*Manchester Guardian*)

HITLER'S WAR ON JUDEA. BERLIN LAWYER SAID TO HAVE BEEN LYNCHED (*News of the World*)

FIASCO OF GERMAN ANTI-JEWISH BOYCOTT, LYNCH LAW AT KIEL (*Sunday Times*)

NAZIS LYNCH JEWISH LAWYER IN PRISON, BOYCOTT TERROR (*Reynolds Illustrated News*)

JEW LYNCHED DURING GERMAN BOYCOTT (*Sunday Dispatch*)

KIEL MOB LYNCH A JEW, BOYCOTT BILLS REMAIN ON SHOPS (*Daily Express*)

[10] *Daily Herald*, 27 Mar. 1933.

EYEWITNESS TELLS OF JEW BAITING TRAGEDIES, NAZI MOB LYNCH LAWYER (*Daily Herald*)

NAZI BOYCOTT OF THE JEWS, BRUTAL INCIDENT AT KIEL (*Observer*)

The *Sunday Referee* had quite the most remarkable presentation, which at least indicated a sound instinct about Hitler's real purpose. Its headlines read:[11]

NAZI DISPLAY OF 'FRIGHTFULNESS' MISFIRES TWELVE HOUR BOYCOTT ENDS WITH ONLY ONE MURDER

There were three interesting exceptions. The *Sunday Express* ignored the Kiel affair, limiting itself to a quotation from an agency message at the very end of its special correspondents' dispatch.[12] This was not because there was no time to do very much about it, since other Sunday papers, in addition to the *Referee*, gave it great prominence. The *News Chronicle* mentioned Kiel in its headlines. Two days later, however, its owner and editor, Sir Walter Layton, had this to say:

By comparison with dramatic acts of this kind [seizure without warning by Party Members of various Government and Trade Union posts] that are taking place all over the country, the anti-Jewish boycott on Saturday was a tame affair. The hidden tragedy of the war against the Jews and its economic implication, are of the greatest moral and material importance to Germany, but it must be admitted as a great testimony to the discipline of the 'Brown Army' [the Party formation] that the day passed off almost without incident.[13]

Most striking of all was the *Daily Mail*. Its story boasted but two headlines limited to a single column:

GERMANY'S JEWISH BOYCOTT
ORDERLY BUT STERN

The Kiel affair was only mentioned at the very end—the actual lynching, admittedly, in bold type.[14] These last three examples help to emphasize that most of the Press did accord a specific significance to what had taken place at Kiel. Very few indeed believed

---

[11] *Sunday Referee*, 2 April 1933.   [12] *Sunday Express*, 2 April 1933.
[13] *News Chronicle*, 3 April 1933; 5 April 1933.   [14] *Daily Mail*, 3 April 1933.

the comparative lack of violence to have been the result of 'Brown Army' discipline. The implications of violence in the April boycott were well understood.

The events of March and April 1933 were of course only one example out of several during the pre-war period, when hatred of the Jews burst out in scenes of physical violence which could hardly help making a strong impression on foreign observers. And the actual incidents in these outbursts were all very much alike—'typical outrages', Sir Harold Nicolson might have called them. The *Manchester Guardian* continued to give the fullest accounts, while various popular papers tended to give exceptional prominence to single incidents which, in one way or another, seemed to them to be especially striking. On the other hand, the *Daily Express* well illustrated its own idiosyncrasy by giving as much space, and as prominent a presentation, to the arrest and expulsion of one of its special correspondents as to any maltreatment of German Jews.[15]

One other event belonging to this period should be mentioned. In March 1936, a book appeared called *The Yellow Spot*. It was an anonymous, but extremely well documented, compilation of a large miscellany of Nazi excesses against the Jews, with a foreword by the Bishop of Durham. This book was given extensive appraisals in most leading periodicals and national organs, whose editors had invited such varied personalities as R. C. K. Ensor, Michael Foot, and Sir Ernest Barker to review it. Naturally, the emphasis varied. Sir Ernest Barker in the *Observer* gave almost as much space to the Greeks and Hebrews of the ancient world and to various philosophic considerations as he did to the incidents which the book actually described.[16] About a third of the review in the *Times Literary Supplement* was taken up with a quotation from the Bishop's foreword.[17] The *Daily Worker* critic's main point was 'the terrifying clarity' with which the book proved 'the putrefaction of capitalism' as expounded by Dimitrov, the Bulgarian Communist and the leading figure in the Reichstag fire trial.[18] Among organs with an even more select readership may be mentioned the *Freethinker*, which could not resist referring to 'the barbarities of the Middle Ages and the tortures of the Inquisition'

---

[15] *Daily Express*, 2 June 1934.   [16] *Observer*, 15 Mar. 1936.
[17] *Times Literary Supplement*, 1 April 1936.
[18] *Daily Worker*, 16 Mar. 1936.

as a useful parallel.[19] The *British Weekly* (Protestant), on the other hand, was inclined to see a parallel in 'the liquidation of the *Kulaks* in Soviet Russia, and the Bolshevik persecution of religion'.[20] Lastly, the *News Review*, with what it fondly hoped was its American 'tough' style, should not be forgotten:

The book is a cram of stories of concentration camp torture, sadist troopers armed with rubber truncheons, is liberally illustrated with spotty, blurred, pictures of blood-curdling incidents.[21]

This statement is less than accurate: a large part of the book does not deal with physical maltreatment at all—and very few of the pictures really depict 'blood-curdling incidents', particularly blurred or spotty. Nevertheless, there is a kernel of truth here: the author of *The Yellow Spot* had understood that acts of violence were the logical and necessary outcome of all the other anti-Semitic acts committed by the Nazis, and the British Press understood this too. During all this period the Press as a whole was fully alive to the violent aspect of anti-Semitism in Germany.[22]

This comparative unanimity becomes even more striking when it is considered from a different angle. Certain specific political factors were operating in those years, which of themselves could well have prejudiced a general acceptance of the more unpleasant details of Nazi violence as literally true. On 19 July 1936, civil war broke out in Spain. The most extraordinarily fierce passions were aroused outside Spain, especially in France and England, and reached their peak when Germany and Italy openly intervened on the side of Franco. The British Press was very much divided over this issue, broadly along expected political lines, and acceptance of atrocity stories accusing one side or the other depended on the political standpoints of the newspaper concerned. It was not surprising that the left-wing Press often connected what the Germans were doing in Spain with what they were doing in Germany. A partisan atmosphere was generated around the whole question of Fascist and Nazi brutality, which might have had most unfortunate results. It was natural that the more doctrinaire used each

---

[19] *Freethinker*, 26 Mar. 1936.   [20] *British Weekly*, 26 Mar. 1936.
[21] *News Review*, 26 Mar. 1936.
[22] Two reviews of *The Yellow Spot* which best expressed this awareness appeared in the *New Statesman & Nation*, 21 Mar. 1936, and the *Spectator*, 20 Mar. 1936.

new German exposure as they did each Spanish one, to propagate their slogans. The *Daily Worker* best illustrates this tendency:

Great applause greeted Jackson's [T. A. Jackson, the party's leading theorist of the thirties] conclusion that the cause of the oppressed Jews in Germany was the cause of the Communist Party . . . a warmly applauded tribute was paid to the services rendered by the *Daily Worker* in exposing the Nazi atrocities.[23]

In May 1934, Rabbi Frankel of Berlin and his daughter succeeding in escaping to England after indignities and physical injuries at Nazi hands. They addressed a meeting in London which was at least partly Communist sponsored, and the *Daily Worker* tried to turn it even more into a straight political issue by stating that 'every effort has been made by interested forces to prevent them from appearing in public'.[24] This was a heartless attempt to use the suffering of two innocent individuals. The details of what they had undergone and the fact that they were to speak in public had been announced in (at least) the *Daily Herald*, the *News Chronicle*, and the *Daily Express* about a week before the *Worker* thought of advertising the meeting in which it was itself especially interested.[25]

Tactics of this kind could have had an effect on Press opinion like those they eventually achieved over Spain: either, that atrocities committed by both sides somehow cancelled each other out, or that it was all political propaganda—and couldn't be believed anyway. Is this first reaction too grotesque if applied to Hitler's other 'war'—that is, against German Jewry? Not at all. We have already seen how at least one section of the Press—non-Fascist, and with influence amongst a substantial English minority—did say that the sufferings of German Jewry must be related to what 'they' (but in the guise of Russian Commissars) were doing to the Christians.

The second reaction, of course, could have been much the more serious of the two. But it is a remarkable fact that all the

[23] *Daily Worker*, 1 April 1933.
[24] *Daily Worker*, 12 May 1934. Speakers at the meeting included Harry Pollitt, General Secretary of the Party, Isobel Brown, leading Party speaker and famous in 'Aid for Spain' rallies, and Professor J. B. S. Haldane, then a strong sympathizer of the Party line.
[25] *Daily Herald*, *News Chronicle*, 8 May 1934; *Daily Express*, 5 May 1934, *Star*, 18 May 1934, printed a full account too, but, admittedly, after the meeting.

attempts to turn the suffering of German Jewry into political propaganda (and there were many) did not shake the general realization of the Press that atrocities, some of them difficult enough to believe, were being committed all the time. Exceptions can of course be found: the *Sunday Chronicle*, for example, gave space to a series of articles by Beverley Nichols on Europe, in one of which he outlined his reasons for thinking that 'the excesses [committed by the Nazis against the Jews] have been wildly exaggerated'. A later editorial comment corrected his more startling blunders—such as that the performers in a Hamburg music hall were all Jewish—but said nothing about his main contention.[26] Occasional letters appeared claiming with surprise or indignation that the individual Jew was perfectly safe in Germany.[27] Two vicars gained temporary fame and considerable space in their local Press by proclaiming from their pulpits that not a single atrocity story was true. One of them subsequently changed his opinion and publicly apologized.[28] The *Liverpool Echo* at a very early stage devoted an article to an exposure of what it called 'exaggerations' and 'fantastic incidents'.[29] But in the main, neither Communist nor Fascist propaganda had any significant effect on British Press attitudes to the reports of Nazi atrocities against German Jewry.

We have seen that there could be no argument about the fact of physical violence during the pre-war period, any more than about other aspects of Hitler's anti-Jewish campaign. Germany was no closed land; no 'iron curtain' veiled her from the rest of the world. However, in the nature of things many descriptions had to depend on anonymous statements or second-hand information. In itself this was reasonable enough. No one could expect a recent victim to provide the Nazi authorities with his name and address when giving evidence of his ill-treatment to a British journalist, and even those safely abroad often had relatives left behind in Germany. But this necessary anonymity scarcely caused the Press to waver in its belief that terrible things were being done in Germany. This was partly the result of the very high (and well-

[26] *Manchester Sunday Chronicle*, 13 Sept. 1936; 20 Sept. 1936.
[27] See a perfect specimen in *The Times*, 3 Jan. 1934.
[28] See *Northampton Echo*, 22 Dec. 1933; *Derby Evening Telegraph*, 29 Dec. 1933, for some references to the one case, and *Glasgow Sunday Mail*, 10 Sept. 1933; *Daily Herald*, 13 Jan. 1936, for the other.
[29] *Liverpool Echo*, 29 Mar. 1933; cf. also *Daily Mail*, 28 Dec. 1934.

deserved) reputation for fair and accurate reporting enjoyed by the *Manchester Guardian* and *The Times*. The appearance in either paper of an account of atrocities from the anonymous pen of 'a correspondent recently in Germany', or of a letter about personal experiences signed with a solitary initial, was accepted as *prima facie* evidence of its truth, and they were often quoted and re-quoted by many others, particularly by the smaller provincial newspapers.

The most obvious examples of continuous and bestial ill-treatment which the Nazis certainly did not publicize were of course the concentration camps—the first and most enduring of all Nazi institutions.[30] Information on what was done there could not very often be first-hand even before the outbreak of war. Visits by accredited Press representatives or others were rarely allowed, and when they were it was difficult to be sure how much a special display was being staged—or how much the visitor was willing to be fooled. One for instance believed he had met with 'enthusiastic praise of the camp leaders' by the inmates of Oranienburg.[31] As a matter of fact, it is probable that faked inspections were arranged even for high Nazi officials who were not within the charmed circle of the *Wirtschaft und Verwaltungshauptampt*—the Economic Section of the S.S.—the body officially in charge, which, from professional jealousy rather than delicacy, guarded the secrets of these institutions.[32] Nevertheless a good deal of information did appear in the Press from the very beginning to the end.

Once again, it is necessary to turn first to the *Manchester Guardian* and *The Times* for much of this information, particularly during the early days. In 1933, for example, *The Times* had a long article on incidents in Oranienburg which earned a much longer reply in a book written by its commandant, including a complete translation and a facsimile reproduction of the headlines.[33]

---

[30] For lists see *Catalogue of Camps and Prisons in Germany and German-occupied Territory September 1939–May 1945*, Arolsen (International Tracing Service, Records Branch) 2 Vols. and Supplement, 1949–1951; IMT XXIII, pp. 208–13; Reitlinger, op cit., p. 451.

[31] Letter in *The Times*, 6 April 1934.

[32] See, e.g., IMT XI, 271. Despite the usual attempt of the witness to exculpate himself by pleading lack of knowledge, it does emerge that the Economic Section did keep all the details it could to itself.

[33] *The Times*, 19 Sept. 1933; cf. W. Schaeffer, *Konzentrationslager, Oranienburg, der Antibraunbuch ueber das erste deutsche Konzentrationslager*, Berlin (1934), pp. 110–24. The whole book is a period curiosity well worth reading.

The *Manchester Guardian*, among its many other excellent reports, had a long general one in 1933 and a special one on Dachau in 1935. The latter was partly reprinted in *The Yellow Spot*.[34] One of the earliest detailed accounts of life in Buchenwald was printed by *Time & Tide*.[35] Of course concentration camp stories appeared throughout the British Press, though few were as carefully written and as convincing as those in *The Times* and the *Guardian*. During the pre-war period they were most frequent in 1938, when the camp population went up steeply during the outbursts which culminated in the Crystal Night, but they never entirely dropped out of the Press and are to be found in all sections of it. One general characteristic was common to all. It hardly needs stressing that no camp between 1933 and 1939 was intended solely for Jews. In fact, until the 1938 pogroms and certainly until the seizure of Austria, the Jews were probably a small minority among the rest of the camp population, which consisted of various sorts of real or supposed political opponents. The British Press generally stressed the fate of the Jewish prisoner.[36] Statistically considered, it was a stress which was totally disproportionate. One reason was that political opponents had been flung into prison and tortured frequently enough in modern Europe, but that this was something new. And there was little disposition to disbelieve editorially what was printed in the news columns.

A few days after the Crystal Night, the *News Chronicle* printed what was described as an eye-witness account of the reception of sixty-two Jews, including two rabbis, into Sachsenhausen. The account was very detailed. It told how the prisoners reached the camp gates escorted by the Berlin police, and how the police were forced to hand them over on the spot to an S.S. unit. All sixty-two were then made to run a gauntlet of spades, clubs, and whips.

Police, unable to bear their cries, turned their backs. As they fell the Jews were beaten further. The orgy lasted half-an-hour.
    Then other prisoners were ordered to carry them away. Twelve of the 62 were dead, their skulls smashed. The others were all unconscious. The eyes of some had been knocked out, their faces flattened and shapeless. The leader of the shock troopers handed a 'receipt' to the police

[34] *Manchester Guardian*, 11 Nov. 1933; *Manchester Guardian Weekly*, 27 Sept. 1935, reprinted in *Yellow Spot*, pp. 268–70.
[35] *Time & Tide*, 20 Aug. 1938.
[36] We have seen that *The Times* occasionally blurred this distinction (see p. 73), but its accuracy in reporting the *facts* was beyond question.

officer to show that he had delivered the correct number, and the police returned to Berlin.[37]

A few days later there appeared an article by Hilaire Belloc which filled a page and a half of the *Weekly Review*. He recapitulated the *News Chronicle* story and continued

> To those who know the Prussian spirit and its traditions, the horrible picture presented here is not impossible . . . on the other hand . . . the story is at least exceptional.
>
> Is it true or false?
>
> . . . At the moment of writing this, no evidence has appeared beyond the bare statement of fact in the *News Chronicle*: with ample dates and figures it is true, but no names. We know nothing of the victims, nor anything of the eyewitness who brought over or sent over this tremendous and decisive revelation of Nazi methods. . . . It won't do.
>
> The truth must be known one way or the other. If the *News Chronicle* fails to make its story good or takes refuge in silence, then we must conclude that a vicious falsehood, dangerous to the conduct of the state, has been forged and uttered. If the Nazis cannot or do not meet the indictment, *they* stand condemned.[38]

There is more than one aspect from which this comment can be discussed. What sort of evidence, for example, would have satisfied Belloc? He himself admitted, later in the article, that 'the *News Chronicle* cannot, obviously, hand over its informant to vengeance by giving his or her name'.

But in any case, here was material for a first-class Press controversy of the kind which was daily taking place over Spanish atrocity stories. Belloc had been aggressive and deliberately so. The *News Chronicle* had a very large circulation and it (or its rivals) could have seized on the issue with enthusiasm for, although the *Weekly Review* scarcely wielded great influence, Belloc's name was very well known indeed, at least as a brilliant publicist, if not as a leader of the English Catholics.

But no one took up his challenge (or supported it); no controversy took place. A fortnight later he wrote:

> I have tried in vain to obtain some confirmation of this story. So far I have received none. The prominent London paper [the *News Chronicle*] which published the original despatch has not said a word about it

---

[37] *News Chronicle*, 23 Nov. 1938.   [38] *Weekly Review*, 1 Dec. 1938.

since. Neither has anyone of the prints which make it their special business in this country to defend the Jews said anything. Neither the *New Statesman* nor the *Manchester Guardian* has, so far as I can discover, said a word. . . .[39]

A month after the original item had appeared, a letter from Belloc, asking substantially the same question, was printed in the *News Chronicle* together with the short and obvious editorial comment that the report had come from a well-informed source which clearly could not be divulged and that there had been no denial in Germany.[40] Finally, seven weeks later, Belloc wrote:

It will soon be three months since the massacre of Jews belonging to the professional classes and including two Rabbis was announced in a leading liberal paper as having taken place in the concentration camp of Sachsenhausen. At first there was debate everywhere whether the news was true or no . . . if it was false it would be such an example of lying on the anti-Nazi side that would make it impossible in the future to believe anything from that quarter without corroborating testimony.

He went on to assert that since no corroborating evidence had appeared, 'the verdict must go by default' and that the 'bulk of readers' would be 'chary of accepting such stories in the future'.[41] But if there was 'debate everywhere', no echo of it had found its way into print.

Why had the British Press failed to take up Belloc's challenge? The simplest answer is that it did not share his belief that the incident had been a 'tremendous and decisive revelation of Nazi methods'. For the past five and a half years there had been innumerable accounts of the most brutal atrocities committed inside the camps and behind the walls of Party headquarters. As far as the Crystal Night itself was concerned, the Press was well aware of the physical injuries which had been inflicted despite the famous declaration that 'not a hair of a Jew's head has been touched'.[42] It simply was not interested in Belloc's private struggle to 'bolt out the truth' as he put it—to 'prove' or 'disprove' that the Nazis were capable of killing and wounding Jews, since it had itself no

[39] *Weekly Review*, 15 Dec. 1938.   [40] *News Chronicle*, 21 Dec. 1938.
[41] *Weekly Review*, 16 Feb. 1939.
[42] See, e.g., *Manchester Guardian*, 28 Nov. 1938. A few months later a Government White Paper proved that running the gauntlet was normal camp reception procedure, see below, p. 98.

doubts about the matter whatever. In one of the few other references to the Sachsenhausen massacre, *Time & Tide* expressed what must have been the opinion of the vast majority when it said that the *News Chronicle* had described 'a characteristic scene'.[43]

On 3 September 1939 Great Britain and France declared war on Germany. So far as readiness to believe in Nazi atrocities went, it will now be realized that this event did not alter the situation so much as might be supposed. In fact, the inclination in some quarters to think that stories of Jews' suffering before the war, just as of their massacre during it, were all part of wartime propaganda against Germany which had much better be forgotten, can most convincingly be refuted by comparing the columns of the British Press before and after the outbreak of hostilities. Nevertheless for the first time the British Government officially recognized and denounced what the Nazis had done and were continuing to do. It should not be forgotten that, until then, it had, as a Government, done nothing of the kind—whatever statements may be placed to the credit of individual members of Parliament, even well-known Conservative ones. Neither Winston Churchill, nor Anthony Eden, nor Duff Cooper, had been members of the Government at the time when their protests had earned them the privilege of being associated by the German Press with the murder of vom Rath, while Neville Chamberlin's 'official' protest was merely a protest against this allegation. Until the outbreak of the war, the only organized investigation and report of Nazi cruelties had been made by a body connected with the British Labour Party, which was mostly concerned with the fate of the German political opposition.[44] Less suspect than the publications of the Communist Party, it was still 'biased'—or could be thought so— and it was indeed fortunate that the Press had no interest in making the question of atrocities a party issue. Now, on 31 October 1939, the Government, still apparently with some reluctance, issued a White Paper which, amidst a quantity of stately diplomatic correspondence between the various British representatives

---

[43] *Time & Tide*, 26 Nov. 1938. There are scarcely any other references. It has already been remarked that there was a tendency to pick one's own atrocity. There was plenty of choice.

[44] Commission of Enquiry of the Labour and Socialist International: *Communications on the Conditions of Political Prisoners*, issued on 22 Dec. 1938. See *Record*, 1 Jan. 1939. (Organ of the T. & G. W., not to be confused with the Methodist journal of the same name.)

in Germany, contained details of actions against Jews as horrible
as any which had appeared in the Press. The details were based
on documents in its possession. The Government had only decided
on publication because of the 'unscrupulous propaganda' Germany was spreading about British treatment of Boer prisoners
during the South African war.[45]

The most shocking descriptions the White Paper contained
were those of incidents in Buchenwald following the Crystal
Night and its aftermath, including a piece of information that
might have set at rest doubts about new arrivals having to run the
gauntlet, which is described as 'more or less usual in all concentration camps'.[46] The great majority of these incidents had never
before appeared in the Press, but they were typical outrages.

This step by the British Government naturally excited considerable attention. Many papers gave it a leading article as well
as extensive mention in their news columns. Press interest was
stirred by this topic more than it had been for some time, particularly since the war itself was then still being fought largely by
propaganda—for example, by leaflet raids over German cities.
But great as the effect was, it was by no means overwhelming.
For what, after all, had been brought to light that had not been
known before? It was only a small minority which chose to speak
of 'revelations' in this context. The main importance of Press
comments does not lie in different reactions to the incidents
themselves as reported in the White Paper—since difference there
was little or none—but in the attitude to the fact of Government
confirmation. In this there certainly was a fundamental division of
opinion. One group could not see much reason for praising the
Government. The *Manchester Guardian* wrote:

Such stories [as in the White Paper] will not be new at least to readers of
this paper. It would have been better, perhaps, if . . . members of the
Government had done more . . . to enlighten public opinion here. . . .
The reason which the Government gives for publishing the White

---

[45] Great Britain, Foreign Office: *Papers concerning the Treatment of German
Nationals in Germany* (London, 1939—H.M.S.O. Cmd. 6120), pp. 3–4. Aside
from this material, the Government was kept continually informed on Jewish
matters in this period, see note 1 to Chapter I above and *Documents on British
Foreign Policy 1933–1939*, London (1956), V, pp. 1, 2, 7, 16, 237 as examples.

[46] *Papers*, p. 29.

Paper betrays some confusion of thought. It says it would not have taken this step but for Dr. Goebbels' propaganda. . . .[47]

Time & Tide took a somewhat similar line but its criticism had a more openly political slant:

It is doubtful whether any good purpose has been served by withholding the official stamp of truth from reports which every sane person knew to be genuine. In the light of the belated White Paper it is indeed all the more unpleasant to recollect that Mr. Chamberlain was fully informed of these horrors when by his signature on the Munich Agreement he extended the area of Nazi sadism to the Czechs.[48]

Not surprisingly *The Times* and the *Daily Telegraph* limited themselves to welcoming the White Paper, and to giving a summary of its contents either in their leaders or in their news columns —although both implied, too, that the facts were not new.[49]

There was a number of minor variations, especially in the more popular sections of the Press. The *Sunday Chronicle* triumphantly published a camp story which it claimed the Foreign Office had forbidden it to print in 1935.[50] The *Daily Express* took this opportunity to sound a note which later acquired a very great significance in the context of Nazi crimes. After heralding the White Paper in appropriately dramatic terms, it chose to introduce a word of caution:

But beware. Do not extend your hatred of Hitler to the German people. Do not confuse them with the Nazis. Remember there is crime and cruelty among the citizens of every nation. It is the misfortune of the Germans that their criminals rule the State. But only a fraction of the German people sympathise with Hitler's methods, perhaps only a fraction know the truth about them.[51]

Without pursuing this fundamental question—to what extent might guilt for the atrocities be rightly spread—it is permissible to ask whether 'crime and cruelty among citizens of every nation' could be compared to the organized horrors of Buchenwald and Dachau.[52]

There were still isolated examples of complete disbelief. A let-

---

[47] *Manchester Guardian*, 31 Oct. 1939. Oddly enough, the word 'revelations' was used in its news columns.
[48] *Time & Tide*, 4 Nov. 1939.
[49] *The Times*, 31 Oct. 1939; *Daily Telegraph*, 31 Oct. 1939.
[50] *Sunday Chronicle*, 5 Nov. 1939.   [51] *Daily Express*, 31 Oct. 1939.
[52] Press attitudes to the question of guilt are discussed below, pp. 132–45.

ter to *Truth*, for instance, claiming that the White Paper material could well be just a Jewish invention, was accompanied by the editorial comment that 'atrocity stories should always be regarded sceptically'.[53] The editor of the *Bristol Evening World*, 'continuing his recollection of Germany in the early days of Nazidom', was glad to report that at Oranienburg there were no 'living skeletons eating unspeakable food and being driven by the lash to labour to the point of exhaustion'.[54] But like Sachsenhausen and Hilaire Belloc, these examples only throw into greater relief the fact that such an attitude was diametrically opposed to that of the vast majority, which was far better expressed by the editorial answer, 'Drivel', to a similar letter in the *Daily Mirror*.[55] The White Paper had perhaps achieved one thing: it had removed the occasional inhibition at seeming sensational, shown by such papers as *The Times*. In the main, however, it had only printed what most sections of the Press had been long ready to print without Government blessing, in spite of all the difficulties of verification, and of the attempt of some elements to turn the whole issue into a party or ideological quarrel of the narrowest kind.

The publication of the White Paper can be said to mark the end of a phase in the history of Jews under Hitler. It told of atrocities, but of atrocities still on a limited and partial scale. It summarized and, as it turned out, 'officially' closed a period when the Nazi purpose had been only torture and physical humiliation of every kind—with death merely as a welcome by-product. The next Government White Paper had a very different tale to tell. It came out in December 1942, and was the first British official account of Jewish 're-settlement', as the Germans called it, that is of the concentration of European Jewry into vast 'reserves' for the purpose of their physical extermination. I do not intend to recount this story in any detail. It has often been told before.[56] But in order to provide a background against which the amounts of information available to the Press may be estimated, and its reactions judged, here is a short outline.

---

[53] *Truth*, 17 Nov. 1939. For more about this paper, see below, pp. 202, 217.
[54] *Bristol Evening World*, 30 Nov. 1939. In the same paper (11 Nov.) there was a very different account of Dachau by an ex-inmate.
[55] *Daily Mirror*, 6 Nov. 1939.
[56] An excellent account is in Reitlinger, *The Final Solution*, to which reference has already been made, and which has been an invaluable guide to much of the background material used for a number of points in this chapter.

Extermination in pursuance of racial theory was first practised not on Jews at all but upon the purest of pure Germans, who had been unfortunate enough to have been declared lunatics or as suffering from certain diseases. As early as 1935, Hitler seems to have expressed the opinion that a war would give him the opportunity of strengthening German stock by this particular method, since the Churches might not then offer so much opposition.[57] By December 1939 there were six institutions equipped with lethal gas chambers for this project, and it was later estimated that by the summer of 1941 about 50,000 of the 'unfit' had been eliminated by this method.[58] Then the killing stopped—for reasons that will be discussed in another context—but the institutions were not closed down.[59] Instead of gassing Germans for being 'unfit', they now began to gas Jews for being Jews. Soon the camps took over the job, giving Auschwitz, Maidenek, Treblinka, and many others their place in the history of our time. Of course this was not the only means of extermination. When the Germans marched into Poland hundreds of Jews were slaughtered by more simple methods, while from the moment Russia was invaded in June 1941 this slaughter was organized as a specific action, aside from the more indiscriminate killing of civilians in general. In fact, the directing extermination cadres, the so-called *Einsatzgruppen* (Special Task Forces), were formed a month before the invasion began.[60] The first great massacre took place in Kiev; others followed along the whole line of the German advance. And from the beginning of the war, trains full of Jews—the 'Transports', as they came to be called—started running from Germany and Austria to the East, while by the end of 1942 the same thing was happening in all the areas captured by the Germans. Mass deportation, mass slaughter—this was henceforth the fate of Jews from Norway to Crete. How much was known abroad, and what were the reactions of the British Press?

It is a remarkable fact that, despite all the obvious difficulties,

[57] So Reitlinger, op. cit., p. 125, quoting one of the Nuremberg defendants. Another defendant claimed that 'the idea only came to Hitler for the first time in the autumn of 1939' (IMT XI, 61). In fact, he may have already thought of it in 1924, see below, p. 94.

[58] A copy of Hitler's own handwritten order starting the process is in IMT XXVI, 169 (document PS630); cf. TWC I, 806, 844.

[59] The reason was actually German public opinion, see below, p. 141.

[60] TWC IV, 136. Their official task was to murder Jews, gipsies, and political commissars.

a great deal of information about Jews in German-occupied territory did appear in the British Press during the whole of the war—long before the advance of the Allied armies had uncovered the truth in its full details. This information partly came from neutral sources (mainly Stockholm), and partly from news reaching the American Jewish Joint Distribution Committee (particularly before America herself entered the war on 7 December 1941). It owed much to the famous 'couriers'—men and women, Jewish and non-Jewish—who succeeded over and over again in making miraculous journeys to and from the Polish ghettos and other Jewish centres in Eastern Europe. And although this news of European Jewry varied considerably in quantity, it covered most of the outstanding incidents, and there is often an understanding of what they really meant.

During the autumn of 1939 and in the early part of 1940, for example, there were a good many accounts of groups of Jewish civilians deliberately massacred as the Germans marched into Poland. They are horrifying enough: wives are forced to see their husbands shot, children flung into the flames of burning houses.[61] Long after the campaign was over, though, the Press was well aware that the slaughter of the Jews went on. 'Although four months have passed since the fighting in Poland has ceased', said one provincial newspaper, 'the campaign against the Jews continues with undiminished ferocity.'[62] This was no figure of speech. At the beginning of 1940, long accounts reached England of the execution and mass murders of Jews in many Polish towns. The Jews were put 'outside the law. Any local Nazi can regard himself as absolute lord of life and death over the Jews and can do anything he likes with them and to them'.[63] From Amsterdam the news was reported that a Munich paper, the *Weltkampf*, had demanded the entire annihilation of Polish Jewry.[64]

It had already been known long before this that Hitler intended to set up some sort of 'Jewish State' in the Lublin area of Poland. Although its eventual purpose was of course not yet clear—the demand for 'annihilation' was not to become an official instruction

[61] Cf., e.g., *Daily Herald*, 8 Dec. 1939; *Manchester Evening News*, 6 Mar. 1940; *Daily Mirror*, 7 Mar. 1940.
[62] *Birmingham Evening Despatch*, 7 Feb. 1940; cf. *Manchester Guardian*, 9 Dec. 1939.
[63] Quoted by the *Manchester Guardian*, 20 Mar. 1940.
[64] *Daily Telegraph*, 8 Feb. 1940.

until March 1941, even in Germany[65]—most sections of the Press had no illusions about the probable results. 'To thrust 3,000,000 Jews, relatively few of whom are agriculturalists', said *The Times*, 'into the Lublin region and to force them to settle there would doom them to famine', and to a later article on the same subject it gave the title 'A Stony Road to Extermination'.[66] The *Spectator* called the plan 'the latest anti-Jewish horror',[67] and there were many stories of the sufferings endured when the resettlement had actually begun.[68] Only *Truth*, in fortunate isolation, wondered whether after the war 'the Jews, having grown accustomed to their purely Jewish surroundings, will not be best left as they are'.[69] Press accounts as a whole made it quite clear what it meant to make the journey to the East, and the word 'transport' quickly acquired a sinister meaning in every European language. More impressive than all these accounts, however, was a cartoon by David Low in the *Evening Standard*. It showed a goods train being methodically loaded with human beings—clearly Jews—tied into bundles. It was not atrocities alone which were being stressed here, but a system—an integral part of Nazi policy. This cartoon was considerably enlarged and reproduced in *Picture Post*.[70]

In the autumn of 1941 there were more reports of Jewish 're-settlement' and of the growth of the 'reservation', including the news that those chosen were classed as 'emigrants' and that thus, according to earlier regulations, their property in the Reich was confiscated.[71] A little later, the *Daily Telegraph* even managed to procure a close-up picture of a woman wearing a yellow star, an old idea now adopted to mark the Jews, largely for the purpose of facilitating 're-settlement' actions.[72] Most of these reports made it

---

[65] For this 'Fuehrer order' see below, p. 98.
[66] *The Times*, 24 Oct. 1939; 16 Dec. 1939.   [67] *Spectator*, 1 Dec. 1939.
[68] Cf., e.g., reports in *Manchester Guardian*, 30 Nov. 1939; 3 Jan. 1940; 13 Mar. 1940; *Daily Mail*, 14 Feb. 1940; *Evening Standard*, 18 Mar. 1940; *Star*, 5 Dec. 1939; *Birmingham Mail*, 7 Feb. 1940; *Glasgow Herald*, 24 Feb. 1940.
[69] *Truth*, 22 Dec. 1939.
[70] *Picture Post*, 20 Jan. 1940.
[71] Cf., e.g., *Daily Telegraph*, 20 Oct. 1941; *News Chronicle*, 8 Nov. 1941. Strictly, this was not accurate, though the results came to much the same. The emigration regulations (*Juedische Nachrichtenblatt*, 17 April 1939, and 2 Feb. 1940) could not apply alone since the 'emigrant' remained in Reich territory. Recourse was also had to an earlier Ministry of Finance decree that property of persons hostile to the State could be confiscated.
[72] *Daily Telegraph*, 27 June 1941. This was actually from Yugoslavia. A regulation for the Reich was not issued until 1 Sept. 1941 (RGBL I, 547).

clear that the intention was to deport the entire Jewish population of Germany and Austria. One of the very few exceptions was a *Daily Herald* headline 'Bombed Nazis get Jews' Homes', which might have given the impression of a slightly different motive, though the report which followed did not.[73]

In the middle of 1942 the Press began to be filled with story after story telling of the actual slaughter of Jews. At first these stories came mainly from the Russian front, where *Einsatzgruppen* activities were having their results. There is no need of a long list. When the Russians began to advance in their turn much more was discovered and reported.[74] It ought to be noted, however, that it was only in this sector that any attempt was made to discount the evidence which was reaching the outside world. It is with no desire to discriminate against a particular section, but rather with regret, that it is once more necessary to turn to an organ of the Catholic Press in England. It was the *Catholic Times* which, on Christmas Eve 1942, while stating that there was 'no doubt about the German persecution of the Jews, nor about its horrible cruelty' thought that certain stories were only 'the horrible product of an unbridled propaganda', such as the Germans in Kiev using Jewish babies as footballs.[75] Perhaps this really was difficult to believe in 1942. It is a little hard to judge now—when we know, for example, that the commandant of a camp in Lwow would take shots at three-year-old children thrown up into the air in front of his balcony, to amuse his wife and nine-year-old daughter. In the next issue the implications of this reluctance to believe accounts of atrocities from the Eastern Front were made clearer:

It is no secret that the recent wave of propaganda about German atrocities against the Jews was Russian-inspired. The interesting thing was the extent to which large sections of the British people distinguished between the facts of German persecution of the Jews (which are well known and appreciated) and the tactical purpose of the present cam-

---

[73] *Daily Herald*, 20 Oct. 1941. For the other reports cf. *Daily Telegraph*, 18 Oct. 1941; *The Times*, 5 Nov. 1941; *Daily Mail*, 20 Oct. 1941; *Evening Standard*, 30 Oct. 1941; *Evening News*, 7 Nov. 1941.

[74] A list of the outstanding atrocities on the Russian Front, mostly reported at the time, appears in IMT I, 48–49. One of the earliest reports was in August 1941.

[75] *Catholic Times*, 24 Dec. 1942. Of course this *particular* incident *may* never have occurred. The *New Statesman*, 26 Dec. 1942, thought the story was 'nonsense'. The point is how the *Catholic Times* used it.

paign. 'What object is being aimed at in this propaganda?' was a question so commonly heard that it constitutes a footnote to present propagandist technique. Propaganda and news are no longer confused in the public mind.[76]

The *Catholic Times* may have had private means of information, but what were the sources for this 'recent wave', as far as the ordinary person could judge from the pages of the British Press? In the middle of June news came of the Vilna massacre. The source was Stockholm, to which a survivor had escaped. His story was reported factually with very little comment.[77] On 27 June the Polish Government in London, scarcely an organ of Soviet propaganda, issued its second 'White Book' of German atrocities with much information about the sufferings of the Jews.[78] Cardinal Hinsley, Roman Catholic Archbishop of Westminster, broadcast about this in the European Service of the B.B.C. No hint of Soviet inspiration is visible here either. The *Daily Telegraph*, certainly expressing a majority Press view, had this to say:

. . . terrible new facts have just come to light about the campaign of extermination against the Jews of Poland. Whether or not the figure of 700,000 victims given in the gruesome chronicle of massacre just made public by the Polish Council in London be accepted as precise, it is wholly in keeping with Hitler's many times avowed policy, and there will be ample means of verification when the time comes for judgment and expiation.[79]

The same point was made with brevity by the *Daily Sketch* in its headline to the report of Cardinal Hinsley's broadcast:

This is the Truth.[80]

At a meeting on 29 June and in a statement on 6 August, the British Section of the World Jewish Congress claimed that the Jews had already suffered more than any other race in the war, with a total of a million dead. The sources of its information were

---

[76] *Catholic Times*, 1 Jan. 1943.
[77] See, e.g., *Evening Standard*, 16 June 1942.
[78] The first had been issued in September 1941.
[79] *Daily Telegraph*, 27 June 1942.
[80] *Daily Sketch*, 9 June 1942.

largely Polish.[81] The headlines all expressed the fact—put in slightly different ways—that a million Jews had died.[82]

On 10 December the Polish Government issued a pamphlet summarizing the references to Jewish atrocities which had appeared in its two 'White Books', together with additional information on the same topic.[83] On 18 December, the Inter-Allied Information Committee published a detailed account of all that was so far known about Jews in German-occupied territory. It told of mass arrests, wholesale shootings, and deportations in Belgium and Holland, in France, Czechoslovakia, and Greece.[84] The Polish pamphlet described what happened to those who reached their destination alive. This entire picture of 'resettlement' followed by extermination was not greatly added to at Nuremberg. Britain, the United States, and the U.S.S.R. made 'a declaration of solemn protest', and members of the House of Commons rose and stood in silence after this had been announced by Anthony Eden.[85]

The effect of this latest information on the Press was profound. There were full accounts of the scene in the House, and long extracts were printed from the Committee's pamphlet.[86] It was not that it contained anything fundamentally new, but that an almost incredible state of affairs in Europe had been publicly and officially acknowledged—much as the state of the German camps had been acknowledged by the White Paper of 1939. The following editorial comment is typical:

The joint declaration issued by the Allies yesterday against Germany's bestial policy and cold-blooded extermination of the Jews says and

[81] The *Daily Telegraph* (30 June 1942) spoke of the same figures based on another source—not the W.J.C.—which was also Polish.

[82] Massacre of Jews—over 1,000,000 Dead since the War Began—*The Times*, 30 Jan. 1942; Greatest Pogrom One Million Jews Die—*Daily Mail*, 30 Jan. 1942; Jewish War Victims More than a Million Dead—*Manchester Guardian*, 30 Jan. 1942; Nazis Have Murdered a Million Jews—*Evening Standard*, 30 June 1942; One Million Jews Killed—*Glasgow Bulletin*, 7 Aug. 1942.

[83] *The Mass Extermination of Jews in German-Occupied Poland*, Republic of Poland, Ministry of Foreign Affairs, London (1942). A particularly impressive report appeared in the *Daily Mail*, 11 Dec. 1942.

[84] Great Britain, Foreign Office. *Persecution of the Jews* (Conditions in Occupied Territories, No. 6), London, HMSO (1942).

[85] *House of Commons Reports* (1942), cols. 2082–7.

[86] For a typical account of the House of Commons scene, cf. *Daily Mail*, 18 Dec. 1942. One of the most vivid appeared in the *Aberdeen Press and Journal*, 18 Dec. 1942. Extracts from the pamphlet were given considerable space for example in *The Times*, 1 Dec. 1942, and the *Sunday Times*, 20 Dec. 1942.

does no more than the facts fully justify. Whatever verification may be forthcoming or lacking for this or that detail, there is no room for doubt that the German Government is responsible for ordering the wholesale slaughter of Jewish people throughout Europe on a scale, and with a degree of inhumanity which makes its actions one of the foulest horrors in recorded history.[87]

Once again it was a Catholic paper which sounded a different note. It declared that 'the unprecedented act of the House of Commons' well expressed British feelings, but went on to say:

even if the reports are exaggerated, a half or a quarter of the accounts should suffice to produce the same reactions. The fact remains that in wartime especially such accounts are apt to be developed [a euphemism for 'embroidered'?] in the uncertain and dangerous transmission, and for the exact truth we must wait until the war is over. The second point is that persecution and the consequent moral reactions should be kept as clear as possible from propaganda. We must recall again that the murder of thousands of Catholics in Russia, Mexico and Spain was passed over almost in silence by those who today rightly lead the campaign to inform the world about what is now happening.[88]

At least it did not repeat this time that those murders of Catholics were committed by Jews in the guise of Soviet Commissars.[89] It is difficult to find many others who were willing to join in this private war with Russia. 'Russian-inspired' information or no— and in the second half of 1942 very little of it was—there was full readiness everywhere to accept facts as facts.

There is one other interesting point. The British Press did not only know the fact of extermination and some of the statistics involved. It also knew the method which became the most infamous of all, and of which every detail was eventually proved—the method of the gas chamber. As early as the autumn of 1939, the *Daily Sketch* had referred to a remark in *Mein Kampf* which Reitlinger has since found very significant:

In the last war [i.e. 1914–18] 10,000 to 15,000 Jews and Marxists should have been gassed at home so that the Government could have carried on the war more vigorously.[90]

[87] *News Chronicle*, 18 Dec. 1942.   [88] *Catholic Herald*, 24 Dec. 1942.
[89] See above, p. 19.
[90] *Daily Sketch*, 10 Nov. 1939 (Reitlinger, *Final Solution*, p. 123; *Mein Kampf*, 1939, English Edition, p. 553).

At the time of the World Jewish Congress meeting in 1942, the *Daily Telegraph* published a report sent to Szmul Zygielbojm, a leader of Polish Jewry who had succeeded in reaching London, of the thousands being killed by carbon monoxide gas in specially equipped lorries.[91] In July a report was circulating about 'a new poison gas discovered by the Nazis following experiments on Jews and political prisoners'.[92] This also turned out to be perfectly true. It was a substance known as Zyklon 'B'—an 'improvement' on the carbon monoxide method—which Rudolf Hoess, the commandant of Auschwitz, was later proudly to claim as his own contribution to the extermination programme.[93]

This question of the gas chambers was not given very great prominence at that time. In many reports of the Congress meeting it was omitted altogether, and only the *Daily Herald* gave it a headline.[94] On the other hand, in the very same month, the *News Review* printed an astonishingly accurate summary of the evolution of the gas chamber:

Death Refined

Bringing their taste for technical refinement into the gentle art of civilian murder, the Germans are using mobile gas chambers for execution behind the front, manned by S.S. and *Gestapo* men.

First introduced by the *Gestapo* to get rid of incurably ill people, gas was taken into special wards and released after patients had received a dose of sleeping-drug, keeping hospitals clear for wounded soldiers.

When war started, large gas stations were set up in Poland to kill off Jews who had been expelled from Germany to Lublin district as well as the Polish Jews who lived there.

No sleeping-drugs were wasted on them. They were just trussed up and finished off. Last winter gas lorries were taken behind the Eastern Front to liquidate guerillas.[95]

There is only one error here. The *News Review* found it hard to believe that the sick could have been exterminated without *some* sort of reason. Hence the reference to 'beds for wounded soldiers'. Aside from this, however, it described very well what was happening. There were numerous other examples of detailed knowledge.

[91] *Daily Telegraph*, 25 June 1942. For the Press and Zygielbojm's suicide a year later, see below, pp. 113–14.

[92] It came from a Russian source through Associated Press and penetrated to many distant corners, e.g. *Western Morning News* (Plymouth), 14 July 1942.

[93] IMT XI, 416. His first experiment had been in June 1941.

[94] *Daily Herald*, 30 June 1942.   [95] *News Review*, 16 June 1942.

An amazingly accurate report appeared in the *Manchester Guardian* of Hitler's 'model' camp—the fortress town of Theresienstadt, to which so-called 'privileged' Jews were sent, but which for many of them was only a transit point for Auschwitz and the gas chambers.[96] As the war continued so did the slaughter of Jewry. But there was this difference: on 31 January 1943, a German Army was trapped and annihilated at Stalingrad. The Russians began to recapture occupied territory and to uncover much fresh evidence of atrocities committed on the civilian population—including Jews. Methodical Government inquiry began to take the place of the individual reports of 'couriers' or escaped persons. In April 1943, some truly horrifying pictures appeared in the Press, obtained by the newly established Russian Commission,[97] and during the rest of the war information from this kind of source became more and more important. The process culminated in the overrunning of the camps themselves by the Allied troops, and the bringing to justice of some of those responsible. In other words, the official material used in the Nuremberg Trials was being accumulated in the last two years of the war.

However, there is one last aspect which cannot go unnoticed at this stage. We have seen that it was known how Jews were being sent from all parts of occupied [Europe for 'resettlement'. We have seen that it was known how, and in what quantities, they were being murdered. It was also known that these actions were part of a deliberate plan to exterminate *all* the Jews under Nazi rule—that it was Hitler's 'Final Solution' to the Jewish 'problem'.

References to the possibility of actual extermination are to be found in the Press at a surprisingly early date. One of the earliest hints appeared in the *Sheffield Telegraph*. In a discussion of where German refugees could go, it asked the following question:

. . . must the Jews of Germany perish in the wilderness as a million Armenians did when deported by the Turks? The question is not fantastic. To the advocates of racial purity remorseless thoroughness is always justified. And indeed they can argue that only the destruction of

[96] *Manchester Guardian*, 17 Sept. 1942. The standard work is by H. G. Adler, *Theresienstadt 1941–1945*, Tübingen (1955).

[97] *News Review*, 22 April 1943. The Soviet evidence was eventually published in two volumes, *Dokumenty Obren'ayut* (*The Documents Accuse*), Moscow-Leningrad, 1943–5, on the authority of the Extraordinary State Commission for the Ascertainment and Investigation of Crimes of the German-Fascist Invaders and their Associates.

the Armenians made possible the new Turkey which everyone praises today.[98]

This was in August 1938. Three months later, at the time of the Crystal Night, the German Press provided more solid material, to which reference has already been made in the previous chapter. *Das Schwarze Korps*, the official paper of the S.S., forecast the following programme for German Jewry:

The Jews must be driven from our residential districts and segregated where they will be among themselves, having as little contact with Germans as possible. Confined to themselves, these parasites will be reduced to poverty. . . . And when we then, as we shall have to, compel the affluent Jews to maintain their poor associates, they will all become destitute and then sink into delinquency. Let no one fancy that we shall stand idly by, merely watching this process. The German people are not in the least inclined to tolerate in their country hundreds and thousands of criminals. We would be faced with the hard necessity of exterminating this Jewish underworld in the same way as under our government of law and order we are wont to exterminate any other criminals—vīz: by fire and sword. The result would be the factual and final end of Jewry in Germany, its absolute annihilation.[99]

This was the first time that the key words 'to exterminate' ('auszuroten') and 'annihilation' ('Vernichtung') had been used so clearly and unambiguously.[1] Extracts from the article were quoted in the British Press, but the *Manchester Guardian* spoke of 'still darker threats' and quoted the significant final sentences, as did the *Daily Herald* and the *Daily Telegraph*.[2] The latter's headlines were the most unambiguous of all:

Threat to Kill off all Jews
U.S. and Britain Warned.

[98] *Sheffield Telegraph*, 6 Aug. 1938.
[99] *Das Schwarze Korps*, 22 Nov. 1938. There is a curious error in *The Black Book*, p. 122, which dates this quotation to 24 Nov., an error which is copied in other places, e.g. by Reitlinger, *Final Solution*, p. 8. The photostat of the *Neue Zuericher Zeitung*, from which *The Black Book* took its quotation, is clearly dated 24 Nov., and under date 23 Nov. says that 'yesterday' there appeared in *Das Schwarze Korps* the following article.
[1] For references to earlier statements cf. some interesting notes in *Wiener Library Bulletin* X (1956), p. 30.
[2] *Manchester Guardian*, 23 Nov. 1938; *Daily Herald*, 23 Nov. 1938; *Daily Telegraph*, 23 Nov. 1938.

Others, such as the *Evening News*, concentrated on the implied threats of a ghetto for the Jews and did not think the extermination threat worth quoting.[3]

At the beginning of 1939 Dr. Wilhelm Frick, Minister of the Interior, and Dr. Robert Ley, the Minister of Labour, made further statements about extermination. The latter was particularly striking: 'The fight against the Jews has not ended,' he said. 'As a matter of fact it will not have ended until the Jews throughout the world will have been exterminated.'[4] The Press reported these statements but still could not take them quite seriously. They were, to quote one typical comment, 'crude and blatant propaganda', and it would take a strong effort of the imagination to believe that any intelligent German could be deceived by it.[5] Even the creation of the Lublin reserve at the beginning of the war seemed at first only to mean extermination either 'accidentally', as it were, by starvation,[6] or in a figurative sense—by the obliteration of all Jewish life in the 'Greater Reich', i.e. Germany, Austria, Moravia, and parts of Western Poland. This last was the sense in which a *Spectator* article headed 'The Annihilation of German Jewry',[7] interpreted extermination. In its estimate of the immediate significance of those early threats, the Press was not wholly mistaken. The Nazis themselves did not decide upon their 'Final Solution' in its real form until some time in March 1941.[8] But the concept of extermination had become thoroughly familiar. Between 1938 and 1942 there were few that had not mentioned that the aim of the Nazis was to put an end to Jewish life in all the lands to which Nazi conquests would extend.

Throughout 1942 it became more and more apparent to the British Press that this was meant in a purely physical sense. In October, for example, the Press reported Himmler's boast that by Christmas not one Jew would be left in Germany. The presentation of this could leave no doubt in anyone's mind that the Press

[3] *Evening News*, 23 Nov. 1938.
[4] These remarks are not to be confused with similar but more violent ones which Ley made on the same topic four years later; see below, p. 100.
[5] *Edinburgh Evening News*, 7 Mar. 1939.
[6] As *The Times* thought in the passage cited above, p. 90.
[7] *Spectator*, 8 Mar. 1940.
[8] The problem of exactly when and to whom the famous 'Fuehrer Order' 'to exterminate all Jews, Gypsies and a-social elements' was issued is still obscure; cf. Reitlinger, op. cit., pp. 80–84.

was aware of the result: immediate death for the great majority.[9] In the event Himmler did not succeed. The great arms factories managed to hang on to much of their skilled labour considerably longer, and there seems to have been something amounting to organized sabotage of 'transports' from Berlin itself.[10] But at any rate the Press knew and printed every major report of extermination activities by the Nazis. In October, the *Manchester Guardian* commented as follows on a recent speech by Hitler in which extermination had been emphasized:

It is easy to take such a passage when first read as just another wild and whirling threat, but that would be a mistake. Hitler means what he says. He aims literally at the 'Extermination' of the Jews in Europe so far as his hand can reach them, and for weeks past reports from country after country have shown that the policy is being carried out with every circumstance of cruelty. When the war began there were perhaps six and a half million Jews in Europe. Half a million are so far safe in the countries free from Hitler. Between one and two millions are believed to have already been destroyed. Perhaps four and a half millions remain, to be, if Hitler has his way, exterminated.[11]

There is one error of fact here—the pre-war Jewish population was probably nearer to nine and a half than six and a half million[12] —but here this is of minor importance. The important point is the unambiguous exposition of Hitler's purpose.

Towards the end of November reports of definite extermination statistics began to reach the State Department in Washington and the American World Jewish Congress. It was said that two million Jews had actually perished and this turned out to be an astonishingly accurate figure. Casting up his accounts at the end of the year, a professional actuary, employed by the Nazis for this purpose, was to make it precisely 1,873,549 with the omission of Russia and Serbia.[13] These reports appeared in practically every

---

[9] Cf., e.g., *Daily Mail*, 12 Oct. 1942; *Daily Mirror*, 12 Oct. 1942; *Daily Sketch*, 12 Oct. 1942. The decree to deport all Jews and to replace skilled workers by Poles was issued on 26 Nov. (IMT XV, 43).

[10] *The Goebbels Diaries*, ed. and trans. L. P. Lochner, New York (1948), p. 294.

[11] *Manchester Guardian*, 27 Oct. 1942.

[12] The generally accepted figure for 1939 for countries later under the Nazis is 9,479,200; cf., e.g., statistical tables in *The Universal Jewish Encyclopedia*, X (1948), pp. 24–25, and table in M. Wischnitzer, *To Dwell in Safety*, Philadelphia (1948), p. 296.

[13] IMT documents, Nos. 5192–4, quoted by Reitlinger, *Final Solution*, p. 490.

section of the Press, and nowhere was it suggested that they were not authentic. The presentation and space allotted varied from the many additional details obtained by *The Times* and *Manchester Guardian*, and the full account of the World Jewish Congress statement printed, for example, by the *Yorkshire Post*, to much shorter announcements appearing in some of the London and provincial papers. Essentially the same effect was achieved: the unambiguous declaration that two million European Jews had perished.[14] The most detailed report of all appeared in an article by Israel Cohen in the *Contemporary Review*; it summarized all that was known from the various sources mentioned, and presented a complete picture of the destruction of European Jewry.[15] Finally, in May 1943, an event occurred which must have removed every possible remaining scrap of doubt about what was going on. This was another speech by Ley, in which he referred to the Jewish question:

We swear we are not going to abandon the struggles until the last Jew in Europe has been exterminated and is actually dead. It is not enough to isolate the Jewish enemy of mankind—the Jew has got to be exterminated.

This was the text as it eventually appeared in the Nuremberg indictment.[16] The Reuter version at the time differed slightly, but the meaning was just as plain. It is interesting to note that, by then, pronouncements of this kind were beginning to lose their news value. Even the *Manchester Guardian* did not give it great prominence, while the *Daily Telegraph*'s main interest in it was as evidence of a last despairing shout by the Nazis before the collapse of their régime.[17] However, it was reported. And it is equally worth noting that the *relative* prominence given such items before the war remained unaffected by the wartime shortage of newsprint—or by the pressure of the war news itself on the space available.

[14] Cf., e.g., *Manchester Guardian*, 25 Nov. 1942; 5 Dec. 1942; *The Times*, 4, 5, and 7 Dec. 1942; *Yorkshire Post*, 2 Dec. 1942; and in contrast *Daily Telegraph*, 2 Dec. 1942; 4 Dec. 1942; *Aberdeen Evening Express*, 2 Dec. 1942; *Bristol Evening World*, 2 Dec. 1942; *Empire News* (Manchester), 29 Nov. 1942; *Northern Whig* (Belfast), 25 Nov. 1942; *Nottingham Guardian*, 2 Dec. 1942; *Sheffield Telegraph*, 25 Nov. 1942; *Evening Standard*, 2 Dec. 1942.

[15] *Contemporary Review*, February 1943.   [16] IMT II, 36.

[17] *Manchester Guardian*, 4 May 1943; *Daily Telegraph*, 4 May 1943; cf. *The Times*, 4 May 1943.

IV

The Jewish Answer

O N 26 March 1933, a small sports car drew up outside the
offices of the Board of Deputies in Woburn House, London. On a placard which dwarfed its tiny windscreen the
following announcement could be read:

JUDEA DECLARES WAR ON GERMANY
BOYCOTT ALL GERMAN GOODS[1]

Similar phrases, when used to imply that the events in Germany
symbolized an equal struggle between Jew and Nazi, instead of a
cold-blooded persecution of one by the other, were of course
utterly misleading. Yet, in a different context, they were both
true and important. From the beginning to the end there were
various efforts to help the victims or exact retribution from the
guilty. These efforts were not confined to England. They were
undertaken by many national and international bodies, both Jewish and non-Jewish. They were the work of a vast miscellany of
groups and individuals. In a very real sense, these efforts constituted a war against one type of Nazi activity long before September 1939. The armed rising of the survivors in the Warsaw
Ghetto, the fight of the Jewish partisans behind the lines on the
Eastern Front, and the last desperate attempt to save the remnant
of the Jewish communities in Hungary, were all part of the same
story. The various trials form the natural epilogue. Atrocities
committed against Jews have formed a substantial part of the
indictment at most of them. Thus, attitudes towards Nazi anti-
Semitism should be taken together with what may be termed the
various answers to it. It is logical to begin with attitudes towards
what was done by the Jews themselves.

The attempt to impose a boycott on German goods was the first

[1] See picture widely reproduced on the following day in London and the
provinces, e.g. in *Birmingham Post*, 27 Mar. 1933.

B.P.N.R.—8

episode in the 'War of Judea on Germany'. By the summer of 1933 there were boycott movements, Jewish and non-Jewish, active in Britain, the United States, France, Holland, Poland, and Sweden. The British Board of Deputies itself, however, never participated —on the ground that German retaliation would make matters worse. It is not easy to estimate what effect the boycott actually had. After a year or two, there is little doubt that it did succeed in damaging German economy, even if not to the extent claimed in some enthusiastic quarters. References to the practical results of the boycott appeared in the Press, but they did not gain a great deal of publicity. In August 1933 there were comments on the boycott as applied to German shipping and on some retaliatory measures (which proved abortive) that the German shipping lines had thought of adopting.[2] Three months later there were references to a pessimistic article in the *Boersen-Zeitung*, the German financial paper, and to a German Board of Trade circular asking British firms for an estimate of how much their trade in German goods had been suffering.[3] The spread of active anti-Semitism in the wake of German expansion caused the boycott to spread as well, and produced a little more publicity about its probable effect. The *Daily Telegraph*, for example, gave some prominence to Italian indignation at a supposed boycott of fruit auctions in Covent Garden, London's central fruit and vegetable market.[4] Trade papers spoke of the serious effects the *Anschluss* with Austria was having on the Viennese fashion houses.[5] The Federation of Synagogues gained a smallish headline when they banned Italian marble for tombstones,[6] and once again there was talk of the boycott on German shipping.[7] An extreme version of the effect of the boycott appeared at the beginning of the period in the *Daily Express* with the headline

JEWS' BOYCOTT CUTS GERMAN EXPORTS
NOW LOWEST SINCE 1918

and an optimistic report by someone described as a 'special representative'.[8] On the other hand, a very cautious report appeared

---

[2] *Southern Daily Echo* (Southampton), 25 Aug. 1933, quoting a shipping trade paper.
[3] *Manchester Guardian*, 28 Oct. 1933.   [4] *Daily Telegraph*, 8 Sept. 1938.
[5] *Women's Wear News*, 17 Mar. 1938.   [6] *News Chronicle*, 8 Sept. 1938.
[7] E.g. *Sunday Times*, 25 Dec. 1938.   [8] *Daily Express*, 31 May 1934.

early in 1939 in the *Scotsman*.[9] Probably the *Financial News* was most accurate in its opinion that it was only certain classes of goods and services which had been affected, for example the Christmas toy trade, and this mainly in exports to the United States.[10]

From one point of view it was not unreasonable that publicity about the effects of the boycott should have been comparatively small. They were difficult to estimate and, in the end, probably not very startling. In any case, if the pre-war period be taken as a whole, the Germans made up many of their losses from the boycott by increased trade with Palestine as a direct result of increased emigration to that country by German Jews. The capital demanded from certain classes of immigrant by the British authorities was permitted to be transferred if it was offset by equivalent Palestinian imports from Germany. A special agency was set up to that end and, by the spring of 1938, it had handled upwards of eight million pounds sterling.[11] At least one paper, quoting 'a Jewish authority', had forecast that Germany might take such steps as an explicit reply to the boycott.[12]

Another point received considerably less attention than might have been expected. On the occasion of the 1939 Leipzig Fair, a provincial paper reprinted a letter from a local firm which had refused to participate as a protest, and commented:

The promoters of the British Industries Fair are . . . expecting a record patronage, but the hopes of those responsible for the Leipzig Fair will fall very considerably if they receive many letters such as this.[13]

The fairly obvious implication—that worse business for the Germans meant better business for the British—was never really taken up. Few links were made between the boycott of German goods and the 'Buy British' campaign which was being conducted at the time, and whose slogans some local boycott committees actually used.[14] The main point of the boycott, however, was symbolic. It was the first act of retaliation by the Jews against their

[9] *Scotsman*, 4 Feb. 1939.   [10] *Financial News*, 28 Dec. 1938.
[11] *Manchester Guardian*, 27 May 1938. This was the 'Haavarah' (Hebrew word meaning 'transfer') established in November 1933, and abolished in 1938, when Nazi hatred outweighed their financial advantage (see TWC XIV, 553). A very interesting and detailed article on the *Haavarah* appeared in *Great Britain and the East*, April 1936.
[12] *Liverpool Post*, 25 Aug. 1933.   [13] *Hereford Times*, 7 Jan. 1939.
[14] See, e.g., report in *South Wales Echo*, 20 Dec. 1938.

persecutors, and its treatment by the British Press must be judged with this point of view in mind.

Press attitudes on the general aspects of the boycott could be described as 'fairly benevolent interest' rather than either violent opposition or support. The *Sunday Referee*, it is true, gave the start of the boycott a big coverage and did its best to encourage it in every way it could. It was even at pains to stress the complete unity of Anglo-Jewry over the issue, which, as has been seen, plain fact unhappily belied.[15] But the *Sunday Referee* was exceptional.[16] A negative approach, so far as it was to be found, implied that boycott and counter-boycott (that is Berlin's April 1st) were both a private Nazi-Jewish affair, with possibly unfortunate consequences for the innocent bystander. Thus, in an early reference, the *Economist* spoke of it with faint disparagement as a 'quarrel between Nazi Germany and world-wide Jewry'.[17] Neither view was representative of the Press as a whole.[18] It was not long before the *Economist* saw that something more serious than a quarrel was in question, and we have noticed already that the tendency, in other quarters, to think of persecution in some such terms was simply the result of efforts to find an original approach at all costs.[19] More indicative of widely held views, but equally rare in actual print, was the rebuke administered by the *Streatham News* to the local vicar, who had exhorted a Rotary Club meeting not to take its holidays in Germany: 'To tour the Rhine by no means suggests the holiday-maker condones anti-semitism or agrees with Pastor Niemoller being in a concentration camp.'[20] But German propaganda made it very clear that 'touring the Rhine' *did* suggest condonation.

A more common and not unreasonable criticism of the boycott was the fear expressed by some trade papers that firms which insisted on continuing business with Germany might be subjected to coercion at home. The *Draper's Record*, for example, said:

Many textile manufacturers and merchants have willingly given the undertaking sought by the association [the Jewish Textile Traders

---

[15] *Sunday Referee*, 23 July 1933; cf. 16 July 1933.

[16] Of course, isolated examples can be found. The *Leeds Mercury*, for instance, gave headlines to the Geneva meeting (2 Aug. 1933).

[17] *Economist*, 1 April 1933.

[18] The *Referee* was for part of this time Jewish-owned, but its exceptional approach was probably intended only to differentiate it from its Sunday competitors.

[19] See above, pp. 20–2.   [20] *Streatham News*, 5 Aug. 1938.

Association—one of the boycott committees] because they sympathise with its cause, but there are some who feel, rightly or wrongly, that they are being coerced into participating in the boycott and that unless their names are enrolled on the list the prospect of further business from members of the Jewish faith will be remote. Mr. Goldstein [secretary of the Association] states that the dispute is between a foreign government and all supporters of individual liberty. It should in that case be dealt with nationally by the Government and not by members of any one faith or race.[21]

Though the fear was not unreasonable, the conclusion was either disingenuous or singularly unintelligent. For who could seriously suppose that the Government had any intentions of 'dealing' with anything of the kind? And was it so wrong, under the circumstances, for the co-religionists of the sufferers to try to take matters into their own hands, seeing that this affair was certainly a threat to basic individual liberties too? A far more plausible criticism was that expressed more than once by the Board of Deputies itself, based on the illusion that a particular course of action by Jews outside Germany could really influence Nazi behaviour for the worse. As late as the end of November 1938, when, it is true, the more obvious folly of 'appeasement' in the broader field of international politics still found plenty of supporters, a provincial paper thought it

doubtful whether those methods [boycott, tariffs, etc.] would produce the desired effect as they would assuredly be represented in Germany as the acts of external Jewry, and it must also be remembered that such action might have a serious reaction on the Jews remaining in that country.[22]

But the fact that no strong dislike of the boycott on any grounds existed is supported by an interesting piece of evidence. No paper ever made derogatory use of the circumstance that the British Communist Party did its best to take as prominent a lead as it could over this issue, just as over that of atrocities. The activities in this field of the Jewish People's Council Against Fascism and Anti-Semitism—a Communist 'front' organization if ever there was one—were as objectively reported as those of any other boycott committee. A mass demonstration held by that body in the East End of London, calling for an intensification of boycott

---

[21] *Draper's Record*, 27 April 1935.   [22] *Lincolnshire Echo*, 22 Nov. 1938.

measures, received, for example, a notice in the far from Communist *Daily Sketch*, from the pen of Sir Antony Jenkinson, almost
identical with the notice in the *Daily Worker*.[23]

Apart from political slants of various kinds, the boycott gained
a certain amount of incidental publicity arising out of three separate aspects. First, the formation of a new local committee was
sure to get an initially prominent mention in the local Press. Thus
the formation of a committee in Manchester, with a name which
could not but strike a sub-editor's imagination—the Watchmen of
Israel—obtained adequate presentation. The *Manchester Daily
Dispatch* spoke of a 'Jews' Black List' and a 'Manchester Boycott
Week', while the *Manchester Evening Chronicle* featured the communal controversy which immediately arose over the boycott
methods which the 'Watchmen' were supposed to have in mind.[24]
The *Manchester Guardian* reports were sober by contrast but they
too were detailed enough.[25]

Secondly, the hesitations of the Board of Deputies earned headlines on one or two occasions, which tended to exaggerate this
point, much as the *Sunday Referee* minimized it. Of course, if the
only bad publicity is no publicity, then this must also be counted
as a positive achievement for the movement. To a report, for
example, of some anti-Semitic propaganda having been scattered
among the Sunday crowds on a Thames towpath, the *Daily
Herald* gave the headline,

JEWS SPLIT
WHILE
NAZIS RAIN
LEAFLETS[26]

This was not entirely an accident, since one of the leaders of the
opposition to the Board's official boycott position was A. L.
Easterman, the paper's chief Foreign Editor.[27] Some months later,
Lord Rothschild's resignation from the Vice-Presidency of the
Board, with headlines that spread over three columns in the *News*

---

[23] *Daily Sketch*, 16 Nov. 1938; cf. *Daily Worker*, 16 Nov. 1938.

[24] *Manchester Daily Dispatch*, 15 Jan. 1934; *Manchester Evening Chronicle*,
15 Jan. 1934.

[25] *Manchester Guardian*, 15 Jan. 1934.   [26] *Daily Herald*, 24 July 1933.

[27] Now (1963) Director of the International Affairs Department, Foreign
Executive, World Jewish Congress.

Chronicle, was connected with the boycott question, though such a connexion was at best doubtful.[28]

Lastly, it is certainly true that the *Daily Herald*, during the whole of this period, gave considerable publicity to the boycott of German goods. But it was publicity of a very specific kind. Not unnaturally, its entire stress was on the campaign initiated by the National Joint Council, by the Labour Party and Trade Unions, and by the international organization—the Non-Sectarian Anti-Nazi Boycott Council—with which these bodies became associated.[29] The *Daily Herald* reports of the inaugural London conference of this Council are remarkable for the fact that the main references to the Jewish aspects of the matter were assertions that the boycott ought not to be, and henceforth would not be, a 'Jewish' one at all. However, it was undoubtedly publicity of a sort.[30] The fact was simply that, despite the undoubted strength and sincerity of the desire evinced by the *Daily Herald* (as well as by the whole Labour Movement) to fight the cruelties of the Nazi régime, it did not give the impression that it really understood the implications of the step which the Jewish community had taken in that direction. And this was the case with most of the Press. Such words as 'retaliation' and 'weapon' appeared now and then,[31] but their significance was not appreciated. After centuries of submission the Jews were preparing to fight, not only, be it said, at the risk of financial loss, but also with the probability of antagonizing many Gentiles in a normally friendly land.[32] They were ready to risk this in a Jewish cause as Jews.

It may be objected that as far as the onlooker went it was, when all is said and done, more a matter of account books. It had not enough drama to interest a journalist. As it happens, an incident

[28] *News Chronicle*, 7 May 1934; for contrast cf. the very quiet reference in the *Evening Standard*, 7 May 1934, to the Board's denial of resignations on this account.

[29] It did, of course, have items on the Jewish movement of occasional prominence (e.g. 5 Oct. 1934) but they were exceptional.

[30] *Daily Herald*, 19 Nov. 1934; 24 Nov. 1934; 26 Nov. 1934; 27 Nov. 1934; 28 Nov. 1934; and similar publicity for the body which grew out of this, e.g. 20 April 1936.

[31] See, e.g., headlines in *Observer*, 29 Oct. 1938; *Daily Sketch*, 27 Dec. 1938.

[32] For example, the *British Trade Journal*, December 1934, pointed out that an effective boycott would injure Germany's mainly British overseas creditors who, it had been agreed, were to be partly repaid from the value of German imports.

did occur which was rather more dramatic, and Press reactions to it are worth describing. On 28 September 1933, the first night of a German play, 'Before Sunset', was disturbed by a furious and obviously planned demonstration directed against Werner Krauss, its leading man, 'hailed', it was said, 'by the Hitler régime as a pattern of Nordic culture'.[33] There was much shouting of slogans, much throwing of stink-bombs and leaflets, and the police had to be called in before the play could continue. The leaflets and slogans left no doubt that the organizers meant to induce a boycott of this type of German goods, and that there was some specifically Jewish initiative behind this. This incident received a uniformly bad Press. From the *Evening Standard*'s 'noisy and malodorous demonstration by hooligans' to an unpleasant remark about 'foreign Jews' which the *Sunday Times* saw fit to make, there was a unanimous chorus of shocked disapproval.[34] The only exception was the *Sunday Referee* theatre critic, who wrote rather unkindly that he had found the demonstration more amusing than the play.[35] It was glaringly un-British to throw stink-bombs at leading actors, and distinguished visitors at that, and even more un-British to mix politics with art. As everyone pointed out with wearisome rectitude, it was the Nazis themselves who were prone to do just this very thing. The general view was expressed in an editorial comment by the *Nottingham Evening News:*

The Jewish sufferers from Nazi fanaticism . . . must keep their retaliatory measures in line with British tradition. They cannot protest against the ill-treatment of distinguished Jews in Germany and at the same time deny a fair hearing to a brilliant German actor in London.[36]

Of course the demonstrators were unmannerly in their attempt to stop an actor from doing his job on the stage, though it is per-

---

[33] Hannen Swaffer in the *Daily Herald*, 29 Sept. 1933.

[34] *Evening Standard*, 29 Sept. 1933; *Sunday Times*, 1 Oct. 1933; cf. *Star* 29 Sept. 1933; *Daily Mirror*, 29 Sept. 1933; *Daily Mail*, 30 Sept. 1933; *Sheffield Independent*, 30 Sept. 1933; *Sunday Dispatch*, 1 Oct. 1933. The *Evening Standard* ended its comment thus: 'With the painless extermination of a group of yelping children and that first act played much more quickly, "Before Sunset" should survive its exciting premiere for a long time.' It would be unfair to stress this, since it was 1933 not 1943, but it shall not escape mention in a footnote.

[35] *Sunday Referee*, 1 Oct. 1933.

[36] *Nottingham Evening News*, 29 Sept. 1933.

missible to ask if their behaviour could seriously be compared with what the Nazis (even by September 1933) had succeeded in doing in similar fields. Nor was Krauss himself responsible for anything the Nazis had done. But how precisely did the rebuke about British tradition apply? Few asserted that this incident, ill-advised and slightly absurd as it may have been, was nevertheless an attempt to make as public as possible the only means of retaliation in fact open to British Jews at that time. This was the boycott of all German goods and services which, as we have seen, never gained all the publicity it might have done. Logically, the connexion should have been obvious enough. The Press did not see it nor did it give the affair the limited sympathy which in its eyes it might have deserved. Traditionally British retaliatory measures were badly shaken by Munich, and finally succumbed on 1 September 1939, when the dropping of the 'Herr' in front of 'Hitler' by *The Times* made good manners to the Nazis no longer obligatory.

From 1939 to 1945, following these boycotts, there were many instances of physical resistance to the Nazis. The best known is the rising in the Warsaw Ghetto, which took place in April and May 1943. This episode made a great impression at the time, and a vast literature has grown up about it since, of which special bibliographies exist.[37] English readers might do worse than begin with John Hersey's *The Wall*, a piece of fiction, but one which brings out with painstaking exactitude every known detail of the struggle, besides giving an excellent picture of ghetto life as a whole.[38] The

[37] E.g. P. Friedman, *Bibliography of the Warsaw Ghetto*, *Jewish Book Annual XI*, N.Y. (1952–3), and various entries in J. Robinson and P. Friedman, *Guide to Jewish History Under Nazi Impact*, N.Y. (1960).

[38] J. Hersey, *The Wall*, London (1950). The novel is carefully based upon accounts by survivors, and upon the diaries and records of Dr. E. Ringelblum, the Ghetto's official archivist, who managed to conceal them in a safe place before his own murder by the Nazis. This material began to come to light from September 1946, and a part of it has been translated and edited by J. Sloan, *Notes from the Warsaw Ghetto*, N.Y. (1958). Other accounts in English include B. Goldstein, *The Stars Bear Witness*, London (1950) (also a translation), and references in general works, e.g. in J. Tenenbaum, *Underground*, N.Y. (1952), pp. 73–166; Reitlinger, pp. 272–80; *Black Book*, pp. 435–44. There is not a great deal in English on the Jewish Resistance as a whole apart from the rather sentimental account by M. Syrkin, *Blessed be the Match*, London (1948). The latest and best accounts are in Hebrew, *The Jewish Partisans*, Jerusalem (1958), and *The Book of Ghetto Battles*, 3rd ed., Tel-Aviv (1956), both edited by various hands under the authority of the Yad Va-Shem Institute.

story of the Warsaw Ghetto is simple enough to summarize. It was physically established in November 1940 as part of the first stage in the policy of concentrating the Jews in certain East European centres. The second stage began on 22 July 1943 when Jews were seized for 'resettlement', that is sent to the gas chambers of Treblinka. This process continued methodically for the next eighteen months. On 18 January 1943, an S.S. squad was attacked while conveying a group to the resettlement transfer point. There were a great many casualties but the survivors were freed. This was the beginning of efforts by the Z.O.B.—an underground group of Jewish fighters, including elements from all the main communal bodies—to hinder resettlement by force.[39] When it became obvious that the results would be small and that the Nazis would certainly succeed in their purpose of liquidating the Ghetto, the Z.O.B. prepared for open resistance. S.S. troops in full battle order marched into the Ghetto on 19 April 1943 and fighting broke out which continued till 16 May. Against Jews armed with a few pistols obtained by fantastic ingenuity from the 'Aryan side', the S.S. were compelled to use tanks, light artillery, and just over 2,000 troops, finally destroying the entire Ghetto area. The Jews fought alone, with very little help from the Polish underground, whose main service was its excellent courier system, through which the London Poles obtained many details of these events as they took place.[40] Under those conditions, the losses suffered by the Jews were very heavy. About thirteen thousand were killed in action, while seven thousand taken prisoner were gassed in Treblinka. Nazi casualties were slight indeed in comparison—fifteen dead and seventy-four wounded—but the moral shock was not inconsiderable. When the rising was officially over (though isolated resistance continued in the ruins till September), Juergen Stroop, the Warsaw S.S. Commander, was so delighted that he had his report printed on seventy-five pages of the finest paper, lavishly illustrated, and bound in the best morocco

[39] Initials stand for 'Jewish Fighter Organization' in Polish (*Zydowska Organizacja Bojowa*).

[40] For example, the full text of the Re-Settlement Order of July 22nd was printed in the Polish *Note* of 10 Dec. to the United Nations (pp. 11–12) (already referred to here, see above, p. 93), as were the figures of resettlement from July to October (*Note*), p. 9. For the paucity of Polish assistance to the Ghetto fighters, see below, p. 123.

leather. He presented it to his superior officer with the title, 'The Warsaw Ghetto is No More'.[41]

In evaluating Press reactions to some of these events, it is obviously difficult to maintain a just sense of perspective. The early months of 1943 were a crucial period of the war. They saw the first really heavy blows by the Allies against the Axis powers. The Russians launched their first great offensive after their victory at Stalingrad. The Americans began on a methodical reconquest of the Pacific. German towns were subjected to continuous day and night air attack. At the very moment that the Ghetto was being destroyed, combined British and American forces were winning their final victories in North Africa and were soon to begin their invasion of Europe by landing in Sicily. At a time when events such as these were taking place, the Press could hardly be blamed overmuch if, with the limited amount of newsprint at its disposal, it gave a comparatively small amount of space to the Ghetto rising.

In fact, apart from the customary accurate and sympathetic reporting in the *Manchester Guardian*, quite a number of instances can be found where presentation and emphasis indicated that the rising did have news value. For example, the Manchester *Sunday Chronicle* gave it headlines with a six-column spread,

WARSAW JEWS DEFY NAZI MIGHT IN LAST STAND AGAINST MASS MURDER
PITCHED BATTLE RAGES IN GHETTO[42]

and the *Evening Standard* printed a prominent feature article.[43] The rising also received a great deal of publicity in the Labour weekly *Tribune*, the most outstanding item being a long review of survivor accounts, which appeared in commemoration of the first anniversary.[44] The *Evening Standard* also had an article showing a most impressive understanding of what the rising meant. It deserves extended quotation:

[41] For a description of this report, see IMT III, 553–8. The original German text is printed in IMT XXVI, pp. 628–94, and the official English translation in *Nazi Conspiracy and Aggression*, III, Washington (1946), pp. 718–75. For a contemptuous comment by the German Regular Army on this fuss over 'a little murder expedition', see G. M. Gilbert, *Nuremberg Diary*, New York (1947), p. 69.

[42] *Sunday Chronicle* (Manchester), 23 May 1943.

[43] *Evening Standard*, 18 Aug. 1943.

[44] *Tribune*, 25 Aug. 1944; a feature article summarizing the history of the rising appeared on 21 April 1944.

Six weeks ago the Wehrmacht laid siege to Warsaw's Ghetto. Men doomed to extermination by Hitler's race decrees determined to sell their lives dearly. With bare fists they fought a modern army in a struggle that could have only one end—undying death in a proud challenge to Nazi tyranny. . . . Three weeks ago . . . the Jews were continuing to resist in a few remaining strongholds. The battle may be raging still; we do not know. What we do know is that brave men have faced death and worse without prospect of succour or victory, but in the hope that the world will be stirred to swifter action against Nazis now seeking to destroy the soul of a nation.

April 19th, 1943, henceforth will be an honoured day among men who love their fellows and cherish the civilised qualities of mercy and toler-ance . . . [the Ghetto] was converted into a fortress of freedom. . . . Jew no longer fights Jew on many fronts for conflicting causes. All Jews fight today on one front—humanity's cause.[45]

But such clear statements were exceptional. It was inevitable that between 1942 and 1944 there should have been a vast pre-ponderance of items referring to the persecution and slaughter of Jewish communities, with comparatively few accounts of Jewish resistance—organized or otherwise. Little information, after all, could be expected to reach the British Press about the skirmishes of partisans in the depths of Lithuanian forest. But the approach to a piece of news, and its general presentation, is at least as im-portant as the amount of information given about it, and is often as good a guide when little information is available. Accounts of Jewish partisan actions, when they did become known, were re-ported as interesting items of war news (which they undoubtedly were) but in a certain matter-of-fact manner with no hint of the extraordinary historical fact that, after many centuries, Jews were fighting their enemies, arms in hand, not as members of the forces of this or that nation, but as Jews.

From 1940 onwards, the full details of the misery and the grad-ual destruction of Warsaw Jewry were reported in the Press, just as the fate of Jewry as a whole was reported. A large picture in the *Sunday Chronicle* gives a vivid impression of early Ghetto legislation, showing Jews wearing a distinctive yellow triangle and compelled to walk in Warsaw gutters.[46] Accounts of food shortage, high prices, and the general worsening of living conditions ap-

---

[45] *Evening Standard*, 2 June 1943.   [46] *Sunday Chronicle*, 31 Dec. 1939.

peared perhaps most frequently in the *Manchester Guardian*.[47] As we saw, the start and the development of the 'resettlement action' was known in London and was reported in a wide variety of papers,[48] with at least one photograph of Jews being marched to the 'transfer point'.[49] The fact that some sections of the Press were under certain illusions until the last moment[50] and some even after that[51] and that the space given to this class of item tended to be somewhat meagre is not so important in the present context. Here, as on the whole question of atrocity and extermination, the Press knew well and printed accurately exactly what was happening. Yet when it came to descriptions of the rising it looked upon that, too, as essentially part and parcel of this destruction of the defenceless, and not as something new. A good illustration of this attitude is to be found in the *Leader*, a very popular weekly of the time. Pictures to mark the anniversary of the rising were either of children 'born in bloodshed and famine' or of old people who had 'almost completed their span and care little what happens now'.[52] The dominant emphasis was on the holocaust of a helpless population and not on the heroism of the few.

Another example ought to be mentioned. On 12 May, while the battle was going on in the Ghetto, Szmul Zygielbojm, the representative of the Jewish Labour Movement on the Polish National Council, committed suicide in a London flat. It was known at the time, and became absolutely clear a fortnight later from the text of the letter he had left behind, that his death had been both a protest against the little that had been done to save the millions of his people in Europe and an act of solidarity with the Ghetto fighters. The second aspect was scarcely mentioned at all. *The Times* and the *Manchester Guardian* printed short laudatory notices of Zygielbojm's achievement for Polish working-class Jewry, and of his part in the defence of Warsaw in 1939. Neither notice

---

[47] Cf. *Manchester Guardian*, 10 Jan. 1940, for an early instance.

[48] Apart from the obvious references items may be noted in *Glasgow Daily Record*, 28 July 1942; *Yorkshire Observer*, 28 July 1942.

[49] *Birmingham Gazette*, 2 Jan. 1943; cf. *News Chronicle*, 21 Sept. 1942, for picture of a general S.S. raid on the Ghetto.

[50] The *Catholic Times*, 5 June 1942, accepted a German newspaper statement that 'elaborate steps were being taken to preserve instead of doom' Warsaw Jews for work on munitions.

[51] *Glasgow Evening News*, 31 July 1942, thought the resettled were being sent to Russia 'to build roads and fortifications'.

[52] *Leader*, 18 Mar. 1944.

mentioned that his death had been by suicide, still less that there had been a purpose behind it.[53] The bulk of *Time & Tide*'s even briefer remarks was concerned with Zygielbojm's adventurous escape from Poland in 1940.[54] Other accounts were longer and more detailed. The *Daily Herald*, as the official Labour paper, had more than one reference, the *Tribune* had a column, and the *News Chronicle* a feature article which included the text of his letter.[55] But it is very striking that scarcely any connexion was made between this last action of a Jewish Pole in London and the last action of his comrades in Warsaw which were taking place at precisely the same moment. The *Sunday Chronicle* was one of the very few papers which in its story of the last stages of the Ghetto rising included a reference to Zygielbojm's funeral. But even there the stress was on the first aspect.[56] Yet both the Ghetto Rising and Zygielbojm's death were acts of resistance—as well as part of the Jewish tragedy of our day.

Some years after it was all over, a reviewer of a book on Jewish resistance by Marie Syrkin[57] said that part of the reason the Allies had done so little to help Hitler's Jewish victims was a possibly subconscious insufficiency of sympathy towards a people which apparently made so little effort to fight their oppressor.

Our imagination refused to take in the idea of six million people docilely entering gas chambers without striking a blow to defend themselves. Even consciously, some of us asked how it was that there was so little resistance among a people who had ample warning of their fate.[58]

We have already seen that not only was this not true as a matter of history, but that there was information enough in the Press to convince even Allied Governments on this point. It may be, however, that the reviewer's analysis had another validity. In spite of all the facts which it printed the Press did not really succeed in altering the traditional picture of the pitiful Ghetto Jew persecuted for centuries—and now 'docilely entering gas chambers'. The majority certainly did go ignorant or unprotesting, and Marie Syrkin (among others) gave reasons for it. But the picture of the

[53] *Manchester Guardian*, 15 May 1943; *The Times*, 19 May 1943.
[54] *Time & Tide*, 22 May 1943.
[55] *Daily Herald*, 13 May 1943; 18 May 1943; 22 May 1943; *Tribune*, 27 May 1943; *News Chronicle*, 1 June 1943; cf. *Sunday Dispatch*, 23 May 1943.
[56] See above, p. 112.   [57] See above, p. 109, note 38.
[58] *New Statesman*, 26 June 1948.

Jewish fighter, although sometimes described in words, was not understood in its full significance. This failure in understanding was simply a failure of imagination.

Apart from direct physical resistance, there were other Jewish groups on the continent of Europe who were by no means passive spectators of their own destruction. There was an attempt to negotiate with the Nazis themselves in order to save the remnant of the Hungarian community. In the summer of 1944, the emissary of a semi-illegal Jewish relief and rescue organization, accompanied by a member of the Gestapo, arrived in Istanbul with an extraordinary proposition. The S.S. Command, he said, was prepared to spare the remainder of Hungarian Jewry in return for various British supplies, mainly army lorries, which would not be used on the Western Front. The offer was immediately and indignantly refused and the British Press showed itself to be unanimously in favour of this reaction.

The British Government know what value to set on any German or German-sponsored offer. They know that there can be no security for the Jews or the other oppressed people of Europe until victory is won. The allies are fighting to achieve that security, and they know, as well as the Germans, what happens when one begins to pay blackmail. The blackmailer increases his price. Such considerations provide their own answer to the proposed bargain.[59]

The main Press emphasis, however, was that the offer was intended to split the Allies.

. . . By exploitation of their humanity, the United Nations, it was thought, might be split. If the Russians would not respond, all the better; the Anglo-Saxons would be so tender-hearted that they would not mind helping Germany with supplies to withstand the 'Bolshevik hordes'; the edge of the combined offensive would be blunted if not turned.[60]

The plan's only purpose was for 'fomenting Russian suspicions'.[61] Moscow was intended to believe 'the Americans ready . . . to save Jewish lives at the expense of Russian lives on the Eastern Front'.[62]

Certainly, one of the intentions behind the offer was to sow dissension between Russia and the West,[63] though there were others, not the least being a desire on the part of higher Nazi officials to acquire a name for moderation when the day of reckoning came. The story of the negotiations is extremely complex; to this day there remains doubt and disagreement even in Jewish circles on many cardinal points, while at the time very little was known about it in England.[64] But on one point there should be no misunderstanding: the men and women who deliberately sought out Nazi officials for this purpose took their lives in their hands and frequently lost them. It was as positive an act of resistance as that of the partisan units and the Ghetto fighters, and nearly as dangerous. It was consciously thought of, by at least one of the leading participants, as part of that same active struggle against the Nazis, and one which culminated in partial success with the limited protection given eventually by the Swedish Legation, Papal representatives, and the Red Cross in Budapest.[65] At the lowest estimate, it was another instance of some Jews not being ready to submit passively to annihilation. It is not unfair to regret that no hint of this aspect can be discerned in Press attitudes. An effort of imagination might have been made to understand that here was an example of Jewish initiative, however tragically mistaken it might have been judged to have been. It could have been mentioned, even in passing, that the Jewish point of view might well have been not whether this offer was genuine or no, but that even a brief pretence at negotiation could have secured the delay, which, with the war clearly drawing to its close, might have resulted in the saving of considerable numbers. Finally, certain remarks could have been rephrased. To speak of 'exchanging Jewish lives for Russian lives on the Eastern Front' was not strictly accurate. It was only a small minority of Jews who had arms in their hands. And the

---

[63] It was not an unsuitable moment. Earlier that year *Pravda* had published a report from its Cairo correspondent of secret negotiations between German and British representatives for a separate peace. For this incident, see W. H. McNeill, *America, Britain and Russia 1941–46* (Survey of International Affairs 1939–1946), London (1953), 413.

[64] At the time of writing, the latest account is A. Weissberg, *Advocate of the Dead*, London (1958), with a very positive approach to the whole affair and the view that the Allies could have saved the remnant of Hungarian Jewry. For contrary views, see *The Black Book of Hungarian Jewry*, ed. L. P. Davis, Zürich and Vienna (1948), pp. 266–73; Reitlinger, op. cit. pp. 434–9, and cf. IMT IV, 368–70.

[65] Weissberg, op. cit. pp. 230–1; pp. 215–16.

Jews were not in the same position as 'the other oppressed peoples of Europe'. They were being methodically exterminated.

It is worth comparing reactions to an example of Jewish initiative nearer home. In the army raised by the London Poles, composed of Poles who had succeeded in escaping from occupied Europe and of volunteers of Polish origin from South America and the United States,[66] there were, at the beginning of 1944, about 800 Jews. Between January and March, 224 of them deserted their units then stationed in Scotland and tried to join the British Army. Two hundred were accepted. The last twenty-four were rejected, court-martialled by the Poles, and sentenced to between one and two years' detention. Their defence had been that open anti-Semitism had made life impossible.

This incident caused some stir. There was a campaign of protest, the twenty-four men were amnestied, and the Poles set up a commission to inquire into the allegations of anti-Semitism.[67] In order to evaluate Press attitudes, it must also be borne in mind that reports of anti-Semitism within Polish units in Britain had already appeared some two years previously with big headlines in the local Press.[68] There had already been one parliamentary debate containing casual allusions to the apparently well-known fact of Allied nationals deserting for this sort of reason in order to join the British,[69] and, by 1944, it was difficult to doubt that life for a Jewish soldier in a Polish unit could be extremely unpleasant. Now, quite apart from the transfer of the 200 which was itself a tacit admission, the Prime Minister told the House of Commons of representations to the Polish Government,[70] while the Poles themselves agreed that incidents 'of a trivial nature' had in fact occurred.[71]

The whole affair received a great deal of publicity. There was profound uneasiness at this glimpse of active anti-Semitism among

[66] This force is not to be confused with that raised by General Anders from Polish prisoners of war in Russia which moved direct to the Middle East. Polish forces in London only became known as Anders' Army after the war.

[67] For the official Polish statement on the court-martial sentences, see *The Times*, 26 April 1944. For the Amnesty Decree, see the statement by the Polish Telegraphic Agency on 12 May (quoted in *Free Europe*, 19 May 1944).

[68] E.g. in *Glasgow Bulletin*, 10 July 1942.

[69] Cf. *The Times* and *Manchester Guardian* reports, 10 July 1942.

[70] Cf. *The Times* report, 27 April 1944.

[71] Polish Telegraphic Agency statement quoted in *Free Europe*, 21 April 1944.

Allied troops on British soil. The *Manchester Guardian*, for example, felt that

The Commons discussion of anti-Semitism in the Polish Army venti-
lated an unpleasant subject, but it should do good. It will impress on
the Polish Government that there is a strongly critical body of opinion
in this country, and that in its own interest it must act with great firm-
ness to crush its anti-Semites.[72]

The *Yorkshire Observer* believed that this was a subject 'on which
there was considerable apprehension in liberal-minded circles
and enough prima-facie evidence is available to justify a British
inquiry'.[73]

This attitude was succinctly expressed in a *News Chronicle* cartoon showing a Polish-Jewish soldier pointing an accusing finger
at a Polish officer with the question, 'Aren't you too a refugee?'[74]

Stronger expressions were also to be found:

Anti-Semitism must be purged from the world. And it now falls especially to Poland to exorcise from its army, and, later, in its own land,
hatreds which are abominable and revenges which are archaic.[75]

The least that the British Government should require of our Allied
guests is that the treatment of their nationals on our soil should not fall
below the minimum that we expect of ourselves . . . the time has come
for both the British Government with righteous indignation and the
Polish Government with patriotic wisdom to say uncompromisingly
that 'This must stop'.[76]

However, responsible Press comment was by no means
unanimous. For instance, the *Spectator* thought that

. . . there has been a good deal of exaggeration in some of the reports
about the troubles of Jews in the Polish Army in Scotland. That there
are anti-Semitic elements in the Polish Army is admitted . . . as to
whether the Jews who deserted had adequate cause for their action is
an arguable question. . . .[77]

Time & Tide, which, as our quotations have abundantly shown,
had an outstanding record in the fight against anti-Semitism,

[72] *Manchester Guardian*, 8 April 1944.
[73] *Yorkshire Observer*, 11 May 1944 (reprinted in *Oxford Mail*, same day).
[74] *News Chronicle*, 13 April 1944.   [75] *Sunday Express*, 14 May 1944.
[76] *Observer*, 30 April 1944.   [77] *Spectator*, 5 May 1944.

was this time considerably more negative than the *Spectator*. It gave a short summary of the events leading up to the courts-martial and then asked,

Can it be that anti-Semitism, extinct in Poland, persists in the Polish Army stationed in this country, and persists, moreover, in so severe a form as to compel Jewish soldiers to seek the desperate expedient of deserting in wartime and on the eve of great military operations? . . .
. . . There was evidently some anti-Semitic talk in the Polish Army, but no more, it would seem, than is to be found in many other armies. So far, the general charge of persecution brought against the Polish Army has not been substantiated . . . no example of physical maltreatment of Jewish soldiers as Jews appears to have been produced. . . . The full truth about the affair is clearly still unrevealed. Was active persecution the cause for the desertions or not? And if there was not sufficient persecution to account for the unusually well-organized desertions, then what is the key to the explanation of what happened? So great has been the stir made by the affair and so intense the feelings it has aroused that a full answer is a matter of public interest.[78]

The important point here is the implication that some conspiracy, and not a genuine grievance, lay at the back of these desertions. This view found its plainest expression in the pages of the *Catholic Herald* whose reporter had the previous day written as follows:

Those Anti-Jewish Charges: A Conspiracy to Malign Poles.
I am able this week to delve even more deeply into the Jewish problem in the Polish Forces and the recent clamour over the trials of a few Polish 'deserters', as the result of contacts I have had with unimpeachable sources, some of them particularly sympathetic towards the 'deserters' themselves.
I can confirm that some malign influence is now at work with two aims in view:
(1) To foment racial trouble (Jewish-Gentile) throughout the world;
(2) To discredit the Polish Government in London.[79]

There is no need to quote any more of this peculiar effusion. It has a strong family resemblance to much else already noted as proceeding from this particular source. However, in a very different sense from that intended here, it was perfectly true that the deserters' case did have very much wider implications (some of

---

[78] *Time & Tide*, 6 May 1944.   [79] *Catholic Herald*, 5 May 1944.

them highly delicate ones) which help to explain why the *Spectator* thought it right to say that reports of anti-Semitic persecution were 'a good deal' exaggerated, and why *Time & Tide* found itself in such strange company.[80]

To understand something of these implications it is necessary to remember how bad Soviet-Polish relations were at this period. In fact, a rival Polish Government was about to be established in the re-conquered territories—the famous Lublin Committee. This was very embarrassing for the British who on the one hand were naturally impelled to support their powerful ally and on the other were equally disinclined to offend their guests—whose forces were being trained side by side with theirs for the coming invasion of Europe. This dilemma was reflected in the Press. Another circumstance made the position even more difficult. From the very beginning, it had been clear enough that the exiled Government exhibited political characteristics of a kind not usually appreciated in Britain, and it was not only the left-wing and Liberal Press that had been moved to some extremely outspoken comment. But it was not easy to distinguish between those who were objecting to Polish reactionary behaviour on principle, and those whose real purpose it was to use various incidents to rally support for every Russian claim at the expense of what was after all the only legal Polish Government in existence. And it was precisely the campaign over the deserters' case that momentarily became the focal point of activities whose objective result could only be the discrediting of the London Poles, and thus, for some at least, a justification of everything that Russia did, or might like to do, in Poland.

It will now be clear why some responsible sections of the Press which were not happy about these wider implications tended to minimize the importance of the deserters' case itself, and why *Time & Tide* found itself in the same camp as the *Catholic Herald*. And it ought to be said in all fairness that the *Herald*'s second point—that here was an attempt 'to discredit the Polish Government in London'—was, in one sense, absolutely correct.

The same diplomatic or political factors which embarrassed

[80] Thus R. Aizenstein, 'The Enemy Within', *Wiener Library Bulletin XIII*, (1959), pp. 58–59, in his short account of the whole affair, somewhat exaggerates when claiming that 'the British press was almost unanimously unfavourable to the court martial sentences'. Of course, it depends on what meaning is attached to 'almost'.

some sections of the Press had precisely the opposite effect on others. These latter would not be in the least ambivalent about their attitude, and would have no inhibitions whatever about attacking the London Poles over a matter which was likely to provide remarkably effective proofs of their reactionary character. This indeed occurred, but the results were not always very good, as far as a reasonable understanding of the actual issue went. In their eagerness to discredit the Poles, some permitted themselves exaggerations which were only too easily rebutted and turned to ridicule. For example, one of the few occasions we can recall when the *Weekly Review* got the better of the *New Statesman* was when the latter had been incautious enough to assert that Polish Army units 'were scarcely less anti-semitic than a division of S.S.'[81]

In this respect the *Daily Worker* was of course outstanding. Its columns were filled with continual references to 'terror' and 'torture' within the Polish ranks practised not only against Jews but also against Ukrainians and Byelorussians; against those, in other words, who ought to be considered Soviet citizens according to Russian claims for frontier adjustments. Reports of some supposed incidents in Scotland were mysteriously quoted from *Pravda* or other Russian sources. At least there could be no doubt where the *Daily Worker* stood.[82] Its campaign was one of the biggest factors in confusing the whole question, and in almost making it an explicit conflict between the supporters of Polish and of Russian claims, or even between Communists (and their sympathizers) and everybody else.

All this was understood well enough, though often with varying emphasis. The *Birmingham Post*, for example, after explaining in a long leading article why little could be done by the British themselves, officially or unofficially and how it was 'unhappily true' that there was a connexion with Polish-Soviet relations, ended with the following comment:

Poland must know perfectly well by now, that her soldiers are going some way to reduce Poland's balance at the bank of British goodwill.

[81] *New Statesman*, 22 April 1944. The *Weekly Review* replied on 27 April 1944.
[82] See, e.g., *Daily Worker*, 24 April 1944 (a *Pravda* report of torture of a soldier); 25 April 1944; 5 May 1944; 8 May 1944; 9 June 1944. The last is a typical *Daily Worker* 'human interest' story: two hospital nurses buy a 'Soviet badge' as their reply to Polish anti-Semitism.

There, so far as Britain is concerned, the matter has to be left. Poland would be wise not to leave it there.[83]

The *News Chronicle*, on the other hand, ended with the same point in a rather more partisan way: 'Unless some sharp hygienic process has been effectively applied there can be little hope of a new "Polish understanding with the Soviet Union".'[84]

Plainest and fairest of all, however, was the *Observer*, in the course of the strong attack on intolerance in the Polish Army from which we have already quoted:

Unfortunately the troubles of Poland have become the plaything of international politics. The treatment of Jews in the Polish Army is seized upon by opponents of the present Polish Government and of its claims to prove the Russian counter-case. . . . The incidents of violence and discrimination have been exaggerated and written up to favour anti-Polish policies.[85]

Such were the factors, then, which helped to create this sharp division in Press comment on the case of the Polish-Jewish deserters. They help to explain why some comment was so obviously inadequate. They do not, however, wholly account for it. An additional cause must be sought in the undoubted fact that it was very difficult for any to understand how 'trivial' incidents became less trivial when they were the latest in a long story of discrimination and persecution. The significance of this argument is best illustrated by the way in which its converse was used in the controversy. The extreme supporters of the London Poles took every opportunity of proclaiming that pre-war anti-Semitism in Poland had never been 'active', and that what anti-Semitism there had been disappeared in the face of a common struggle against the German enemy.[86] If this were accepted all these incidents were indeed 'no more than are to be found in many other armies'.[87]

The first contention was just plain nonsense. Any pre-war year would have provided a depressing quantity of evidence to show that Polish anti-Semitism was not in the least 'inactive'. In 1937, for example, there was a nation-wide boycott in which many Jews were injured, while Warsaw University decided to introduce a separate seating system for Jewish students. Neither event was a secret;

[83] *Birmingham Post*, 27 April 1944.   [84] *News Chronicle*, 16 May 1944.
[85] *Observer*, 30 April 1944.   [86] E.g. *Weekly Review*, 27 April 1944.
[87] *Time & Tide* as quoted above, p. 119.

both were widely reported in the British Press.[88] Nevertheless, the heights since attained by the Nazis had rather put these amateurish efforts in the shade, and this was why such a contention could be risked at all. And while these facts about pre-war Poland were well known, an imaginative understanding of them was, by 1944, often missing. There certainly were Press references to the obvious connexion between the Jewish lot in a Polish unit and that in a pre-war Polish town, but the emotional significance of such a connexion for the Jewish soldier himself was seldom adequately emphasized.

The second contention—that Polish anti-Semitism had become extinct in the common struggle against the Nazis—was almost as easy to disprove. It is true that Jew and Pole had fought side by side against the Germans in 1939. But then neither had had much choice in the matter. It was true that there were stories of Jews (particularly children) who owed their lives to the protection of a Polish neighbour or whose escape from Poland had been accomplished through some non-Jewish assistance or other. One Jew had, indeed, reached London not long before, fervently proclaiming that he owed everything to the Polish underground.[89] But just a year before the deserters' case, the Warsaw Ghetto had perished in flame. The Ghetto fighters had died in their unequal struggle and any evidence that they had received substantial material help, much less genuine co-operation, from non-Jewish sources was extremely thin.[90] The general impression was that little had altered in Polish attitudes, and an understanding of this was essential in any approach to the case of the deserters from a Polish unit.

The main point was this: whatever the truth of Polish co-operation may or may not have been, the Jews of the Warsaw Ghetto, like the Jews in other ghettos, and the Jewish partisans, had risen and struck back at their enemies. We have seen that this

[88] See, e.g., *Manchester Guardian*, 3 Mar. 1937; 14 Sept. 1937. *The Times*, 6 Oct. 1937; 27 Nov. 1937.

[89] See interview in *Evening Standard*, 21 Oct. 1943.

[90] A photostat copy exists of Stroop's private opinion that help from 'the Polish population was of no consequence' (Reitlinger, p. 276). He should have known. So should General Komarowski; his claim of Home Army help was very modest (interview with *Manchester Guardian*, 2 June 1945). It seems that, in total, the Z.O.B. received from this source fifty revolvers and fifty hand-grenades, the rest was bought and paid for (Friedman, *Martyrs and Fighters*, pp. 208–9).

was well known and that it commanded great sympathy (if not much else). The incidents in Scottish barrack rooms were considerably less dramatic, but there was this much in common—Jews had come considerable distances, and at some risk, in order to do precisely the same thing, that is, to fight their enemies. It was their contribution to the 'Jewish answer'. They had met with a reception which, in however 'trivial' a manner it may have been expressed, could not but remind them of the fate of their brothers in Poland, nearly three million of whom had by then been most certainly exterminated. Their own 'answer' could hardly be effective under such circumstances, and they endeavoured to make it so in the only way that seemed possible—by getting into surroundings where the struggle against the Nazis could be a genuine reality for them. The fact that this endeavour was used for all sort of propaganda made not the slightest difference to its essential meaning, and no comment on their case could be adjudged adequate that did not point to the connexion between the Jewish 'deserter', the Jewish partisan, and the heaps of Jewish dead. Such unambiguous comment was rare. One of the best was an editorial in the *Daily Worker*,[91] but unfortunately its only effect was to encourage others to take a different line at all costs. In other words, comment on the deserters' case was one of the few instances when a question of anti-Semitism during the Nazi period became inextricably mingled with a general political controversy.

Nevertheless, there was a wider failure, too. It seemed very difficult for the Press to think of Jews as fighters, as individuals with a positive stand of their own, as anything other than helpless victims.

It is shameful that the surviving members of a community wiped out by the Nazis in Poland should still be insulted and ill-treated by people who themselves are also victims of the same oppressor,

said the *Observer*,[92] while the *Economist* thought that such behaviour was 'an extraordinary instance of moral and political perversity'.[93] This was undoubtedly the best representative comment by those, at least, who saw that the true emphasis ought not to be on the complexities of Polish-Soviet relations. It was shame-

[91] *Daily Worker*, 28 April 1944.   [92] *Observer*, 9 April 1944.
[93] *Economist*, 6 May 1944.

ful indeed, and morally perverse—but that was not the whole of the story. The insults and the ill-treatment were not merely disgusting in themselves as affronts to the helpless, but actually a danger—as a hindrance to fighters.[94]

Finally, this picture of Jewish resistance and the reactions it evoked would be incomplete without some discussion of the reactions to the part played by Palestinian Jewry in the British war effort. This had significance because there was, from first to last, no military conscription in Palestine. What Jews did or tried to do there was a positive and deliberate contribution to their own struggle against the Nazis, and comment on it has to be considered, first and foremost, in that light. Of course neither the Jewish Agency for Palestine nor the Zionist movement generally ever concealed the belief that the greater the volume of Jewish recruitment, the more explicit its effective employment as a Jewish element, on a level with all the other national elements within the Allied armies, the better would be the chance of influencing Mandatory policies both immediately and in any post-war settlement.[95]

The moment war was declared the Agency called for volunteers, and, by the middle of 1940, had willingness been the only factor, the great majority of able-bodied men and women of the Jewish population of Palestine would have been in uniform.[96] Unfortunately the British authorities understood the political implications of such a result just as well as did the Agency and did their utmost to prevent it.[97] Little by little the military situation compelled them to accept Jewish recruits (since Arabs rarely came forward), but they tried to restrict them to anything but com-

[94] For further references to the Polish-Russian background to the whole affair, see McNeill, op. cit., pp. 415, 418, 433.

[95] See, e.g., the advice to use this argument in a variety of contexts by the American Zionist Emergency Council, *Press Book on Palestinian Jewry's Contribution to the War Against the Axis*, New York (n.d.), (probably summer of 1944).

[96] For Palestinian Jewry and the war, see J. C. Hurewitz, *The Struggle for Palestine*, New York (1950), pp. 124–33; D. Trevor, *Under the White Paper*, Jerusalem (1948), pp. 52–84; J. Gill, *The Jewish Brigade*, Tel Aviv (1950) (in Hebrew). The official British account is by G. Kirk, *The Middle East and the War* (*Survey of International Affairs 1939–1946*), Oxford (1952), pp. 228–50; 306–33.

[97] For some amazing examples of obstruction, including concealment of the address of the recruiting centre and physical assault on the Jewish officials, see Trevor, op. cit., pp. 56, 59, 67, 81–82.

batant duties.[98] Finally, after a bitter struggle, the authorities capitulated and permitted the formation of a Jewish Brigade in time to play its part in the last stages of the Italian campaign—just as those Palestinian Jews who had managed to get to a fighting front earlier had played theirs in Abyssinia, North Africa, and Greece.[99]

However, another group of events stood in sharp contrast to the official policy of obstruction. Between 1936 and 1939 the authorities had appointed Captain Orde Wingate to train elements of the existing Jewish defence organization—the *Haganah*—in order to help in the crushing of a serious Arab revolt.[1] Between 1940 and 1942, these same elements—not now Wingate-trained but in the Wingate tradition—became a guerrilla force to act in the event of a German occupation of Palestine, and led the British thrust into Vichy-held Syria.[2] In April 1944, Wingate, now a Major-General and famous, was killed in Burma. Not long before he had advocated the formation of an independent Jewish force.[3]

Press treatment of all these events provides some interesting comparisons. On the one hand, the figures of recruitment and the details of service (actual and proposed) could all be found in *The Times* and the *Daily Telegraph*, acquiring not surprisingly a much greater emphasis in the *Manchester Guardian*. *The Times* record was as usual so full and so accurate that it could be used as a reliable source in subsequent histories.[4] On the other hand there were remarkable omissions and inadequacies—not always capable of a simple anti-Zionist explanation. In the spring of 1944, for example, the normally intelligent *World Review* continued through two issues (a total of eighteen pages) a discussion of the Mandate without a single reference to the Jewish war effort. It is true that the explicitly stated intention was to 'put the Arab case', 'a small effort to redress the balance' (of Zionist propaganda).[5] But the

---

[98] Ibid, p. 118.   [99] Hurewitz, op. cit., p. 127.

[1] On the Mandate 1933–9, so far as it concerns this survey, see below, pp. 182–3.

[2] Hurewitz, op. cit., pp. 127–8; Trevor, op. cit., p. 61.

[3] If we say nothing of a third group of events—the achievements and heroism of Jews in British uniform behind the enemy lines, typified in such names as David Raziel and Hannah Senesch—it is because this was obviously unknown in our period and thus could not give rise to any Press reactions.

[4] E.g. Hurewitz, op. cit., p. 341, on figures of volunteers, on details of Syrian campaign, etc., quotes *The Times*, 6 June 1942; 9 Dec. 1942; 4 Mar. 1943.

[5] *World Review*, May and June, 1944. (The old *Review of Reviews*, see *Register of Newspapers & Periodicals*, below, p. 215.)

emphasis of that propaganda was, at the time, precisely on this Jewish contribution, and some comment, if only by way of casual refutation, might have been expected. Earlier that same year, the *Illustrated* printed a somewhat similar feature, of course on a much more popular level. Here the attitude was highly sympathetic to Zionist aims. Both the text and the photographs tried to present the most favourable picture of the Jews in Palestine. But again there was virtually no reference, in five full pages, to their war activities, with the possible exception of the following caption to a photograph:

Fighting on the side of the United Nations against the Nazi tyranny is this officer of the Czech Army. He made a most adventurous escape to avoid the enemy and reach Eretz Israel where he is continuing to soldier.[6]

Just then it was possible to obtain excellent information on the whole subject without even the trouble of glancing at files of *The Times* or the *Manchester Guardian*. There was in the centre of London an exhibition of 'Jewish Palestine at War', whose existence was certainly not ignored by the Press. But some provincial newspapers of standing contented themselves with printing what was obviously no more than a condensed version of the exhibition's Press release.[7]

The same sort of inadequacy became strikingly obvious in reactions to the news of Wingate's death. It was not that scarcity of space coupled with a natural preference for matters of immediate rather than of historical interest inevitably limited comment to Wingate's mastery of guerrilla tactic in Burma. On the contrary, his childhood, his eccentricities (real or invented), the smallest details of his private life, were discussed from every imaginable angle in the news columns, the editorials, and the feature pages of practically all sections of the British Press. There was one outstanding omission. Wingate's work in Palestine, that is, his first military success, received only the most cursory mention. Probably the most offhand remark of all appeared in the *Yorkshire Post*, whose sole reference to Wingate in this context in a leading article on his death was that 'Wingate had learned his scouting by

---

[6] *Illustrated*, 4 Mar. 1944.
[7] For example, the *Scotsman*, 22 Mar. 1944; *Yorkshire Post*, 22 Mar. 1944; *Birmingham Post*, 23 Mar. 1944.

aeroplane in the Sudan, Palestine and Transjordania . . . like Lawrence of Arabia he had a flair for working with the natives. . . .'[8] The *Daily Telegraph* leader was not far behind with its solitary comment that 'Palestine and Abyssinia gave him opportunities in commanding mixed troops which he turned to wonderful purpose'.[9]

It is difficult to say whether this was better or worse than the editorials which managed to avoid all mention of Wingate in Palestine (*Sheffield Telegraph* and *Nottingham Journal*[10]), those which limited themselves to mentioning that Wingate had cleared Palestine of terrorists (*Great Britain & The East*, the *Glasgow Herald*, and *Western Morning News*), or feature articles in three instalments which said equally little (*Manchester Sunday Chronicle*).[11] Some gave a little more detail—not always very felicitously expressed. The *Daily Mail*, for example, described in a feature article how Wingate had

enlisted the fanatic fury of the Zionists—sole Jews to hold their ancestral land. He trained them, gave them a stiffening of professional British soldiers, taught them and led them, always by night.[12]

A slightly belated feature in the *Daily Express* gave a rather better account of Wingate's work[13] while *The Times* obituary on the whole reached its expected standard of accuracy.[14] But the general impression remains that this side of Wingate's life was touched upon as lightly as possible. On its connexion with Palestine Jewry and the war, the touch was lighter still, indeed there was almost complete silence. References to some practical results of his work —for example the response of *Haganah* units in 1940–2, the whole 'Wingate tradition' which took on a great importance for the Jew in the armed forces, and references to his own advocacy of a Jewish army, are hard to find, although the facts were well known. The use of *Haganah* men in Palestine and Syria had been officially

[8] *Yorkshire Post*, 1 April 1944.   [9] *Daily Telegraph*, 1 April 1944.

[10] *Sheffield Telegraph*, 1 April 1944; *Nottingham Journal*, 1 April 1944.

[11] *Great Britain & The East*, 22 April 1944; *Glasgow Herald*, 1 April 1944; *Western Morning News*, 1 April 1944; *Sunday Chronicle*, 2 April 1944; 9 April 1944; 16 April 1944.

[12] *Daily Mail*, 11 April 1944.

[13] *Daily Express*, 11 April 1944.

[14] *The Times*, 1 April 1944. Shorter, but reasonably accurate references appeared in *News Chronicle*, 1 April 1944; *Observer*, 2 April 1944.

noted in Parliament more than once.[15] Yet the constant implication was that nothing need be said of Wingate and Palestine after 1939. This was carried to such lengths that even mention of Wingate's participation in the Quebec Allied Staff Conference often omitted his main plea there: that he should once again be allowed to lead Jewish troops.[16] To all this there were only two outstanding exceptions: the *Manchester Guardian* and *Time & Tide*. There Wingate's true significance for fighting Jewry was really made clear. The connexion was brought out between the night squads of 1938 and the Syrian victories of 1941, between the man who successfully persuaded a reluctant War Office to permit him to organize Jewish defence against Arab terrorists, and the man who failed to get permission to organize the same Jews against the common Nazi enemy.[17]

But the British Press as a whole was not prepared to stress the possibilities of Palestinian Jewry as a genuine independent fighting force. The immediate reason is obvious enough. Any emphasis on Jewish fighting qualities or achievements in Palestine would mean a certain support of the campaign for a Jewish Army (as would, of course, any mention of the fact that the hero of the hour had been in favour of it). The political implications were known well enough and a large section of the Press was strongly opposed to them. The point at issue was put quite unambiguously by *The Times*:

In view of chronic and basic political problems, which at present are only temporarily solved, it is far more important to keep Palestine internally quiet . . . than to upset the whole situation either by conscription or by favouring the nationalistic ambitions of one of the rival races.[18]

It was equally well understood by the *Manchester Guardian*—one of the very few to support the campaign from beginning to end.[19]

---

[15] *House of Commons Debates*, 374/2019; 381/194; 382/1271, 1273.
[16] Particularly striking examples are: *Daily Telegraph*, 1 April 1944; *Daily Express*, 12 April 1944. *The Evening Standard*, 1 April 1944, left it as 'He prayed that he might lead a Jewish Army'—but did not mention that his prayer was not to heaven but to the Allied Command. Small news items did occasionally appear connecting Wingate's name to wartime Palestine. But the total effect is not impressive.
[17] *Manchester Guardian*, 1 April 1944; *Time & Tide*, 22 April 1944.
[18] *The Times*, 30 May 1942.
[19] See among much else its leaders on 10 Nov. 1941; 6 Aug. 1942. The campaign was also supported by *Time & Tide* (see, e.g., issue of 17 Jan. 1942) and by the *New Statesman* (see, e.g., 28 Jan. 1942).

When the Brigade was formed, it recounted some of the background and asked,

Why then was the British Government so reluctant to accept [the offer of an independant Jewish force]? The reason is not far to seek. The Government and, still more, the Palestine Administration feared that to allow the Jews of Palestine to serve as Jews with a Jewish flag in their own units would be to acknowledge their right to nationhood and would annoy the Arabs. Since it is the declared policy of the British Government, reaffirmed by the successive Ministries and maintained by Mr. Churchill, to establish a Jewish National Home in Palestine, this fear does not seem reasonable. . . .[20]

No serious evaluation of Press attitudes to the question of Palestinian recruitment can be made at all without an equally serious investigation of attitudes to the Zionist case as such—something which would fall entirely outside the scope of the present survey, just as in the context of Palestine and the refugee question to be discussed later, it is arguable that a great deal depended on the view taken of the purpose and responsibilities of the Mandate, i.e. whether the true emphasis was on 'keeping Palestine quiet' or 'building a Jewish National Home'. But this was not the whole of the story. Attitudes to the concept of a Jewish Army, to the facts of the war effort made by Palestinian Jewry, cannot be judged simply as attitudes to Zionism. For these events were not merely the expression of 'the nationalistic ambitions of one of the rival races', but had an intrinsic importance for the whole of Jewry in its hour of trial. The fact that this other aspect was so rarely understood was much more significant than any lack of sympathy for Zionism. For example, the point was not infrequently made that 'proposals for the segregation of Jews into a special army may be represented as a concession to Hitler's own argument',[21] that such a concept 'retains the spirit of the Ghetto, the separatism which has caused so much suffering'.[22]

The eventual formation of the Brigade did get a sympathetic Press, and some of its officers even achieved the distinction of a glossy picture in the *Tatler*.[23] But there was little allusion to what had actually been happening. *The Times* printed a favourable

[20] *Manchester Guardian*, 20 Sept. 1944.
[21] *Western Morning News*, 4 July 1944.   [22] *Tribune*, 22 Sept. 1944.
[23] *Tatler*, 22 Nov. 1944.

leader blandly remarking that the delay had been the result of shipping difficulties, and that the Brigade was a 'concession to the fine response of the Jews of Palestine to the call for volunteers'.[24] It did not think it necessary to recall either its own or the Mandatory's characterization of that 'fine response' as the 'nationalistic ambitions of one of the rival races'. The fact that it went on to speak of the symbolic importance of the Brigade did little to efface the impression made by this omission. It was once again left to the *Manchester Guardian* to stress what had really been at issue: a Jewish force which 'in the dark days of 1941 and 1942 would have been an encouragement to active Jewish resistance throughout Europe'.[25] A hint or two to the same effect could be found in other places,[26] but the Press as a whole failed to grasp the true meaning of the war effort for Palestinian Jews.

[24] *The Times*, 22 Sept. 1944.   [25] *Manchester Guardian*, 20 Sept. 1944.
[26] Cf. *Time & Tide*, 1 April 1944, and a moderately approving interview with the editor of the *Palestine Post* in the *Evening Standard*, 26 April 1944.

V

The World's Answer

THE world answered Hitler at Lake Success when the Great Powers agreed to the resolution which gave legal sanction to the establishment of an independent Jewish State—the State of Israel. Whatever other criticisms may be made, this positive act must always be remembered and appreciated. Within the field covered by this inquiry, however, the world's answer was confined to acts of retribution: the indictment, trial, and punishment of some of the guilty. This was the one effective achievement —and attitudes towards it may be usefully compared to those towards the specifically 'Jewish answers'. Such an inquiry has to be considered against a wider background. The question of retribution, whether in theory or in practice, was only part and parcel of the whole question of German guilt; a question which was being debated long before the end of the war and which, in a sense, was but the continuation of an older debate begun before 1918.

As we have seen, one of the most common attitudes to the particular question of responsibility for pre-war anti-Semitic outrages in Germany was to turn it into a general one, and to embark on historical, psycho-analytical, or even theological discussion about the German character. At its crudest it could produce the 'Hun' of the Great War as the guilty party, at its most refined a recondite combination of pseudo-scientific evaluations which raised many more difficulties than it solved. For all that, in one sense this attitude was valid and was responsible for a useful principle: whether the trouble was caused by culture, economics, religion, or anything else, some of the responsibility for what had happened in Germany was German; it had to be sought in Germany, and not in any other country. It was not surprising that this principle persisted and gained ground, especially when Nazi policies began to affect others than Jews. Thus the outbreak of war

in 1939 caused wide sections of the Press to proclaim in no uncertain manner that this was 1914 all over again—the German
beast had once more destroyed the peace of Europe. The crudity
of some of these formulations should not obscure the genuine need
felt by the Press to state and re-state a simple fact: the seizure of
the remnant of Czechoslovakia and the invasion of Poland were the
deliberate actions of a powerful German State—whatever the support it might have commanded among German people as a whole.
No one could deny some meaning to the concept of German responsibility.

Thus the *Sunday Express* printed features with such headings as

Why all this bosh about being gentle with the Germans after we have
beaten them when ALL GERMANS ARE GUILTY!

and felt that the German mentality was 'a bog of mental evil'.[1]
The *Sunday Dispatch* opened its columns to Lord Vansittart,
whose name became synonymous with a policy of uninhibited
national retribution.[2] On the other hand, one must remember that
a substantial element in the Press continued to the end to make
some differentiation between German and German; if not between
the Nazi party and the rest, then between the 'Prussians' or the
'military cliques' and the population as a whole. Such was the
sense of another, more representative article in the *Telegraph*, and
such too the favourite topic of most responsible papers.[3] However,
the broad attitude of the majority was summed up well enough by
a *Daily Express* Giles cartoon, which appeared after the European
war was over. It shows a British soldier in the midst of a fine
selection of German civilians: 'Now,' he says, 'that we can all
fraternise I think we'll start by telling you what I think about the
—— Germans.'[4]

At the same time, a strong minority strove to place final responsibility elsewhere. It consisted of those who, like the *Tribune*,
blamed capitalism in general and the Western powers in particular

---

[1] *Sunday Express*, 7 Mar. 1943; 22 Oct. 1944.
[2] E.g. *Sunday Dispatch*, 26 Mar. 1944; cf. *Daily Telegraph*, 22 May 1945.
[3] *Daily Telegraph*, 29 Mar. 1945; presumably this was also the *Observer* view
since the article was by its editor J. L. Garvin. Cf. *The Times*, 24 Oct. 1945;
Spectator, 15 Oct. 1943; *Evening Standard*, 12 April 1944.
[4] *Daily Express*, 18 July 1945.

for encouraging Hitler in the thirties,[5] and of those who blamed some such abstraction as Man's inclination to war.[6] However, the Press as a whole was perfectly clear that responsibility for German actions must be sought in Germany.

Attitudes to the question of actual punishment were similar. It was only a minority that was wholly against it, though ideas of what was suitable, or possible, varied enormously from suggestions that expressions of strong moral disapproval might be sufficient to those envisaging complete political annihilation (put forward by, among others, the *Weekly Review* which despite its Italian and Spanish sympathies was always ferociously anti-German).[7] There were many to point out the practical difficulties of wholesale sanctions[8] and some preached a 'forgive and forget' policy.[9] The vast majority, however, plainly believed that something was wrong in Germany which needed putting right—whatever degree of punishment or coercion to achieve this might be thought desirable.

It is against this background that the specifically Jewish context has to be evaluated. Generally speaking, the division of opinion was much the same. The majority attitude was that those directly responsible had to be punished and that responsibility could justly be extended to wider circles: certainly to the Party leadership, possibly to Party members and sections of the German army, perhaps to the German people as a whole. As the suggested circle of responsibility widened, so the numbers suggesting it tended to decrease. When the story of mass extermination was first fully known the inclination to blame 'the German' for it was very much stronger. For example, Low showed a train of open trucks loaded

[5] See, e.g., *Tribune*, 28 July 1944; 11 Aug. 1944; 15 June 1945; *New Statesman*, 3 Aug. 1946; Hannen Swaffer in the *People*, 23 July 1944, and most issues of the *Daily Herald* in 1944–5. It is interesting that one left-wing newspaper disagreed. The *Daily Worker* made little distinction between 'German Fascists' and 'German People' calling for condign punishment on them all; see especially a most revealing article on 18 Nov. 1944. In this, of course, it did agree with Stalin who at the Teheran Conference said that the best post-war plan for Germany would be to begin by executing 50,000 officers and technicians 'as a safety precaution'. See McNeill, op. cit., p. 360.

[6] See, e.g., a cartoon in *Punch*, 22 Aug. 1945.

[7] See, among much else, its call for the destruction of Germany after the war ('Delenda est Germania') on 26 Oct. 1944.

[8] See, e.g., *New Statesman*, 7 Oct. 1944; *Manchester Guardian*, 22 June 1945.

[9] See, e.g., article in *Contemporary Review*, November 1945 (by the same gentleman who had compared the Nazi régime to a public school eleven years previously in the *Spectator*—above, p. 4). For the case of Victor Gollancz, see below pp. 139–40; 15.

with 'Jews for the slaughter house'. 'I've settled the fate of Jews,'
cries Hitler. 'And of Germans,' replies the figure of Nemesis
while writing on a scroll marked 'the horrors to be repaid'.[10] A
Daily Mail cartoon showed a group of Jews facing an execution
squad composed of ordinary German soldiers without a hint of
party insignia. The commanding officer is making a list of his
victims, and, behind him, the figure of Justice is making the same
list.[11] It was essentially this attitude which was expressed in the
editorial comments of two papers so obviously differing widely in
every conceivable respect—the *Daily Sketch* and the *Spectator*.
The latter prophesied with gloomy accuracy the main difficulty
which would confront future judges striving to apply some criteria
of differentiation:

When the day of reckoning comes there will, of course, be a *sauve
qui peut* from the Nazi Party, everyone who does not happen to be
called Hitler, Himmler, or Goering protesting passionately that anything they did they did under orders and utterly against all their desires
and instincts.[12]

It was this attitude which was undoubtedly behind the wide Press
approval given to the Archbishop of York's denunciation of what
he called 'unchristian sentimentality' towards the fact that 'the
worst barbarities committed by pagan conquerors had been re-
vivified and intensified by the Germans', and his demand that 'the
German people' should be told 'solemnly and repeatedly' that
'sure retribution awaits not only the master criminals who have
ordered these horrors, but also their brutal underlings who are
carrying them out, often apparently with zest'.[13]

As the *News Chronicle* put it, though at a somewhat later date,

. . . the whole German nation stands convicted of acquiescence in these
crimes against civilisation.[14]

Of course, it was obvious that, when thought of in a practical
light, there could never be any question of supporting the view that

[10] *Evening Standard*, 14 Dec. 1942.   [11] *Daily Mail*, 14 Dec. 1942.
[12] *Spectator*, 28 Dec. 1942; cf. *Daily Sketch*, 18 Dec. 1942.
[13] Cf. reports and comments on his Leeds speech in *Daily Telegraph*, 15 Mar.
1943; *Daily Express*, 15 Mar. 1943; *Yorkshire Evening News*, 15 Mar. 1943;
Northern Echo, 15 Mar. 1943. Cf. similar attitudes expressed editorially in
Yorkshire Post, 5 Oct. 1943; *Time & Tide*, 1 July 1944.
[14] *News Chronicle*, 31 Aug. 1944.

all Germans were responsible in terms of actual retribution. Few would ever be found to agree with the *reductio ad absurdum* of Vansittartism proclaimed in February 1943—that retribution was not class conscious (whatever that meant), that it would not recoil from numbers however great if really guilty, that these numbers included the Gestapo and the German Army, and that the German Army was the German people.[15] These opinions were expressed, in fact, in relation to the fate of European Jewry, and their extreme nature led most of the Press, not surprisingly, to reject them, just as it had rejected the concept of universal German guilt. But just as with the wider question, there was a stronger kind of reaction which manifested itself in the inclination to discourage talk of retribution or punishment at all. To some extent this was the result of a sincere conviction that the only path towards a sane Europe was that of forgiveness and understanding. This was the sense of a leading article in the *Inquirer*, the organ of the Unitarian Christian Movement.[16] But this attitude was not confined to the religious Press. It could be found, for example, in the *Manchester Guardian*, seeing that publication of the views of its regular contributor 'Artifex' were an editorial responsibility.[17] Views with this sort of motivation—and they were not very widespread—could not but command respect if not agreement.

There were others, superficially similar, which are hard to discuss with becoming detachment. The *Catholic Herald*, too, had declared that 'the way of education, mercy and conversion, not of punishment, we believe, is the way of Christianity'. But this happened to be the last sentence of the leading article to which we have already referred, speaking of the details of extermination as 'apt to be developed in the uncertain and dangerous transmission', which had been unable to avoid its King Charles' head:

We must recall again that the murders of thousands of Catholics in Russia, Mexico and Spain was passed over almost in silence by those who today rightly lead the campaign to inform the world about what is now happening.[18]

The whole thing left a slightly unpleasant taste, but was it representative of anything besides the *Catholic Herald*? Not so long

---

[15] Lord Vansittart in the House of Lords, see report in *The Times*, 12 Feb. 1943.
[16] *Inquirer*, 2 Jan. 1943.   [17] See, e.g., *Manchester Guardian*, 24 Apr. 1945.
[18] *Catholic Herald*, 24 Dec. 1942; see above, p. 94.

after this the dying Cardinal Hinsley was to speak with a very different voice in his message to a great protest meeting organized by the World Jewish Congress.[19] That inimitable publication *Truth* had equally unexceptionable reasons against indiscriminate retribution: 'We do not turn against all the strangers in our own midst because a few commit murder and rape and outrage. . . .'[20] This piece of fairmindedness must not be forgotten when considering *Truth*'s comments on a particular section of these 'strangers' —the Jewish refugees from Nazi rule.

It is strange but true that a close parallel to the attitude of the *Catholic Herald* was found in a section of the Press diametrically opposed to it in every other respect. 'Revenge is sour,' declared George Orwell in the *Tribune* three yeas later, describing a visit to prisoners' cages reserved for former concentration camp commanders and their immediate assistants. But it was not only 'revenge' that he meant. He kindly forgave 'a little Viennese Jew' who kicked an S.S. man to attention, but thought that the 'obvious need' of this Nazi (who, as Orwell himself believed, had been quite certainly in charge of camps and had presided over tortures and hangings), was 'not for punishment but for some kind of psychological treatment'.

Then Orwell spoke of 'the monstrous peace settlement now being forced on Germany' and of 'Allied crimes' in East Prussia.

Only the minority of sadists who must have their 'atrocities' [Orwell's quotation marks] from one source or another, take a keen interest in the hunting down of war criminals or quislings. If you ask the average man what crime Goering, Ribbentrop and the rest are to be charged with at their trial, he cannot tell you. Somehow the punishment of these monsters ceases to seem attractive when it becomes possible: indeed, once under lock and key, they almost cease to be monsters.[21]

Now Orwell was a novelist, a brilliant journalist and above all a man of highly individual views and methods of expressing them. Yet it is not unfair to speak of the quotation above as a *Tribune* view, too. Orwell was at the time one of its foremost regular contributors, and this particular contribution did not differ in essentials

---

[19] See reports in *Catholic Times, Universe,* and *Catholic Herald* itself, 5 Mar. 1943.
[20] *Truth,* 27 April 1945.
[21] *Tribune,* 9 Nov. 1945.

from the *Tribune*'s general trend of opinion on the subject. On the contrary, apart from its interesting suggestion that by then few knew what the War Crimes Trials would be about, the article is an excellent expression of the logical conclusion of a trend which was not, of course, confined to the *Tribune* (or to the Left): i.e. that the only criminals are the Allies.[22] Both with this type of analysis, as with that favoured by the *Catholic Herald*, the boundaries between ordinary right and wrong have almost vanished, to be replaced in the one case by some sort of Marxist derivative, and in the other by a disingenuous combination of one aspect of Christian doctrine with a mass of virulent anti-Russian prejudice.

The Orwell line could also be seen as the extreme form of a rather more widely held view, examples of which become far more striking when considered in relation to the actual extermination programme—the 'Final Solution'. This was the view which claimed that the real guilt was to be sought outside Germany—whether by that term the Party, the Army, or the whole nation was intended. The trial of Josef Kramer, commandant of the Belsen Camp, inspired two cartoons which illustrate this well. In the first, behind the man in the dock (whose personal villainy is emphasized by the artist) stands the figure of 'world monopoly and big business intrigue'. The caption reads, 'The other man in the dock . . .'.[23] In the second, as background to a similar representation of Kramer, a pre-war British upper-class family is shown at home proclaiming its support for various aspects (including, though not stressing, anti-Semitism) of the Hitler régime.[24] This type of explanation is pitifully inadequate. 'Big business', monopolies and a reactionary upper class were no new factors in 1933; indeed they are still with us. But the slaughter of six million Jews has (so far) been a unique phenomenon, and no apportionment of guilt or estimate of punishment was or ever will be adequate, which does not repeatedly stress the equally unique factor that a substantial number of individuals took, and maintained, the deliberate and freely made decision to exterminate a whole community for the sole crime of its existence.

It was fatally easy to forget this last point and to draw parallels

---

[22] Cf., e.g., Professor V. I. Galbraith: 'The Allies will forever stand at the bar of history for their treatment of conquered Germany. To justify their actions in the eyes of posterity, no trouble can be too great to establish the facts . . .' *The Times*, 21 April 1945). There was no hint that Germany might need justifying.
[23] *Daily Mirror*, 19 Sept. 1945.   [24] *Daily Herald*, 18 Sept. 1945.

where none existed, as did the leader writer of a daily paper which at that time enjoyed the biggest national circulation:

What happened to the Jews, happened to others. Catholics, Communists, Liberals, Socialists—all were persecuted. Their sole desire was liberty to express a point of view. . . .[25]

But the Jews were *not* murdered for any 'point of view'—however true or untrue this may have been of the others. They were murdered for one reason and one reason only: because they fitted Hitler's definition of what a Jew was. It was this uniqueness of their fate which was insufficiently appreciated—the fact that this tragedy had *no* parallel, that their deaths could *not* be cited as simply one more instance of a dictatorship acting against its real or fancied opponents.[26]

Another point of view must not go unrecorded. Shortly after the 1942 declaration, Victor Gollancz published a pamphlet entitled *Let My People Go*.[27] It was a moving plea to the Allied Powers to save what could be saved of the remnant of European Jewry, and will be referred to again in connexion with the question of attitudes to the refugee problem.[28] But it also contained another plea: a special plea against emphasis on retribution and punishment. It was based upon much the same motives as we have already noted in the case of the *Inquirer* and of 'Artifex' in the *Manchester Guardian*. However, Gollancz insisted on a curious dichotomy. Rescue operations, he claimed, would be hampered, both in intention and in execution, to the extent that vengeance was stressed. That these operations *were* inadequate, indeed practically non-existent, was unfortunately indisputable, but the connexion between the two questions was by no means so. Gollancz's stand was taken up by many responsible papers, and undoubtedly encouraged a hazy feeling that unduly stern judgement somehow meant a lukewarm attitude towards helping the

---

[25] *Daily Mirror*, 3 Aug. 1945. Very similar comments can be found in the *Tribune*, 27 April 1945.

[26] Even the *Manchester Guardian* helped to perpetuate the same fallacy when it stressed 'that the primary victims of Buchenwald were Germans' (28 April 1945) without troubling to mention that a large proportion of those were Jews—explicitly *not* classified as 'Germans' by the authorities.

[27] V. Gollancz, *Let My People Go*, London, 1943.

[28] See below, p. 181, n. 25.

potential victims of the criminals who were to be judged.[29] Thus
an additional illogical element was added to a debate which already
lacked logical qualities. It still seems hard to understand why
there should have been any inherent contradiction in the following
simple proposition, which a proportion of Press opinion certainly
accepted: to make it clear that wrong-doing would be punished,
to win the war as soon as possible, and to offer all possible protection and encouragement to those who tried to escape.[30]

Before proceeding to discuss attitudes towards the practical
result of all these theories and prophecies—the Nuremberg Trials
—it will be useful to consider some reactions to an earlier event:
the capture of Buchenwald camp on 11 April 1945, and its inspec-
tion a few days later by a parliamentary delegation. These reactions were important, because they illustrate the most widely
discussed aspect of the whole controversy over 'German guilt'.
The question that Buchenwald posed for many was very simple:
did the local inhabitants know what was going on behind the wire,
and, if they did (and, thus, if others did in similar localities), could
they be blamed for not having done anything about it? It was, in
short, the question of responsibility in its most concrete form.
A substantial proportion of newspapers had no doubts whatever
about the matter.

There was never what there should have been with a people with a
sense of civic responsibility—resignations in the Civil Service and the
teaching professions and in every branch of the State machine—*at whatever cost*—[italics in the original] against the perpetration of these fear-
ful things. It is on this criminal acquiescence that history must condemn the German.[31]

The German stood convicted of 'callousness or cowardice'.[32] He
must 'learn the first law of freedom: that a man may surrender all
else but not his conscience',[33] said the *Manchester Guardian*.
Others were not so sure. Apart from the left-wing Press in general
which stressed, quite rightly, that the best elements *had* protested
and had perished many years earlier, there was, for example, a

---

[29] E.g. *Observer*, 10 Jan. 1943; cf. *Economist*, 20 Feb. 1943, and some sections
of the religious Press, e.g. *Christian World*, 14 Jan. 1943 (though the dichotomy
is less stressed) and many comments in the Quaker *Friend*.

[30] An exceptionally clear statement to this effect was made in a leader in the
Derbyshire Advertiser, 19 Feb. 1943.

[31] *Time & Tide*, 28 April 1945.   [32] *Glasgow Herald*, 28 April 1945.

[33] *Manchester Guardian*, 25 April 1945.

reasonable and sober survey of the question in *Picture Post* which gave due weight to fear, the effects of propaganda, and natural human inertia. It evoked letters from some members of the parliamentary delegation, which mainly supported its view.[34]

The theory that fear provided some sort of excuse was more or less explicitly stated in more than one quarter, for instance in the *Manchester Guardian* itself, only three days after the appearance of the remarks just quoted:

We must be careful, therefore, before we spread the responsibility for these crimes too wide. The German civilians who now say that they did not know what was going on behind those grim walls are not wholly lying. If they did not know they guessed—and feared.[35]

On the other hand the *New Statesman* view was perhaps the most concise expression to be found of the persuasive *tu quoque* method:

I wonder, incidentally, how many of those who criticise the German people for ignorance or docility or condemn them for passive complicity would have raised their voices against the government in this country had they known that death or torture were the penalties for criticism. 'What could I have done?' the German pastor of a village near Belsen is reported to have said, 'Had I preached against the régime or denounced the camps, the immediate result would have been that I, my wife and my children, would have been sent to one of them.'[36]

However, a piece of evidence does happen to exist on the question of public knowledge and of public protest—particularly on the initiative of local clergy and quite apart from any question of the dedicated political few. The village pastor's query was by no means as rhetorical as it seems to have sounded in the *New Statesman*'s editorial ear.

In giving a factual background to the discussion on attitudes towards the 'Final Solution', mention was made earlier of the Nazis' first experiments in gassing their victims, who were originally drawn from among the insane, or from others considered unfit to live in the new Germany, but who were very largely of impeccable Aryan ancestry.[37] This first phase came to an abrupt end in August 1941. The reason was that the local inhabitants near one of these institutions—Hadamar, near Limburg—knew what was going on after little more than a year of operation, and publicly

[34] *Picture Post*, 5 May 1945; 12 May 1945.
[35] *Manchester Guardian*, 28 April 1945.   [36] *New Statesman*, 28 April 1945.
[37] See above, p. 95.

protested to the Nazi authorities. There was something like riot-
ing in the streets of the little town as the blacked-out buses carried
their loads to their destination. The Churches, both Protestant and
Catholic, joined in, and on 13 August 1941 the Bishop of Limburg
made a solemn pronouncement of his horror and disgust. All this
was reported in a number of papers, including the *Manchester
Guardian* and the *Catholic Universe*.[38] How many suffered for this
protest we do not know, but the fact remains that Hitler gave a
direct order and the extermination team left to take up other
activities.[39] Hadamar proved that effective protest of a mass type,
and in time of war, *was* possible. And, after making due allow-
ances for obvious differences between the two cases, some comment comparing the people of Hadamar in 1941 to the people of
Weimar from 1934 to 1945 might have been appropriate.[40] Of
course there were not only Jews in Buchenwald, and, for that
matter, in other camps where the gas chambers functioned. Yet it
is difficult to avoid the feeling that here, too, one is up against that
same uncomfortable factor so often misunderstood—the uniqueness of the Jewish tragedy.

There is a second reason for giving the Buchenwald reactions
special attention. The camp was overrun on 11 April 1945. From
that date, as reports of what was found there began to come in,
there was a widespread and mounting horror, which culminated
with the publication of the report of ten Members of Parliament
on 27 April.[41] Much of the national Press reprinted the text in
full; some had special articles by individual members of the delegation, elsewhere there were more or less complete summaries.[42]

[38] Complete Press reference, *Keesing's Contemporary Archives* (1940–3), IV,
p. 4903.
[39] See above, p. 88. For the text of the Bishop of Limburg's protest, see
IMT XXVI, 165–7; for the subsequent history of Hadamar IMT V, 364–7,
cf. Reitlinger, pp. 132–3.
[40] The Hadamar case came up at the American 'Wiesbaden Trial' (see IMT
XXXII, 426–9), but it was very poorly reported in England, and, so far as we
are aware, the obvious moral was never drawn.
[41] *Buchenwald Camp: The Report of a Parliamentary Delegation*, London
(1945), HMSO, Cmd. 6626.
[42] The full text was reprinted in, for example, *The Times, Daily Telegraph,
Manchester Guardian*, and *Daily Worker* (all of 28 April 1945); articles by delegation members appeared in *Reynolds News*, 29 April 1945, and the *Spectator*,
4 May 1945. The evening papers mostly printed summaries, e.g. the *Star*,
27 April 1945. The *Daily Mail* published the photographs in pamphlet form,
Lest We Forget, London, Associated Press, 1945.

Buchenwald received more publicity than any other story in the field of Nazi anti-Semitism, with the possible exception of the 'Crystal Night'. The general tone was the obvious and expected one of profound disgust at every detail of degenerate sadism,[43] with some interesting modifications appearing here and there. There was one which was undoubtedly not representative of Press comment, but of certain sections of public opinion. The author was that pillar of *Truth*, Sir Ernest Benn:

These horror pictures look very different to most of the world than to us. The Spaniard who finds his recreation in the gory game of Bull Baiting, or whose recent personal experience includes the massacre of helpless harmless religious communities, will pass them over with the thought that, after all the Germans might as well have a taste of what was common form with him. The gentler Viennese, who has been the eye witness throughout his life of periodical pogroms, will not experience such a shock to his sensibilities as could be desired; those who know something of the ghetto in Warsaw will take a less excited view of Buchenwald than the comfort loving folk of Boston. Our Russian Allies will be able to appreciate the murder machines with a knowledge that is happily denied us ...

In, therefore, ruminating on all the implications of the disgusting news from Germany, we should remember that it rises directly from the action of war criminals, but indirectly from the tacit assent of inferior, official-ridden human beings. In the long catalogue of nations between the Hun and ourselves there are many different grades, few if any of them able to aspire to that full measure of human value which we have long since attained.[44]

That was all there was to it: both the murderers and the victims had the misfortune of being foreigners. British standards simply did not apply. The last sentence deserved a place of honour in any collection of 'This England' extracts, but it was by no means a mere caricature of some basic English attitudes.[45]

More representative were two approaches very different in origins and intention, but united in more or less strongly disapproving of the publicity given to the discoveries in the captured

[43] See, e.g., leaders in *Daily Telegraph*, 28 April 1945; *Manchester Guardian*, 28 April 1945; *Scotsman*, 28 April 1945; *Yorkshire Post*, 28 April 1945—to take a few at random. Cf. also comment on Press attitudes as a general 'wave of bitterness' in *News Review*, 3 May 1945; a fair evaluation.

[44] *Truth*, 4 May 1945.

[45] For some similar 'letters to the editor', see below, pp. 196–7.

camps, especially the official sanction given by the dispatch of a parliamentary delegation. Certain sections of the right-wing Press took the view that the whole affair was a deliberate indulgence of morbid instincts which could only benefit 'cads in our own country who exploit such happenings to stimulate a class war'.[46] The purpose of all the publicity, particularly the official part of it, was to 'teach hate'.[47] We have already noted very similar opinions in the pages of the *Tribune*—in spite of the probability of its being an organ of those very 'cads'.[48] Now Left and Right met in cordial agreement. Publicity about atrocities had an ulterior motive. The only dispute was about its nature. The Left was not so categorial as the the Right but had no doubt *something* was wrong:

But why, I repeat the question, the fuss *now*? For six years prior to the war the facts relating to concentration camps were known in this country, but broadly speaking, publicity was given to them only in the organs of the Left . . . the papers of the Right knew none of those things. Was it because the victims were only German Jews, Liberals, Social Democrats, Communists or Pacifists, or was it because the policy of the Right was to cultivate good relations with the Nazis at all costs?[49]

This argument was based upon an initial fallacy. We have shown how, precisely in contrast to the stock attitudes towards Spain, the question of Jewish sufferings seldom depended on this or that political approach for its formulation. Similarly, the arguments of the Right stood on shaky ground. It scarcely needed morbid instincts to horrify the average reader with what was found at Buchenwald. But the important point was not the validity of Left or Right-wing attitudes. It was that the irrefutable proof of the 'Final Solution' should be made known as widely as possible. For, as the *Yorkshire Post* put it, unquestionably expressing the majority view,

The world needs to learn much more of what happened during the 12 evil years of Hitler's rule. The full appalling truth about Nazism must be faced and studied as doctors study the worst symptoms of some dreadful disease—in order to investigate its cause and possible cure.[50]

But criticisms such as those quoted were made by a not uninfluential minority of the Press. In other words, even before the war

[46] *Weekly Review*, 26 April 1945. [47] *Sphere*, 28 April 1945.
[48] It will be remembered how Orwell stressed the sadistic impulses—of the Allies (above, p. 137).
[49] *New Statesman*, 28 April 1945. [50] *Yorkshire Post*, 30 April 1945.

was well over, various ill-defined ideas began to get about that the exposure of Nazi crimes was inspired by biased or impure motives. This development was taking place on the very eve of the Nuremberg Trials, and should be borne in mind when Press attitudes towards these are being considered.

The story of the war crimes trials has been told many times and commented on from many angles. Apart from the numerous volumes of the trials themselves, there exists today a very large literature on the subject.[51] We will recall only some salient facts. The first of these trials was held by the Russians, when they recaptured Kharkov. Three Germans and a collaborator were very expeditiously tried, convicted, and executed for their part in the gassing activities of the *Einsatzgruppen*. The Soviet Film Agency made a news-reel of these events and had it shown in England. A typical reaction was that it was a pity the four could only be hanged once for what they had done.[52] In August 1945 the United Nations War Crimes Commission agreed to set up an International Military Tribunal to try those whose activities could not be limited to a specific area. The rest were to be handed over to countries in whose territories particular crimes were said to have been committed. The Tribunal began its work at Nuremberg on 20 November 1945 and concluded it on 1 October 1946. There were twenty-four defendants, of whom eleven were executed. It is common knowledge that of the real leaders only Ribbentrop, Rosenberg, and Streicher ever reached the hangman, that Hitler and Goebbels were already dead in the famous Berlin bunker, and that Goering, Himmler and Ley managed to commit suicide while in Allied custody. The Nuremberg Tribunal was, of course, not the only series of trials to be held. The British conducted their own, under Royal Warrant, notably of the commandant of Belsen and his staff,[53] while the Americans, in a separate series of trials, were responsible for bringing to justice highly important figures in

---

[51] For bibliography, see Robinson and Friedman, op. cit., pp. 190–203. A good standard work is W. R. Harris, *Tyranny on Trial*, Dallas (1954); see also A. W. Cooper, *The Nuremberg Trial*, London (Penguin Books No. 598). (1947).

[52] James Agate, *Tatler*, 19 July 1944, made this point with apposite Shakespearian quotations, e.g. 'I would have him nine years a-killing,' and 'O, that the slave had forty thousand lives! One is too poor, too weak for my revenge.'

[53] There were nine of these trials. Their full record has been printed in the *War Crimes Trials*, ed. David Maxwell Fyfe, London, 9 vols. (1948–52).

Nazi administration.[54] The trials continued and are still going on; but the later ones, like the Eichmann Trial, are outside our scope.

We have already discussed varying views on guilt and retribution in general and on the Jewish issue in particular. We have now to place beside them some Press reactions during the period when theoretical possibilities turned into practical problems, and when the indictment and trial of actual individuals became the news of the day. An interesting contrast can be found. There were very few indeed who were prepared to cast any serious doubts on the wisdom of holding trials, or on the correctness of their procedure while they were being held. This was in spite of the fact that two sorts of difficulties, which may be fairly called 'technical', unquestionably did exist. One was the problem of how traditional concepts of war crimes, basically confined to mistreatment of prisoners or of civilians in conquered territory, could be made to cover some of the most outstanding misdeeds of the régime, for example the murder of German nationals or of those of countries not conquered in war, such as Austria and perhaps Czechoslovakia. When the War Crimes Commission was set up this difficulty was clearly seen, and it seems a pity that the following extremely straightforward solution, suggested by the *Observer*, was not adopted:

Its [the Commission's] task is simply to reassert the law, which has been flaunted with impunity. The very words 'war crime' are misleading. There is no particular kind of 'war crime' punishable as such. There is only ordinary crime, as defined in the penal codes of the civilised countries. Hitler, for instance, cannot be tried for having caused the war. He can be tried for ordering the mass murder of Jewish, Polish, Russian or Yugoslav civilians, and if found guilty, can be executed as a common murderer.[55]

We do not pretend to judge how sound this argument may have been in law, but it is worth noting that two years later, when the details of the indictment were known, the same point was made by that great constitutional historian, Sir Lewis Namier, in a special *Manchester Guardian* article:

[54] Printed in *Trials of War Criminals before the Nuremberg Military Tribunals under Council Control Law No. 10*, Washington, 15 vols. (1951–2). [Cited as TWC.]
[55] *Observer*, 14 Oct. 1943.

. . . But the real objection to this part of the prosecution [waging of aggressive war] is that it is better suited for historical treatment by independent scholars than for argument in an international court of law. . . . Much more suitable for criminal prosecution is the record of the German mass-murders, culminating in 'genocide'.[56]

A substantial section of the Press thought it sufficient to emphasize this second part: the charge of plain murder—from murder on the smallest to murder on the largest scale.

The other difficulty was of a more fundamental kind. Since, by the time the trials took place, many incontestable facts had been common knowledge for a considerable period—first and foremost the partial success of the 'Final Solution'—it seemed absurd to claim that there could be an 'impartial' procedure in the traditional British sense, if there could only be a foregone conclusion. The Russian delegate in 1945 made this point when he stated bluntly that the major war criminals had already been officially and explicitly named as such by the heads of the Allied Governments, and that the sole task for a tribunal could only be to fix suitable punishments for various individuals.[57] Not surprisingly, this was the enthusiastically expressed attitude of the *Daily Worker*. Nuremberg was an unfortunate but necessary formality, useful as a record of the names of the guilty, whose role could only be to pass in at one door in front of their judge and out of the other to face their executioner.[58]

How was it conceivable, for example, that the Tribunal should appoint defence counsel for those whom the Governments responsible for that very Tribunal had just correctly described as criminals whose like the world had seldom seen? What line, moreover, could such counsel adopt which would not be farcical—or, on the other hand, not offensive to the memory of the victims? At the Belsen Trials, in fact, counsel for Josef Kramer did make use of very unfortunate phrases which another procedure might have avoided:

[56] *Manchester Guardian*, 20 Nov. 1945. The term *genocide* was coined by Prof. Raphael Lemkin of Duke University, North Carolina, and was officially adopted in the indictment. Those who dislike using hybrid neologisms are fully entitled (as Reitlinger, p. 8) to go on calling it 'Race-murder'; cf. an interesting article on legal meaning of 'genocide' in *Nineteenth Century*, Nov. 1945.

[57] An English version of the Russian delegate's contention is to be found in Harris, pp. 16–18.

[58] See, e.g., a badly drawn but quite unambiguous cartoon in *Daily Worker*, 25 Aug. 1945.

The type of internee who came to those concentration camps was low and had very little idea of doing what he was told, so that the control of those internees was a great problem.[59]

The *Daily Worker* version of these remarks was considerably more unpleasant, but the line adopted by counsel was perfectly clear: some of the means used in the camps were to be justified by the plea that order could not otherwise have been maintained. If the original Russian view of the matter had been accepted, then the *Daily Worker*'s reaction to this legally unexceptionable defence would have been logically inescapable:

> After the Belsen Trial is concluded it would hardly be out of place to proceed with a trial of the defending counsel on a charge of spreading Fascist propaganda.[60]

We have deliberately chosen an extreme example of something which was bound to occur once the principle of defence was accepted at all. Counsel had to do his job—though admittedly he did not have to do it as Kramer's had done. But whatever he did could, on a strict interpretation of the Russian view, only appear as a defence of Nazism.

The majority of the British Press did not believe anything of the kind. Its main emphasis was on the proposition that, however heinous the offence, the accused had to be accorded a scrupulously fair trial. Most papers endorsed the view expressed by the British leader of the prosecution at Nuremberg, a view favourably commented upon by both *The Times* and the *News Chronicle*: the Nuremberg Tribunal 'will provide a contemporary touchstone and an authoritative and impartial record to which future historians may turn for truth and future politicians for warning.'[61] For this, if for no other reason, there had to be a full trial: the full traditional formula had to be gone through so that, as far as humanly possible, there should be no doubt in anyone's mind that here was no act of political vengeance, but a true example of the operation of impartial justice against proved and convicted torturers and murderers. The words just quoted were echoed at different levels of the Press in different tones, but the intention

[59] *Trial of Josef Kramer and 44 Others* (The Belsen Trial), *War Crimes Trials*, II, London (1949), p. 149.

[60] *Daily Worker*, 11 Oct. 1945.

[61] *The Times*, 21 Jan. 1946; *News Chronicle*, 26 Mar. 1946.

was one and the same. The *Daily Mirror*, for example, had a cartoon which stressed that the very thing which the accused had most to fear was, in fact, a fair trial, and the same thought was variously expressed by cartoons appearing in *Punch* and in *John Bull*.[62]

If there was anything that worried the Press from the spring to the autumn of 1945 it was that the accused were being too gently treated, that the trial was being dangerously delayed, and that some major criminals might yet escape their just fate—a fear which was to prove not altogether unfounded.[63] At the time, too, there was some reason for anxiety. There were not a few Press agency messages which stressed such items as Goering sympathetically discussing the Jews of the Old Testament with the Lutheran Lieutenant Eggers of the United States Chaplaincy, or the Catholic Captain O'Connor's discovery about the Nuremberg prisoners as a class: 'There are no Al Capones or tramps here', he was reported as saying, 'they are intelligent individuals whatever they have done.'[64] There were stories, certainly exaggerated but disquieting nevertheless, of special cells and luxury dinners. 'Justice Must be Swift', demanded *Picture Post* in a two-page feature,[65] 'Time Lag arouses Public Anger', cried *Cavalcade*[66] and the *Sunday Express* had a particularly brilliant Giles cartoon showing how a cosily reclining and well looked-after Goering did not mind the delay in the least.[67] Nearly a year previously, *Illustrated*, not a very serious organ of opinion, had underlined a serious enough aspect of every delay—all trials and punishments after the signing of peace treaties might be fatally hindered by infinitely complex problems of extradition.[68] And on an issue such as this, the attitude of the *Daily Worker* does not need elucidation.[69]

Not much need be said about the Press and the reporting of the actual trials, whether at Nuremberg or elsewhere. There were few variations from the view that justice was at last being done. However, it should not be forgotten that for the professional journalist

[62] *Daily Mirror*, 31 Aug. 1945; *John Bull*, 3 Nov. 1945; *Punch*, 28 Nov. 1945; and cf. *Cavalcade*, 24 Nov. 1945.
[63] See below, p. 152.
[64] E.g. British United Press message as in *Manchester Guardian*, 17 Oct. 1945.
[65] *Picture Post*, 23 June 1945.
[66] *Cavalcade*, 26 May 1945; cf. a cartoon in *News of the World*, 8 July 1945: 'Chief War Criminals to be tried—some day'.
[67] *Sunday Express*, 27 May 1945.   [68] *Illustrated*, 16 Sept. 1944.
[69] See especially cartoon 17 May 1945.

the trials were, obviously, not only an exhibition of justice but also an event containing perhaps more concentrated news-value than anything that had happened within newspaper memory. Six hundred correspondents from all over the world reported the progress of the main trial, and, not unnaturally, did their utmost to supply, in addition to their factual accounts, something exceptionally original and exciting which might give them an advantage over their competitors. There were the inevitable 'peeps behind the scenes' to show, as one paper put it, 'the private life of the Nuremberg stars between sessions of the court'—that is, of the prisoners in their cells.[70] And on one occasion the *Evening Standard*, in what must have been a desperate hunt for an effective sub-headline, discovered that Streicher was being defended by someone called Marx.[71] But just as the opening of the Nazi era had defeated all attempts to make it seem even more 'sensational' than it was, so did its close. Little could be done to give Nuremberg some specific angle or interest in the journalist's sense—the event was too big.

As far as attitudes to verdicts are concerned, it is necessary to make one basic distinction. On attitudes to war crimes trials as such it is impossible to make any very useful comment because they are still going on. The final verdict on Press attitudes can only be attempted, or even seriously discussed in this context when the final verdict has been pronounced (and sentence has been carried out) by some court, somewhere, on the last of the Nazi criminals. It would then be possible to take a broad survey of Press attitudes to this group of events as a whole, and attempt general evaluation. On the other hand, one important conclusion can be advanced here. The preliminaries, the conduct, and the result of the main trials at Nuremberg can be treated as one connected whole, and about that the great majority of the British Press had no doubts whatever.

Of course there continued to be minority points of view in which queer identifications of opinion manifested themselves between newspapers which could hardly have been supposed to have had very much in common. Once again *Truth* and *Tribune* found themselves on the same side of the barricades. Orwell's comments on the unfortunate inhabitants of the prisoners' cages[72]

---

[70] *Illustrated*, 5 Jan. 1946.   [71] *Evening Standard*, 9 Nov. 1945.
[72] See above, p. 137.

were echoed some years later by *Truth* which, when reviewing the Belsen volume in the War Crimes series, concluded that nothing *alleged* against the accused had been as bad as the *actual* treatment of concentration camp staffs by American security units.[73] In 1947 the *Spectator* printed an article the purpose of which was to arouse sympathy for interned S.S. men.[74] It elicited one expression of support which, although it is in no sense an example of Press opinion, we cannot refrain from quoting:

These camps [for the S.S. internees] are excellently run but the injustice is horrible. Man after man whom we interviewed was clearly guilty of nothing worse than of doing what at the time he conceived to be, *and what in fact often was* [our italics] his patriotic duty. Nuremberg is retrospective legislation of the cruellest and most reactionary kind. . . . The young fellow who joined the Waffen S.S. at seventeen in exactly the same spirit in which an Englishman might have joined the Guards will become, at any rate for some considerable period, a stigmatised criminal —unless he can prove, as of course he cannot, that he did not know the Jews were being persecuted.[75]

The writer was Victor Gollancz. And there is an echo here of an earlier *Spectator* article, a quotation from which appeared as the first one in this inquiry—the article that sought to compare the new Germany to some giant English public school.[76] Similar Press opinions, though not often so individually (or so honestly) expressed, grew and spread during the post-war era, which saw changes in the attitude towards Nazi criminals just as it did towards much else which during the war, and at its close, had been more or less accepted. Worries about the Russians came to the fore; worries about the Germans, whether in the guise of Nazis or 'neo-Nazis', sank more and more into the background. We have no intention of pursuing Press attitudes into the regions of the 'cold war'. But it is worth saying that while the minority viewpoints and eccentricities we have noted were almost certainly independent of those developments, the new climate was reflected in responsible comment on the war criminals issue. As early as October 1946 the *Statist* praised a statement by Dean Inge, the Dean of St. Paul's whose political pronouncements had enlivened a generation, that Russia had been as big a war criminal as Germany, and should have been in the dock at Nuremberg with her—not in

[73] *Truth*, 11 Mar. 1949.   [74] *Spectator*, 5 Sept. 1947.
[75] *Spectator*, 19 Sept. 1947.   [76] See above, p. 7.

the seat of judgement.[77] But finally one clear impression emerges: during the period of the main trials, Press comment was largely united. The partial extermination of European Jewry had been one of the greatest crimes of the Nazi régime, and those that could be had to be caught, tried, and punished.

It would be encouraging to conclude this aspect of the inquiry here, but that would only be permissible if Nuremberg and subsequent trials had really been a final answer to Nazi anti-Semitism in Europe. Everyone knows, however, that unfortunately this was not so. Apart from the fact that many have so far escaped justice, and that many others have gained substantial remissions,[78] there was no finality. Most of the Nazis had gone, but not a little of their work remained. Even while the trials were being held, fresh manifestations of anti-Semitism arose in Germany, to such an extent that at least one responsible commentator in an equally responsible journal suggested that the Allies must beware of allowing individuals to hold important administrative positions who might 'introduce racial or ideological feelings'.[79] In Poland there was an old-style pogrom when forty-five Jews died as the result of a ritual murder accusation.[80] From the end of the war, until long after war crimes trials had dropped out of the front pages, there was a continuous series of items in the Press which might have made anyone doubt that the Nazi régime had really been overthrown. The following specimen headlines, taken entirely at random, are a fair illustration:

ANTI-SEMITISM IN HOLLAND, Effect of Nazi Propaganda
ANTI-SEMITISM IN GERMANY, Growing Campaign
POLISH JEWS FLEE FROM NEW TERROR.[81]

It is against this background that it is necessary to consider Press reactions to an incident in the British sector of West Berlin, about two years after the Nuremberg verdict. On 20 and 21

[77] *Statist*, 5 Oct. 1946.
[78] See lists in Reitlinger, op. cit. pp. 502–17. Such lists continue to appear; cf., e.g., *Wiener Library Bulletin*, X (1956), pp. 28–29; 47; XI (1957), p. 17.
[79] *Sphere*, 17 Nov. 1945; cf. *Contemporary Review*, which exactly a year previously had printed a much more explicit statement on the same lines, and a very forthright rejoinder to this kind of thing in the *Leader*, 4 Nov., 1944.
[80] This was at Kielce, see, e.g., account in *Manchester Guardian*, 13 July 1946.
[81] *Manchester Guardian*, 23 April 1945; *Manchester Guardian*, 21 April 1950; *News Chronicle*, 10 Dec. 1945. The connexion between this and the problems of post-war refugees is discussed below, pp. 190–2.

February 1949 a crowd of about fifty Polish and other 'displaced' Jews stopped the showing of the British film *Oliver Twist*, claiming that the portrayal of Fagin was an incitement to anti-Semitism. No German Jews were involved. The agency accounts of this affair, and that of *The Times* were objective enough,[82] but there was also a strong element of hostile and remarkably unpleasant comment. It was not surprising that *Truth* should speak of 'Jewish Ingrates' and 'arrogant aliens preying like vultures on the misfortunes of the defeated Germans'—for whom the Fagin character was 'too near the mark'.[83] Nor was it odd that the *Catholic Herald* thought the demonstration to be a result 'of the prolonged cult of pro-semitism'.[84] But this kind of approach was not confined to the specialized minority from which similar quotations have been drawn throughout this study. Scarcely milder attitudes were to be found in more unexpected quarters. These were references in the provincial Press to 'aggressive and cock-a-hoop postwar Jewry', and to the desirability of the Jews 'acquiring thicker skins'.[85] The *News Review* took this opportunity to expatiate on 'the most exclusive black market in Germany which is run almost entirely by Jews'.[86] This was echoed by the *Daily Telegraph*, which began its story with the words 'Fewer than 100 Polish Jews, many who are known as black market operators, again stopped the showing of . . . *Oliver Twist*', and went on to lament the loss that 'British prestige has suffered by allowing the film to be twice forced off the screen by an organized demonstration of a handful of foreigners'.[87]

These were some Press reactions to the *Oliver Twist* episode. Of course neither Charles Dickens nor the Rank Organization had had any intention of inciting anti-Semitism. Yet there are two serious points on which judgement can hardly be suspended. The first is the tone of Press comment on so small an incident. In its bitterness and unpleasantness it provided a sour contrast to what had been printed far and wide at the time of Nuremberg and earlier. The second point is more specific. After all, 'organized' or no, black marketeer or harmless refugee, German Jew or Polish Jew, these people had been demonstrating in a city which had

---

[82] Reuter and British United Press in *Manchester Guardian*, 21 Feb. 1949; *The Times*, 21 and 22 Feb. 1949.
[83] *Truth*, 25 Feb. 1949.   [84] *Catholic Herald*, 25 Feb. 1949.
[85] *Edinburgh Evening Dispatch*, 1 Mar. 1949; *Dundee Courier*, 23 Feb. 1949.
[86] Two items, 3 Mar. 1949; 17 Mar. 1949.   [87] *Daily Telegraph*, 22 Feb. 1949.

recently been the administrative centre of an extermination programme intended for all Jews, whether they were now 'foreigners'
or respectable citizens of the British Sector. This was surely
something that ought to have been taken into consideration. It
might have helped to explain the passions aroused by a mere piece
of entertainment. For in the eyes of European Jewry Fagin could
not but bear a frighteningly close resemblance to Streicher's
archetypal Jew—and Streicher's ideas had not disappeared.[88] The
commentators who chose to hint at this background were very few
indeed.[89] It seems that in a short space of time it had become even
harder to understand what it was like to be a Jew under Nazi rule.

[88] This was the point most forcibly made in a Board of Deputies letter to the
Daily Telegraph, 24 Feb. 1949.

[89] An honourable exception was an editorial appearing in two slightly differing
versions, in the *Northern Despatch*, 21 Feb. 1949, and the *Oldham Evening
Chronicle*, 24 Feb. 1949; cf. also *British Weekly*, 5 Mar. 1949.

VI

The Refugees

FROM 1933 to 1945 the British Press was virtually unanimous in its denunciation of what was happening to Jews under Nazi rule. In order to test how seriously this was meant by different sections of the Press at different periods, it is necessary to consider various reactions towards any practical steps that were taken to halt the persecution or mitigate its effects. Such steps can only fall under two heads: the destruction of the régime, and the succour of its actual or potential victims. Obviously Press reactions under the first head, that is, reactions to the war itself, cannot be a fair test of attitudes towards Nazi anti-Semitism. Only a mono-maniac on the subject (and of those Britain had not many) would have insisted that the war was being fought 'for the Jews'. As far as the ordinary citizen was concerned, there were, after all, a good many other reasons for hostility to Germany between 1939 and 1945. It is only in regard to the second step—activities connected with Jewish refugees—that Press reactions are a real test of the strong feelings consistently expressed over Nazi treatment of the Jews under their rule.

The total number of Jewish refugees during the entire period, excluding those that finished up in Russia, was something like three-quarters of a million.[1] Of these, the United Kingdom took not more than 65,000,[2] Australia about 9,000, Canada and South

[1] Statistical surveys of the Jewish refugees 1933–45 are to be found in Werner Rosenstock, 'A Survey of Jewish Emigration from Germany 1933–1939', *Leo Baeck Year Book*, I (1956), pp. 373–90; A. Tartakower, 'The Jewish Refugee', *Jewish Social Studies* IV (1942), pp. 311–48; M. L. Wischnitzer, *To Dwell in Safety*, Philadephia (1948), pp. 175–259; 289–94. For the United Kingdom in particular, see *Dispersion & Resettlement* (Association of Jewish Refugees in Great Britain), London (1955). A bibliography appears in *Leo Baeck Year Book*, I (1956), pp. 401–2. The basic German document is the 'Korherr Report', an actuarial statement submitted to Himmler; cf. Reitlinger, op. cit., pp. 490–2.

[2] Tartakower, op. cit., p. 316. The more usual figure for the United Kingdom is 50,000; cf., e.g., *Dispersion & Resettlement*, p. 61.

Africa 8,000 each,[3] while the rest of the Commonwealth took very much smaller numbers. Palestine was a special case which has to be discussed separately.[4] It naturally varied as the result of obvious external circumstances. Between the spring of 1933 and the summer of 1938, that is from the seizure of power by the Nazis to just before that rise in the pitch of persecution which culminated in the 'Crystal Night', the biggest year was the first, when about 37,000 Jews left Germany—74 per cent. of them for other European countries, mainly France and Holland, with comparatively few for the United Kingdom.[5] During the next four years the numbers fell to an average of 23,000 a year, the highest (25,000) being recorded in 1936—immediately after the promulgation of the Nuremberg Decrees.[6] The biggest emigration took place between August 1938 and September 1939, when the United Kingdom also received the highest proportion of its final number—40,000 from Germany, 2,000 from Austria, and 1,000 from Czechoslovakia.[7] The condition of entry into the United Kingdom, for the vast majority, was prior acceptance in the immigration quota of some other country. Stay was meant to be temporary, and only the outbreak of the war prevented the fulfilment of this explicit intention. And for the vast majority entry depended on a financial bond deposited by a resident of the United Kingdom. The war did not immediately halt the movement of refugees from Nazi territory. Legal emigration continued from Germany itself until 1 October 1941, and from unoccupied France until 11 November 1942[8]—that is, until the distinction between the two sections of that country was obliterated as a reaction to the Allied landings in North Africa. Thus the possibilities of escape existed—if only there was somewhere to go—for much longer than is, perhaps, generally realized.[9] Of course there was one great difficulty almost from the very beginning. Year by year the refugee was permitted to take less and less of his possessions. The famous 'flight tax', which first made its official appearance in December 1933, was extended by various additional regulations until practically no personal belongings, and little more than 6 per cent of his cash, could possibly remain at

[3] Tartakower, ibid.; Wischnitzer, op cit., pp. 292–4. The latter gives a far lower figure for Australia (6,475). All estimates *exclude* post-war emigration.
[4] See below, pp. 182–92.   [5] Rosenstock, op. cit., pp. 377 and 379.
[6] Ibid., p. 377; see below, p. 167.   [7] Ibid. p. 387.
[8] Reitlinger, op. cit., pp. 28–29; cf. IMT VII, 27–28.
[9] See below, p. 180, and cf. Rosenstock, op. cit., p. 373 (note 2).

the disposal of the intending emigrant.[10] This was true until the summer of 1939; after that anything that was left had to be expended in bribes to Nazi officials.[11] It was thus not only a Jew and 'refugee that the world was called on to accept, but an utterly destitute individual as well,[12] for whom, in addition, someone had to stand financial guarantor.

In the first year of the Nazi régime refugees got little publicity. We know one reason for this: a general disinclination to believe that Hitler was really serious over his anti-Semitism, and thus to accept the possibility that this intensification of Europe's refugee problem would be anything more than temporary. A *News Chronicle* editorial on the subject, for example, placed the whole matter within a broad historical context. The refugee had always been the oldest and most difficult of problems that nations had ever had to face: it was to be hoped that its latest form 'would not become a political question'.[13] Another reason was that by December 1933, there were only 3,000 Jewish or other refugees in Britain, while by the following April their number had decreased to 2,000.[14]

Nevertheless, it was precisely over this small number that the first cleavage of opinion appeared. The great majority of these first arrivals belonged to the professional classes, especially to the university world,[15] and in May 1933 an Academic Assistance Council was set up with the object of absorbing them into their appropriate fields, without, very properly, injuring the position or prospects of their British colleagues. This body had the immediate blessing of *The Times*, with all the expected scholarly references to previous instances of persecution in one country which inadvertently bene-

---

[10] See, e.g., the decree of 17 Apr. 1939, published in the official gazette *Juedisches Nachrichtenblatt*, 25 April 1939 (photostat of German text, *Black Book*, p. 124; translation, p. 510).

[11] Long a substantial source of income for the S.S.; cf. Reitlinger, pp. 29–30.

[12] This was the general picture. On the occasionally ambivalent acts of the Gestapo which even at a later stage was known to encourage emigration to the extent of permitting the taking out of possessions, cf. A. Prinz, 'The Role of the Gestapo in Obstructing and Promoting Jewish Emigration', *Yad Va-Shem Studies* III (1959), pp. 205–18.

[13] *News Chronicle*, 7 Dec. 1933.

[14] *Report of Permanent Commission for Refugees (Jewish and Other)* (*The Times* and *Manchester Guardian*, 3 May 1934).

[15] It will be remembered that the first discriminatory laws applied to the universities and the Bar. Members of the latter profession, however, had probably the least chance of all in England because of the fundamental differences between its legal system and practically all Continental codes.

fited learning in many others, from the sack of Constantinople on wards. A similar approach could be seen, naturally enough, in the columns of such papers as the *Manchester Guardian*, the *New Statesman*, and the *Observer*.[16] The more general question, too, had an equally favourable reception in sections of the provincial Press, even in industrial areas where fears of additional employment problems would not have been surprising. The very small numbers of refugees involved and the strict Home Office rules for labour permits were emphasized, while, even as early as September, it was stressed that some had already left England for other countries.[17] In Scotland the *Edinburgh Evening Dispatch*, after opening its columns to as virulent a set of anti-Semitic letters as could have been found anywhere outside Germany itself, printed a leading article which left no doubt about its own opinion. All questions of expediency apart, justice, conscience, and divine command alike dictated the reception and succour of the Jewish refugee.[18]

There was another point of view altogether, which attached little importance to principle, to the mechanics of absorption, or, for the matter of that, to the type of refugee who had actually come. The Home Office might say what it liked; one more job for a refugee meant one less for an Englishman. From beginning to end examples of this attitude can be found without any difficulty. In that first year they were largely confined to the provincial Press which no doubt felt that warnings of this sort indicated its readiness to protect local interests.[19] However, one national newspaper with sufficiently large circulation expressed the same attitude— but in a peculiarly misleading way. In April 1933, the *Daily Express* spoke with appropriate headlines of the arrival of two Jewish refugees as 'the first of 60,000 of their race who had fled from Germany'.[20] The implication could only be that the whole 60,000 were on their way to England and that they were all Jews. From the

---

[16] *New Statesman*, 27 May 1933; *The Times*, 24 May 1933; *Manchester Guardian*, 24 May 1933; *Observer*, 28 May 1933. On the academic refugees, see N. Bentwich, *The Rescue and Advancement of Refugee Scholars*, The Hague (1933).

[17] See, e.g., *Coventry Standard*, 16 Sept. 1933.

[18] *Edinburgh Evening Dispatch*, 20 May 1933, and see below, p. 197.

[19] See, e.g., *Bolton Evening News*, 23 Aug. 1933; 6 Oct. 1933; *Nottingham Guardian*, 6 Oct. 1933; *Bournemouth Daily Echo*, 24 Aug. 1933.

[20] *Daily Express*, 21 April 1933.

figures already quoted it will be seen that this was a fantastic exaggeration. In October, an *Express* news item began as follows (in bold type):

BRITONS—
HELP
BRITONS;

British Jews are actively resisting the influx of foreign refugees who take jobs which British Jews should hold.

There are many unemployed British Jews. Their slogan is: 'Britons—Help Britons'. . . .[21]

At this point, the bold type ended. Those who troubled to read further would have discovered that the secretary of the Catering Trades Association, whose membership was stated to be 10 per cent Jewish, had sent the *Express* a request he had received from the Jewish Refugees Committee to help one case of theirs, with the comment that this was very unreasonable since there were thousands unemployed in his industry already. We are not concerned in judging this attitude. The point is that there were no 'Jews actively resisting' anything whatever, and not a sign of a slogan. All this existed only in the special world of the *Express*. And yet it had a valid enough importance. It was eminently suited to give a convincing picture of floods of German Jews, ready to threaten the hopes of the unemployed and the prospects of the precariously employed.

This attitude was never expressed in so extreme a form by more than a minority, but it must always be taken into serious account for any accurate appreciation of the reaction of the British Press to the Jewish refugee.

It must be admitted that in a more moderate form this attitude was by no means a minority one. As the difficulties for the Jew in Germany showed no signs of decreasing, there was increasing pessimism about the re-settlement of an ever-growing number of the penniless, and, from the end of 1935, of the stateless. As that number grew, so did the apparent dilemma between economic compulsions and the claim of ordinary human feeling. This was at no time more simply put than by a *Scotsman* editorial in January 1936:

[21] *Daily Express*, 3 Oct. 1933.

It appears that there may be a conflict between two duties—the duty imposed by humanity to help the refugees, and the duty to keep our own people at work.[22]

The same day, the *Manchester Guardian* expatiated on the apparently insoluble financial problem involved.[23] Occasional hints from the Nazi authorities of a relaxation of the restrictions on refugee property (hints which were later to culminate in the 'Schacht Plan') were always linked to the explicit condition of a pro-rata preferential treatment for German exports. No British Government in an era of economic depression could accept such a condition; neither did any British newspaper support it. The alternative perpetually posed was between taking in a refugee for whom work or maintenance had immediately to be assured, or affording him greater initial security at the cost of some damage to British trade or industry. Either way, home employment seemed bound to suffer. Such was the difficulty facing the responsible majority, which did not, in contrast to what has been cited, ever suggest that each refugee admitted automatically meant an Englishman unemployed.

In order to judge the correctness of such an analysis, one must consider the development of the situation as it affected the refugees after the first few months of the régime and until the crisis of 1938–9, together with Press reactions to this development. In October 1933 the League of Nations had appointed a 'Permanent Commission for Refugees (Jews and Other) Coming from Germany'. To avoid German objections, this body had had to be set up on a non-League and, indeed, on a non-Governmental basis. Its funds had to come from private sources. Its members had no power to pledge their Governments to anything whatever, representing them, as they did, in only a formal sense, and its High Commissioner, James MacDonald, could make his approaches for assistance in no capacity save his own. The first result of this step was a marked increase of publicity for the refugee issue, particularly since the Commission's headquarters were almost immediately transferred from Lausanne to London. Its first full meeting in January 1934 was widely reported and, in one respect at least, all the reports were alike. There was very little

[22] *Scotsman*, 11 Jan. 1936.   [23] *Manchester Guardian*, 11 Jan. 1936.

reference to the inherent limitations of such a body. This attitude was, perhaps, best expressed by *Daily Herald* headlines proclaiming '12 Nations plan aid for Nazi victims. World Envoys meet in London today'.[24] The fact that no nations as such were planning anything at all was not immediately apparent even from more sober accounts—and still less was there any comment on the possible results of this 'unofficial' attempt to deal with a very 'official' difficulty.[25] In May the Commission published its first statistics on refugee distribution and this, too, was reported fairly optimistically by most of the national Press. In September, the difficulties facing the Commission began to be highlighted by the Press. Five million dollars had been raised (95 per cent from Jewish sources) and progress had been made in resettlement, but it was becoming more and more obvious that no 'unofficial' method could possibly deal with the situation.[26]

The refugee question as affecting England in particular also began to receive publicity. The first 'human interest' stories began to appear, whose intention it was, on the whole, to arouse sympathy for the refugee.[27] At the same time, however, there was a growing emphasis noticed on the negative side. While the anniversary of the Academic Assistance Council caused both *The Times* and the *Manchester Guardian* to print a full-page feature (by Professor Trevelyan and Lord Rutherford respectively),[28] and while the *Daily Telegraph* stressed that refugee absorption into the university world had on no occasion injured a single British student or lecturer,[29] the same period saw a very different spirit arising in other, equally respectable professional quarters. The *British Medical Journal* began to give space to acrimonious correspondence on refugee doctors,[30] and *The Times* itself had something similar regarding a university appointment (a correspondence initiated, it must in fairness be admitted, by an English Jew).[31] A striking incident was a controversy over the success of a refugee architect in a local competition. The publicity it aroused was not confined to professional journals. One of them, indeed,

---

[24] *Daily Herald*, 30 Jan. 1934.   [25] See, e.g., *The Times*, 31 Jan. 1934.
[26] *The Times*, 6 Sept. 1934.   [27] E.g. *News Chronicle*, 14 June 1934.
[28] *The Times*, 2 May 1934; *Manchester Guardian*, 2 May 1934.
[29] *Daily Telegraph*, 7 July 1934.
[30] *British Medical Journal*, 16 Dec. 1933; 30 Dec. 1933; 13 Jan. 1934.
[31] *The Times*, 14 Dec. 1934.

got more than it wanted by reprinting (though with excellent motives) an article on the subject from the *Fascist Week*.[32]

From 1935 onwards the whole refugee question began to receive even more attention. By September, the Nuremberg Decrees made 'official' much of what had been hoped was 'unofficial' within the Nazi régime. It began to seem likely that the refugee would not remain a relatively minor phenomenon—one of a number of unfortunate consequences from a period of revolutionary excesses. The world was faced with a steadily increasing stream of Jews from Germany, and suggestions began to be made that one or more countries might soon be forced into accepting responsiblity for the entire half-million of German Jews. Such views found their most pessimistic expression towards the end of the year. In December, James MacDonald announced that he could no longer continue as High Commissioner, and Press comment on the refugee issue was naturally concentrated around that event. The main point made by MacDonald in his letter of resignation was that the refugee problem, specifically in its Jewish context, was only soluble if international pressure caused a change of heart on the part of the German Government.[33]

The letter received considerable publicity. Practically all important organs, national and provincial, printed substantial extracts, if not the whole text. The *Sunday Referee* gave it headlines with a four-column spread, including pictures of MacDonald and Goebbels in suitable apposition,[34] and other sections of the popular Press were not far behind.[35] In that sense, MacDonald's action had had a positive and beneficial result. But a very brief analysis shows that the bulk of comment on MacDonald's letter was either naïve or bewildered, and sometimes quite astonishingly misleading. *The Times* was most optimistic:

It is scarcely credible that the leaders of Germany can themselves remain much longer insensitive to the movement of opinion in Europe and America or to the injury which is being done to German interests abroad.[36]

---

[32] For the fullest reference to the whole incident, see the *Architects' Journal*, 15 Feb. 1934; 22 Feb. 1934.
[33] For the text of letter see *The Times*, 30 Dec. 1935.
[34] *Sunday Referee*, 5 Jan. 1936.
[35] Cf., e.g., *Daily Mirror*, 30 Dec. 1935; *Daily Herald*, 30 Dec. 1935.
[36] *The Times*, 30 Dec. 1935.

It is hard to understand on what *The Times* based its conviction—which appeared as the final paragraph of a short, but highly accurate, survey placing the responsibility for the situation on 'Nazi fanaticism'—unless it was based on its long-held illusion that there was a valid distinction between this fanaticism and the German Government. The *Daily Telegraph*, on the other hand, merely 'hoped' that Germany would not 'neglect to consider the advice of world opinion',[37] while the *Leeds Mercury* could only

watch and pray for the early accession in the rulers of Germany of that wisdom and tolerance without which no State, however materially strong, can long remain in health.[38]

The *Star* more or less implied that Hitler might be disposed to take note of specifically British moral disapproval, which could outweigh any good impression made by visits of German football players or ex-soldiers.[39] An approach practically parodied by the *Newcastle Evening Chronicle* (a paper with a solid northern circulation) which devoted almost the whole of its leading article —*Civilization and Tyranny*—to proving England's peculiar excellence in contrast not only to Germany but also to America, whose 'gangsters, kidnappers, bootleggers and grafters' were compared to the Nazi conditions which the MacDonald letter described.[40] The *New Leader*, an organ of non-Communist ultra-left opinion, declared that a 'moral appeal' to Germany was useless. Only the overthrow of capitalism could solve the problem.[41] The most inept comment of all, perhaps, came from the *Nottingham Guardian*:

. . . that there is occasion for some sort of an investigation no one can doubt.[42]

In contrast, the *News Chronicle* was refreshingly sure of the outcome. Whatever the League could or could not do, 'Mac-Donald's indictment will provoke a reaction throughout the world not excepting America—which Herr Hitler will ignore at his peril'.[43] This confidence is harder to understand than that of *The Times*. The *News Chronicle*, after all, had never been inclined to

[37] *Daily Telegraph*, 30 Dec. 1935.   [38] *Leeds Mercury*, 31 Dec. 1935.
[39] *Star*, 30 Dec. 1935.
[40] *Newcastle Evening Chronicle*, 30 Dec. 1935.
[41] *New Leader*, 3 Jan. 1936.   [42] *Nottingham Guardian*, 31 Dec. 1935.
[43] *News Chronicle*, 30 Dec. 1935.

distinguish between Nazi and Nazi. *The Times* and the *Telegraph* might speak quite sincerely of Germany and the European community, but the *News Chronicle* had had no such illusions in a reasonably comparable situation, when Mussolini's Abyssinian campaign had proved that 'provoking a reaction throughout the world' was not such a very perilous affair.

This sketch of representative views on MacDonald's thesis that there was no alternative to an appeal to the Nazis, shows something more than various degrees of illusion about the fundamental character of Nazi anti-Semitism. It shows, first and foremost, a great measure of agreement over MacDonald's main point: the refugee problem as such was insoluble whether it were attacked by private philanthropy, by Governments, or by an international body. A high proportion of the refugees already created by Nazi policy could only be resettled with the greatest difficulty, and if that policy continued to create more there was little prospect of further success. This was the reason why, quite apart from misunderstanding or ignorance, there was such a strong compulsion to believe that the Nazis could be influenced. Some papers did not even think it necessary to add a comment on the alternative to an appeal to the Nazi Government, while those that did made it plain that it was no alternative at all. *The Times* spoke of 400,000 Jews 'facing hunger and helplessness abroad'.[44] The *Daily Telegraph* stressed 'the stern difficulties of unemployment and of heavily burdened finances'[45] and the *Star* used almost exactly the same phraseology,[46] while the *News Chronicle* said that 'the neighbouring states are no longer able to harbour the flood of penniless refugees'.[47]

There were, of course, other newspapers with a rather more positive approach but general sympathy was more in evidence than methodical discussion of what might be practically possible. A number of Liberal and left-wing journals were unanimous in proclaiming that it was the job of Governments rather than of philanthropic groups or individuals however devoted, without, however, making any concrete suggestions. Essential (and remarkably well-known) data were either completely left out of account or only very casually mentioned.[48]

[44] *The Times*, 30 Dec. 1935.   [45] *Daily Telegraph*, 30 Dec. 1935.
[46] *Star*, 30 Dec. 1935.   [47] *News Chronicle*, 30 Dec. 1935.
[48] E.g. *Daily Herald*, 30 Dec. 1935; *Manchester Guardian*, 4 Jan. 1936; *Time & Tide*, 4 Jan. 1936; *New Statesman*, 4 Jan. 1936.

In the first place, very little statistical reference was ever made to certain relevant figures which must by that time have been available. At the beginning of 1936, the total number of Jewish refugees stood at 81,000. Of those, more than 20 per cent had settled in Palestine, while nearly 25 per cent had been successfully absorbed in other parts of the world outside Europe.[49] It is not easy to say precisely how many of the remainder were still unabsorbed, but MacDonald himself, who could hardly have wished to minimize his difficulties, put them at 15,000. The immediate practical problem, therefore, was the placing of, at most, 15,000 German Jews; but neither this basic fact, nor the general statistical picture, was ever directly put before the reader. But surely it was a problem which need not have been automatically considered insurmountable by the combined resources of the non-Nazi or non-Fascist world—even in relation to the economic conditions of the day. No journalist, however wedded to his style, need have allowed himself to call 15,000 Jews 'a flood' in relation to the population of Europe—nor 81,000 in relation to that of the world.

Secondly, there was very little reference to what was then extremely recent history. While there has been more than one occasion in this survey to criticize insufficient Press awareness of the uniqueness of the Jewish situation, it now becomes necessary to criticize its apparent unawareness of the fact that, as refugees, the Jews were anything but unique. The problem of the refugee was not new. At the end of the first World War the Russian and Turkish revolutions had caused a movement out of their territories which could more properly be described as a flood than could the refugees of 1933–6. Russian refugees alone numbered little short of a million, while Armenians and Assyrians brought that number up to considerably over that figure. I am not trying to make the sufferings of these people appear less than they were, but the fact remains that in a relatively short time the vast majority was absorbed into fresh areas of settlement—during a period immediately following the most destructive war that Europe had yet seen—and that, for example, France alone took nearly half a million Russians without noticeably damaging her internal eco-

[49] These figures are adapted from Rosenstock, p. 377, who took them from League of Nations reports and other contemporary official sources that could hardly have been a mystery to the ordinary journalist.

nomy. Now it may be true that this view is misleading because the 1929 slump brought about an entirely new set of circumstances, under which absorption of the refugee had become an infinitely more difficult matter. However, the point is that the bulk of Press comment nearly ignored this background altogether, particularly the outstanding fact that without fantastic exertions the world had succeeded in absorbing refugees to the amount of almost three times the entire German Jewish community.[50]

The small group of existing Press references to this topic supports the present argument. The comparatively successful settlement of the refugee problem after the first World War had been partly due to the invention of the famous 'Nansen' passport, which gave a stateless person an identity, and which the League of Nations had succeeded in persuading most civilized countries to recognize. At the beginning of 1936, the League announced that the Nansen office would be closed. Its task was done, and after MacDonald's resignation the 'new' refugee question would be put into the hands of some sort of inter-Governmental committee. On the whole, Press reaction was unfavourable. There was recognition of what Nansen had achieved, and a feeling that this was hardly a suitable moment to dispense with the useful tool he had created.[51] There was at least one suggestion that the League ought to go on issuing an international passport, whatever name it chose to give it.[52]

Yet there was little attempt to relate the statistics of the refugee problem caused by the Nazis to the substantially greater problem of the 'Nansen' period, thus putting it into a more reasonable perspective. And hardly anyone seemed to appreciate one very simple fact: lack of legal identity was, after all, only a part of the troubles of the refugee. His main trouble was often to gain acceptance as a potentially useful element (at the least not a potentially harmful one) within a community, in the way in which, for instance, the Russians had by and large been accepted. And,

[50] The only paper, as far as we know, to point this out was the *Manchester Guardian*, 10 Sept. 1938.

[51] E.g. *News Chronicle*, 20 Jan. 1936.; *Northern Echo*, 10 Jan. 1936; cf. also the *Glasgow Bulletin*, 11 Jan. 1936, which opposed the closing on the grounds that this would leave political, as distinct from Jewish, refugees unprotected. On the whole its implication was that the new body would adequately deal with the latter.

[52] *News Chronicle*, 7 Jan. 1936—a feature article.

inevitably, the immediate point at issue was whether a particular Government was willing so to accept him, something which no amount of international documentation could ever guarantee. In this respect, there is no doubt of the contrast between post-1918 and post-1933 Governmental attitudes. Why did the Press make so little reference to this noticeable difference? One of the very few exceptions was the *Daily Sketch*, which said: 'What the Nansen Office did, probably the Jews could do for their oppressed if they had the same amount of official sympathy.'[53]

There was thus a basic identity of approach between the irresponsible and antagonistic elements quoted earlier in this chapter, and the generally friendly ones representing the more responsible sections of the British Press. Stripped of polite circumlocution this approach expressed the opinion that the German-Jewish refugee was already a serious menace to living standards, and that he was likely to become a more serious one if the Nazis continued their anti-Semitic policies. No denunciation of these policies, however trenchant, no pity for the individual sufferer, however sincere, could disguise the fact that the real question at issue was an apparently insoluble practical economic problem which the German Government unhappily persisted in thrusting on a reluctant world.

In remarkable contrast to this near-panic atmosphere was the calm, bordering on indifference, during the subsequent two years. After MacDonald and Nansen had lost their news value and before Austria had acquired hers, the amount of space given to the refugee question was small and the type of item that did appear tended to be of a colourlessly informative nature.[54] The effects of the Nuremberg Decrees had not borne out MacDonald's prophecy. In 1935 21,000 Jews had left Germany. In 1936, the number was 25,000, in 1937, 23,000, while the picture in 1938 would have been a similar one if the figures until just before the events of the autumn be taken as a reasonable indication—even in spite of the addition of Austria as a new source.[55] This absence of a crisis was reflected in the Press. The amount of space and type of presentation ac-

[53] *Daily Sketch*, 11 Jan. 1936.
[54] The occasional feature article or piece of sensationalism could be found; cf., e.g., *Sunday Express*, 6 July 1937, on 'the moving heart-cry of a refugee', and, in contrast, the *Manchester Guardian* was exceptional in carefully chronicling every development.
[55] See above, p. 156.

corded to the refugee problem from the early months of 1936 to those of 1938 was a sign that the British Press was coming to accept the wanderings of the refugees as part of the ordinary European or even the English scene; so much so that during 1937 the *Spectator* even ran a regular column in German. But this new attitude was no more justifiable than the old. Before very long, Nazi actions changed all this: between the summer of 1938 and the outbreak of the war Great Britain received between three-quarters and four-fifths of her final refugee population.[56] The Press again began to be filled with refugee stories, and gave publicity to various attempts at dealing with the new crisis.

The general picture was not encouraging. 'Dreadful, dreadful, are the afflictions of the Jewish people,' lamented the *Daily Express*—but maintained that there was no room for them in Britain.[57] The *Evening News* said:

Every country is privately determined not to become the spiritual [*sic*] home of the Great Unwanted. . . . Money we will provide, if need be, but the law of self-preservation demands that the word 'Enter' be removed from the gate.[58]

The *Sunday Express* was even plainer:

In Britain half a million Jews find their home. They are never persecuted and, indeed, in many respects the Jews are given favoured treatment here. But just now there is a big influx of foreign Jews into Britain. They are overrunning the country. They are trying to enter the medical profession in great numbers. They wish to practise as dentists. Worst of all, many of them are holding themselves out to the public as psycho-analysts. A psycho-analyst needs no medical training, but arrogates to himself the functions of a doctor. And he often obtains an ascendancy over the patient of which he makes base use if he is a bad man. . . . Intolerance is loathed and hated by almost everybody in this country. And by keeping a close watch on the causes which fed the intolerance of the Jews in other European countries we shall be able to continue to treat well those Jews who have made their homes among us, many of them for generations.[59]

Perhaps this was only what the *New Statesman* called 'just the Beaverbrook press enjoying its continuous silly season with its

---

[56] Depending on whether the higher or the lower figure be taken for the English total, see above, p. 155.
[57] *Daily Express*, 2 Sept. 1938.   [58] *Evening News*, 13 July 1938.
[59] *Sunday Express*, 19 June 1938.

usual irresponsibility'.[60] There was certainly little difference between the menacing, Svengali-like figure evoked here and the ordinary Nazi picture of the Jewish doctor corrupting some trusting Nordic maiden.

Unfortunately similar implications, if not in the same highly individual style, were to be found in other sections of the Press:

Most of the alien doctors and dentists are Jews who are fleeing from the terror in Germany and Austria. . . . And the methods those aliens are bringing into England are not always in accordance with the professional etiquette of this country.[61]

The question of refugee doctors was also stressed by the *News Review*, which gave favourable publicity to certain hostile pronouncements by the Medical Practitioners' Union—in a manner calculated to give the casual reader the impression that that body had as great an authority as the British Medical Association.[62] The *Daily Mail* turned to the wider question and, under the headline *Aliens Pouring into Britain*, reported with hearty approval a sentence of hard labour passed on an illegal immigrant,[63] an approach paralleled in the *Daily Mirror* (Manchester) with its four-column spread in bold type:

SMUGGLING OF EXILES ALARMS BRITAIN [64]

The *Glasgow Herald*, while paying homage to the 'moral obligation of civilized nations to do all within their power to alleviate the misery of the unfortunate people who for reasons of politics or race have been exiled from their countries', pointed out that many of them were Jews and that Jews were not 'universally welcome'.[65] *Reynolds Illustrated News* allowed itself to spoil an extremely sympathetic article on the problem with an unpleasant cartoon of a refugee family, with every Jewish facial characteristic as conceived by Streicher exaggerated to the fullest extent.[66] Finally it must be noted that one organ enjoying a much higher reputation for responsibility than most of the foregoing—the *Observer*—commented as follows:

[60] *New Statesman*, 27 Aug. 1938.　　[61] *Everybody's Weekly*, 17 Sept. 1938.
[62] *News Review*, 14 July 1938; 11 Aug. 1983.
[63] *Daily Mail*, 20 Aug. 1938.　　[64] *Daily Mirror* (Manchester), 27 July 1938.
[65] *Glasgow Herald*, 6 July 1938. This particular note had been sounded earlier; cf. *East London Observer*, 4 Nov. 1933.
[66] *Reynolds Illustrated News*, 11 Sept. 1938.

A typically baffling illustration of the difficulty is the fact that Britain now has more Jews than Germany ever had. If a further accretion of, say, 100,000 of them come into the country, how could the danger be averted of an anti-Jew feeling here? [67]

The most obvious question that arises here is how far such pessimistic forecasts could be supported by the actual state of British public opinion in regard to the Jews—whether alien or native—and to this an answer will be attempted in the context of other questions of public opinion.[68]

However, two comments must be made at this point. Firstly, statistics were being treated somewhat casually. The estimate of the *Daily Express* that half a million Jews had found their home in Britain and the assertion of the *Observer* that, by the summer of 1938, there were more Jews in Britain 'than Germany ever had' (i.e. more than 550,000), were both statements bearing but a sketchy resemblance to the one statistical source available—the *Jewish Year Book*, which gave the Jewish population of Britain at the end of 1938 as 370,000.[69] Secondly, one basic assumption emerged, whether all its implications were consciously understood or not. If more Jewish refugees meant, or might eventually mean, more anti-Semitism in host countries, then the cause of anti-Semitism was—the Jew. And since anti-Semitism, at least in its more virulent form, was clearly wrong and barbarous, the only course was to prevent any notable increase in one's own Jewish population. Whether the Jew was a potential corrupter of medical morality or, more politely, just 'not universally welcome' (as the *Glasgow Herald* put it), the inescapable inference was that some characteristic of his, at least as much as any of his persecutor's, lay at the roots of the anti-Semitic disease. The Jew carried the seeds of his condition with him and to admit him in any great quantities was to risk spreading the infection. Of course, it would be wrong to suggest that such attitudes exemplified all that the Press had to say about the refugee—but equally wrong to forget that they existed.[70]

[67] *Observer*, 31 July 1938.   [68] See below, pp. 199–200.

[69] *Jewish Year Book*, London (1939), p. 345. Although the *Year Book* figures were based on explicitly non-official estimates, the least that might have been done would have been to give the evidence for so widely differing from the only known figure: in the case of the *Express* by 130,000, and, in that of the *Observer*, by presumably something nearer 200,000. In the absence of such an indication, these statements can only provide an example of tendentious exaggeration.

[70] See also Chapter VII.

Two more examples may be given of a swing from unfounded pessimistic evaluations to an equally unfounded optimism. At a conference held at Evian in the summer of 1938, thirty countries declared their inability to admit refugees except on the basis of individual cases separately considered. An organization was established to systematize this procedure and to seek relaxations in German restrictions on refugee capital. Although this was a very modest result—essentially no more than an international blessing on the *status quo*—it was welcomed by the Press. *The Times* was especially clear:

> ... Evian has done its work admirably ... it has devised machinery which, if not blocked by the countries of origin, should transform the haphazard flight of destitute Jews into the orderly exodus of not wholly impoverished emigrants.[71]

No other paper was quite so optimistic, but there was wide agreement that anything more than the Evian plan was out of the question.[72] Even the *Manchester Guardian* appears to have been under the same illusion that there was still some practical point in insisting that the chief responsibility lay with the one country which had proved over and over again its firm intention to make the problem harder.[73] One of the very few exceptions was the *Daily Herald* which asked, 'If this is coming to the help of the refugees, then what would the nations do if they meant to desert them?'[74]

The second example comes from the 'Crystal Night' period. A few days after the pogrom, the British Government announced that, to cope with the expected increase in refugees, it would call a special meeting of the Evian powers and investigate possibilities of settlement in various colonies. Immediate admission would be limited to children to be trained for re-emigration—anything more would encourage 'the making of a definite anti-Jewish movement'.[75] This announcement had a good reception. The *Daily Telegraph* claimed that '32 Powers plan swift aid to Refugees'.[76] *The Times* rebuked those who might have expected 'a grandiose scheme' and affirmed that the Government were doing

[71] *The Times*, 18 July 1938.
[72] Cf., e.g., *Scotsman*, 6 July 1938; *Leeds Mercury*, 7 July 1938.
[73] *Manchester Guardian*, 10 Sept. 1938.
[74] *Daily Herald*, 26 Aug. 1938.
[75] Parliamentary Report in *The Times*, 22 Nov. 1938.
[76] *Daily Telegraph*, 22 Nov. 1938.

'their utmost for a solution'.[77] Many concentrated on the one immediate step—the admission of refugee children—and thus achieved a positive slant to their presentation,[78] while even the *Manchester Guardian* certainly did not give a pessimistic impression.[79] The *Evening News* was exceptional in stressing with unctuous approval the Government's reference to the risk of anti-Semitism[80] —but then, on the other hand, so was the *News Chronicle* with its headline

PREMIER'S PLANS FOR REFUGEES DISAPPOINT M.P.'s.[81]

The financial aspect was widely stressed—the Government was right to be cautious for that reason if for no other.[82] The Government's attitude was, in the words of one provincial source, 'sympathetic but business-like'.[83]

In contrast to this picture the *Spectator* saw what was involved:

The immediate necessity is that any Jewish refugees who do reach these shores should be admitted and found temporary accommodation of some kind and that the Government should not merely keep in step with the other Governments represented at the Evian Conference, but do its utmost to stimulate that body to effective action.[84]

And the *Daily Herald* roundly declared:

Until emigration of whole families on a large scale is arranged, humanity —and particularly, the British Empire—will not have done its duty by the German Jews.[85]

The clearest understanding was shown by the *Manchester Guardian*, in spite of its optimism about the Government statement. A week later it quoted the Nazi prediction of how 'the end of Jewry and

---

[77] *The Times*, ibid.

[78] E.g. *Daily Express*, 22 Nov. 1938; *Daily Mail*, 30 Nov. 1938; *Daily Mirror*, 3 Dec. 1938; *Eastern Evening News*, 3 Dec. 1938; *South London Press*, 25 Nov. 1938.

[79] *Manchester Guardian*, 22 Nov. 1938.

[80] *Evening News*, 22 Nov. 1938; but on 2 December it was equally favourable to admission of the children.

[81] *News Chronicle*, 22 Nov. 1938.

[82] E.g. *Daily Telegraph*, ibid., cf. *Nottingham Guardian*, 22 Nov. 1938.

[83] *Wolverhampton Express*, 22 Nov. 1938.

[84] *Spectator*, 25 Nov. 1938.   [85] *Daily Herald*, 22 Nov. 1938.

its annihilation' would be attained.[86] It then proclaimed its own unambiguous position:

> To these threats, which are not vain, there is only one answer. The Jews in Germany must be rescued from that country and rescued quickly. A thin trickle of emigrants through the narrow, normal channels is no way of meeting this challenge thrown to the world to save a defenceless and innocent people. . . . If Governments can but regard themselves as the executors of their people's consciences they will show greater energy and give greater help than they are now doing to the Jews who seek to escape a country whose rulers are determined to destroy them.[87]

Reactions to Evian and the 'Crystal Night' refugees prove that a substantial proportion of the British Press did not appreciate that aspect of the refugee problem which had become fundamental even earlier—its urgency. It did not seem to see the difference between re-settlement and asylum, the fact that the choice was *not* between a difficult but fairly stable life under the Nazis and dependence on charity elsewhere, but between rescue and destruction. This inadequacy was partly the result of an innate incapacity to understand phenomena for which there was no modern European precedent. But it was also the result of something more practical, which cannot be too often repeated. It was the result of a conviction that the refugee was a danger to British standards of living. Of course there were those, led by the *Manchester Guardian*, who continually tried to expose this fallacy.[88] At any rate it should have been clear that the direct costs of absorption were always and everywhere borne by the Jewish community itself. But the negative attitudes described above persisted unchanged during that last year, until the outbreak of the war automatically ended various sorts of theoretical possibilities for large-scale immigration. Whether expressed in the inimitable manner of the *Evening News* or the *Daily Express*, or, more suavely, by the *Daily Telegraph*, this attitude remained clear and unmistakable. Sympathy was unbounded, but little more could be done than was being done already, and nothing at all could be done quickly. Above all, there must not

---

[86] *Das Schwarze Korps*, 24 Nov. 1938; for general Press attitudes to this passage, see above, pp. 97–8.

[87] *Manchester Guardian*, 29 Nov. 1938. The *Economist*, 26 Nov. 1938, and the *Star*, 22 Nov. 1938, were also critical. The *New Statesman*, 26 Nov. 1938, thought the Government 'had been extremely cautious', but said little else.

[88] See especially an article on 13 July 1938; cf. *Time & Tide*, 26 Nov. 1938.

be the least risk of a 'flood'.[89] The minority went on proclaiming that sympathy was not enough—but it was a minority.[90]

In short, there was a fairly general agreement during this period to welcome, and to persuade the Government to welcome, what was thought of as 'the desirable Jewish refugee'. This attitude was no cynical one and it would be wrong to minimize its positive character. At the same time, it would be just as wrong to minimize its inevitable implications. The principle of selection meant, for the unlucky ones, life under the Nazis, and support for this principle, however unpleasant this formulation may sound, meant support for that alternative too. Few British journalists would have declared in so many words that such a penalty was appropriate for even the least 'desirable' of Jews, but then there were very few who were capable of imaginatively grasping that alternative.

The outbreak of war obviously meant the immediate abandonment of existing plans for the refugees. The 'refugee attitude', therefore, ceased to be found in what may be called its 'pure' form after that decisive year for Jews under Nazi rule—from the summer of 1938 to the summer of 1939.[91] After that it became, first, the attitude to the resident alien in time of war, then a brief (though sincere enough) anxiety about the chances of saving the remnant of European Jewry, and finally a particular element in attitudes to the post-war 'displaced person' and to the struggle in Palestine—where it was involved in all sorts of other considerations, and influenced by political factors quite outside the purpose of this inquiry. Nevertheless, provided that these reservations are borne in mind, the attitude of the Press to refugees between 1939 and 1945 is still worthy of analysis. For in whatever guise he might appear the object of these attitudes was still the same person—the Jewish refugee whose identity and history could never be in doubt.

At the beginning of 1940 there were 238,000 aliens living in

[89] See, e.g., *Daily Express*, 7 July 1939, and a particularly nasty article in the *Sunday Express*, 14 May 1939, approvingly cited by *Truth*, 19 May 1939; *Evening News*, 30 Mar. 1939; 15 June 1939; *Scotsman*, 6 July 1939; *Daily Telegraph*, 11 Aug. 1939.

[90] See, e.g., *Time & Tide*, 11 Feb. 1939; 15 July 1939; *Manchester Guardian*, 3 Aug. 1939.

[91] For an extended discussion of this point, see the interesting essay by J. Tenenbaum, *The Crucial Year 1938*, *Yad va-Shem Studies II* (1958), pp. 49–77.

Britain, of whom about a third came from enemy territory. Of those, between 60,000 and 65,000 were immediately placed in 'Category C'—'friendly alien'—while out of that number between 51,000 and 55,000 were officially classified as 'refugees from Nazi oppression',[92] a high proportion of whom were quickly absorbed in industry, the professions, and the army.[93] The great majority were Jews. This is a reasonable inference from a comparison with either of the estimates for Jewish refugees in Britain,[94] which is confirmed by a survey taken in 1940 with the result of a proportion of 82 per cent.[95] Attitudes to this category of alien were attitudes to the Jewish refugee—a circumstance recognized by many sections.[96]

There were few doubts about the *loyalty* of this category. Both the Government and the local Aliens Tribunals which implemented its policy recognized that a German Jew was likely to be friendly to Britain.[97] And the Press as a whole accepted the official attitude. In March 1940 *The Times* expressed this view in two leading articles, and it was echoed not only by the *Manchester Guardian*, the *News Chronicle*, and the *Daily Herald* but also by the *Daily Express*.[98] It is interesting, moreover, that even those minority sections by then 'traditionally' unsympathetic rarely thought it worth while to worry about the security aspect. The *Weekly Review* actually declared that it was simply irrelevant since the Jew 'had the inherent right to stand apart from the present war which does not concern him and for whose tragedies he is not responsible'.[99] *Truth* ignored all 'categories' and persisted in talking about 'enemy aliens' without distinction. Yet in its eyes, too, the risk was not treachery but

[92] For a comparison of different estimates and for a most useful survey, see H. Jaeger, 'Refugees Internment in Britain, 1939–1940', *Wiener Library Bulletin*, IX (1955), pp. 31–33; 49–51.
[93] In 1941, at least 2,000 held important positions; cf. *Spectator*, 26 Sept. 1941. For the refugee in the armed forces see N. Bentwich, *I Understand the Risks*, London (1950).
[94] See above, p. 155.   [95] Jaeger, op. cit., p. 49.
[96] See next quotation and below, pp. 178–9.
[97] However, for some extraordinary Tribunal questions, see e.g. *New Statesman*, 30 Dec. 1939: 'So you are a Jew and a well-known doctor in Berlin. Why did you leave your practice, doctor?'
[98] *The Times*, 14 and 23 Mar. 1940 ; *News Chronicle*, 23 Aug. 1940; *Daily Herald*, 23 July and 23 Aug. 1940; *Daily Express*, 23 Aug. 1940. *Manchester Guardian*, 11 Jan. and 26 June 1941.
[99] *Weekly Review*, 19 Sept. 1940.

xenophobia rising quickly and fiercely, a development for which the refugees have only themselves to thank ... many are boorish, insulting, arrogant and unbelievably ungrateful.[1]

Between the citizen and the alien there was thus an unbridgeable gulf—a far more serious assertion than any momentary panic about security. This attitude was not confined to the minority Press. A *Sunday Dispatch* cartoon depicted the astonishment of two Englishmen meeting in a London street overrun with aliens of revolting appearance,[2] and the same paper spoke of the 'unhappy irritation' caused by badly behaved aliens.[3]

This simple method of proclaiming the alien's unacceptability by insisting that everyone knew he was personally a very unpleasant fellow (a method essentially no different from one type of pre-war approach) may be contrasted to another, more serious attack upon the alien, which was an adaptation of a second type of pre-war approach, also discussed earlier. Just as in the thirties, so now, he was represented as an economic danger. Since it could hardly be denied that the immediate wartime problem was lack of manpower rather than unemployment, the old allegations were altered to place the emphasis on something to fit the altered situation. In the opening of new shops and businesses, which of course was governed by a host of regulations, priorities, and so forth, the authorities, it was said, deliberately favoured aliens at the expense of British people serving in the forces. During September and October 1943, for example, a good deal of publicity was accorded to such statements emanating from two districts in South London. The *Evening News* carried a number of items with such headlines as 'Alien Traders: London Business Men Call for a Ban; Banning Aliens in New Shops',[4] and devoted a leading article to the subject.[5] The *Daily Sketch* had a similar leader, while its corresponding news item that day printed in bold type the suggestion made by traders' organizations that aliens should only be allowed to open a shop after at least ten years' residence.[6] It is not surprising that the local Press should also have had a number of items on the subject.[7] The distant *Yorkshire Post*, too, had a paragraph, albeit of a fairly objective kind.[8] Nor was the

---

[1] *Truth*, 28 July 1939, but its wartime attitude was identical.
[2] *Sunday Dispatch*, 10 Jan. 1943.   [3] *Sunday Dispatch*, 15 Aug. 1943.
[4] *Evening News*, 15 Sept. 1943; 13 Oct. 1943.
[5] *Evening News*, 17 Sept. 1943.   [6] *Daily Sketch*, 17 Sept. 1943.
[7] E.g. *Brixton Free Press*, 17 Sept. 1943; *South London Press*, 22 Oct. 1943.
[8] *Yorkshire Post*, 16 Sept. 1943.

reader left in doubt of what this perturbation was about. The returning soldier would either find his business in the possession of an alien, or his prospects of livelihood from it diminished by the incursion of alien competition. The Briton would be squeezed out.[9]

The fact (vouched for by the *Evening News* itself) was that from 1 January 1942 to 30 June 1943 thirty licenses to open shops had been granted to aliens, while during that same period British traders had collected 2,969.[10]

Of course there were plenty of protests raised against such an attitude. The *Spectator*, for example, sought to demonstrate by statistics the numerical insignificance of the entire alien element,[11] and there was no dearth of items praising the alien contribution to the British war effort.[12]

Nevertheless, the other attitude was there too, and it cannot be ignored. For while in the majority of cases the deliberate propagation of anti-Semitism was quite obviously absent, it is difficult to exculpate some newspapers from the responsibility of understanding that despite every disclaimer, the normal interpretation of an attack on the 'alien' could only be that it was an attack on the Jew, since that is what he usually was—and was known to be. Sometimes there was more specific encouragement for such an identification. Ever since the Russo-Jewish immigration at the beginning of the century, for example, a typical and well-known demand of the anti-Semite had been that Jews ought to be forbidden to adopt 'English' names. Now the alien was attacked in precisely the same context: 'The habit of strange people suddenly acquiring such names as "Percival Selby Lowndes" or "Henry York" must be stopped', said the *Sunday Dispatch* (in heavy type), 'if British unity and fairness of mind' were to be safeguarded.[13]

For many years the Jewish shopkeeper had also been attacked for keeping open on Sundays instead of Saturdays. Now the *Evening News* gave one of its reports on the South London protest the headlines

[9] *Evening News*, ibid.; *Daily Sketch*, 31 Aug. 1943.
[10] *Evening News*, 22 Sept. 1943.   [11] *Spectator*, 28 Jan. 1944.
[12] See, e.g., *Evening Standard*, 21 July 1942; 26 Apr. 1943; 24 Aug. 1945; *The Lady*, 12 Nov. 1942; *Catholic Herald*, 26 Feb. 1943; *Newcastle Daily Journal*, 2 Dec. 1939. The *Star*, 9 Oct. 1942, even stressed that where the alien failed to help as he might he was most likely to be a 'friendly' alien, i.e. neither German, nor Austrian, and thus, by implication, exculpated the Jewish refugee.
[13] *Sunday Dispatch*, 15 Aug. 1943.

FOOD SHOPS OPEN ON SUNDAY
ALIENS TAKE UNFAIR ADVANTAGE[14]

The *Daily Mirror*, with its enormous circulation, printed what its columnist 'Cassandra' called 'a short piece' about the alleged malpractices of Jewish traders, and then, after a *Jewish Chronicle* complaint, a defence of why such an attack had been desirable, even unavoidable:

What then are we to do? Print the crimes of Gentiles in the millions of copies of the national press and allow Jewish offenders to be publicised only in the relatively tiny circulations of their own papers? And this charge of emphasising the Jewishness of culprits. The moment their names are mentioned their race is apparent.[15]

The effect of all this was to encourage division, not only between Briton and alien, but also between Briton and Jew—whether German, Austrian, British, or any other. Although when the alien was discussed in the British Press (particularly when discussed in a derogatory manner) the word 'Jew' was never used and rarely hinted at, there were newspapers which saw and deplored the inevitable identification, in contrast to those which persisted in ignoring (or denying) that any such thing was intended. At the end of the war some ladies connected with an organization called 'The Fighting Fund for Freedom' petitioned Parliament 'that aliens of Hampstead be repatriated and that, meanwhile, they could be housed in army or prisoner-of-war camps'.[16] The *Sunday Express* commented that 'Hampstead is feeling the presence of so many foreigners somewhat oppressive because of the housing shortage'.[17] Neither the *News Chronicle* nor the *New Statesman* had any doubts that the petition was loaded with anti-Semitic implications.[18] Those journals which felt it necessary to issue warnings or demands about aliens were doing so about one particular sort of alien—the Jewish refugee from Nazi terror.

The significance of this salient fact will become even clearer if approached from a somewhat different angle: the altered situation. It is from this angle that all arguments must be judged, and it is

---

[14] *Evening News*, 12 Oct. 1943.   [15] *Daily Mirror*, 30 Jan. 1941.
[16] Cf. *Hampstead & Highgate Express*, 12 Oct. 1945.
[17] *Sunday Express*, 26 May 1946.
[18] *News Chronicle*, 27 Oct. 1945; *New Statesman*, 27 Oct. 1945.

this factor which must influence all evaluations of attitude. Just as in the critical year of 1938, the difference between a more sympathetic and a less sympathetic approach, often in itself distinguishable by little more than a difference of emphasis on one or other of the basic issues just mentioned, took on a very much harsher colour in the light of the events of the Crystal Night and the published threats of annihilation. Exactly the same observation may be made, but with a great deal more force, about wartime attitudes. Just as 1938 was not only the critical year for German and Austrian Jewry but also a critical test of peacetime attitudes to refugees, so the period between the summer of 1942 and the summer of 1943 was the critical wartime period. By 1938, no section of the Press could have been in any doubt about what the refugee was fleeing from in the way of peacetime anti-Semitism, and evidence has also been brought to prove that by June 1942 it was equally plain what the wartime conclusion of that anti-Semitism had turned out to be, and that during the following twelve months the British Press knew the fate of Jews under Nazi rule down to the last detail. Whatever confusions or misconceptions the British Press may have had about the origins and meaning of Nazi anti-Semitism, it never had any about its practical results. It is against this background that certain Press reactions to the refugee problem during these important months must be set.

In the first place it becomes obvious that accounts of attacks on aliens, so often hard to distinguish from attacks on Jews, took on an especially unfortunate character when the same paper described what 'the Nazi terror' actually meant for those same aliens' co-religionists, or even relatives. References to this or that piece of alleged Jewish misbehaviour had an especially sinister character when read in conjunction with detailed reports of the slaughter of Jews in Warsaw or Vilna. Between talk of an 'unfair' Jewish shop-keeper or an 'arrogant' German-Jewish refugee, and advocacy of the gas chamber, there was certainly a long enough road, but in that critical year when the gas chamber had become a common item of news, there was nevertheless an uncomfortable parallel between the two. It was this parallel which was so pointedly illustrated by one of David Low's best-known cartoons: 'How the Beastly Business Begins'. In the foreground stand two housewives, complete with shopping baskets. 'It must be the fault of the Jews,' they are saying. The background is filled with scenes of the holocaust.[19] But some papers could not or did not wish to see his point.

There was another, more practical aspect in which this period became a test of attitudes. Just as after the 'Crystal Night' it was possible to make a rough distinction between those who realized that urgency was the main factor and those who devoted quantities of print to discussing long-term proposals, so, after the House of Commons declaration, there was a similar division of opinion over what, if anything, could be done to save the remnant of European Jewry. Once again this division of opinion was over whether the Government was doing everything possible or not. In 1938 Government action, apart from the admission of children, had begun and ended with Evian. In 1943 it began and ended with an Anglo-American Conference on Refugees in Bermuda, and once again speed was not the striking characteristic. The declaration in the House of Commons had been made in the middle of December 1942. At the end of January, the United States was asked to consider measures 'to cope', as the language of the British *aide-memoire* put it, 'with what might be an unlimited demand for accommodation by refugees threatened by German extermination policies'. At the end of March the two countries agreed to hold a conference, which took place during the last ten days of April. The sole practical result was a statement that there would be a committee with greater powers than those which the Evian participators had enjoyed.

The world was now at war, and the majority of the threatened Jews were to be found in enemy-occupied territory. But as before, the neutral countries to which Jews could occasionally escape were unwilling to let them in, while the Allies were equally unwilling to take the responsibility of encouraging them to do so—or to relax their own entry regulations in any substantial degree. It was true that, as in 1938, responsibility was common to the whole non-Nazi world, and could not be pinned on Britain alone. But it continued to be the separate responsibility of every part of that world. Therefore, Press attitudes in Britain to Government action or inaction can be fairly used as a test of practical sincerity in denunciations of Nazi anti-Semitism.

One other parallel is apposite. Again there was a tendency to hope for some external event which alone could provide a real

[19] *Evening Standard*, 18 June 1943.

solution. In 1938 it had been a change of heart, voluntary or forced, on the part of the Nazi authorities. In 1943 it was a victorious conclusion to the war. Both propositions were, of course, perfectly logical, but too great a stress on either tended to go with the attitude that nothing much could be done about the problem itself, and that thus the Government could not be criticized greatly for not doing much.

Between January and May 1943 several papers did not see the need for any very radical criticism. The *Daily Sketch*, for example, seems to have been quite enthusiastic over the preliminaries of Bermuda, and gave a House of Lords announcement on the subject the headline,

BRITAIN AND U.S. HAVE NEW PLAN TO SAVE JEWS[20]

The *Daily Telegraph* was also optimistic and felt that Bermuda would ensure 'a sympathetic and practical treatment of a very difficult problem',[21] an estimate supported by both *The Times* and the *Yorkshire Post*.[22]

There were others who were less satisfied. The *Economist*, *Time & Tide*, and the *Scotsman* expressed their strong disappointment.[23] The *News Chronicle* pointed out that while Governments debated the slaughter of Jews went on—perhaps at the rate of 14,000 a day.[24] The most forthright expression of all came from the *Observer*:

Today, on April 11, 1943, it must be stated that the British Government has not so far found it within its power to rescue and shelter from cruel death one single Jewish man, woman or child . . . to arrange for a conference with these terms of reference is only a cruel mockery.[25]

But even in those months there were some editorial fears that rescue plans might actually succeed—that Britain might have to accept more Jews.[26]

[20] *Daily Sketch*, 24 Mar. 1943.   [21] *Daily Telegraph*, 13 April 1943.
[22] *The Times*, 20 May 1943; *Yorkshire Post*, 20 May 1943.
[23] *Economist*, 1 May 1943; *Scotsman*, 21 April 1943; *Time & Tide*, 22 May 1943.
[24] *News Chronicle*, 12 Mar. 1943; cf. *Manchester Guardian*, 22 April 1943; 15 May 1943; *Glasgow Herald*, 24 Mar. 1943; cf. also *Daily Worker*, 7 April 1943; *Reynolds Illustrated News*, 21 April 1943.
[25] *Observer*, 11 April 1943; cf. 25 April 1943. And this was the essential (and incontrovertible) point of Gollancz's pamphlet.
[26] See, e.g., editorial comment in *Yorkshire Observer*, 25 Jan. 1943; *Sheffield Telegraph*, 12 Feb. 1943.

Finally, we must consider attitudes towards Jewish immigration into Palestine. These are exceptionally interesting for two reasons. Firstly, Palestine presented a striking contrast to most other countries before the war. Instead of a slump, it had a boom; instead of unemployment, a labour shortage. And the Zionists (largely responsible for this prosperity) were naturally striving to increase the Jewish population. The efforts of the Jew to escape his tormentors were equalled by the efforts of the Jewish Agency to bring him to Palestine. Secondly, the refugee's fate in Palestine depended much more plainly than anywhere else on considerations of national policy. Britain ruled Palestine under a 'League of Nations Mandate', with a specific reference to the Balfour Declaration promising the Jews a 'National Home', and unspecific ones to the safeguarding of Arab rights. Various promises had been also made to the Arabs (because of help against the Turks) which might conflict with Lord Balfour's promise. At the same time, Palestine was considered as strategically vital; Italian and German propaganda there was thought to endanger Britain's whole position in the East. All these factors naturally resulted in variations in policy on Jewish immigration. Until 1936 interpretation of the Mandate had been moderately favourable to Zionism, and immigration policy had been governed more or less by economic factors. After that, a serious Arab revolt and increased anxieties about Hitler's and Mussolini's colonial intentions made it more and more pro-Arab—and purely arbitrary restrictions on immigration increased. Between 1935 and 1939 Palestine's share of the total of refugees dropped from 36 per cent to 10 per cent.[27] Immediately after the 'Crystal Night', the Jewish Agency's request for 100,000 immigration certificates, whose holders would be transported and maintained entirely at Jewish expense, was categorically refused. In 1939 a Government White Paper declared that only a further 75,000 Jews would ever be allowed to enter—to be spread over five years. From 1944 all entry would depend on Arab consent.[28] Now, while it is perfectly true that all this admits of a multitude of highly controversial interpretations, and while it may be claimed that selection and presentation here is by no means 'objective' (the

[27] For 1935 the figure was 61,854, for 1938 and 1939 together 40,419; Wischnitzer, op. cit., p. 290. For the total figure in the latter period see Rosenstock, op. cit., pp. 381–2.

[28] On the White Paper, see *The Times* Parliamentary Report, 18 May 1939.

present writer is certainly not so: he is a Jew and a Zionist who has settled in Israel), one indisputable fact does emerge. Palestine was the one place where British policy actually clashed with the efforts of those who were striving to save potential victims. And so Palestine became an interesting test of attitudes to refugees.

It was over the connexion between Mandate policy and the refugee problem that the most salient characteristic of British Press attitudes manifested itself. From the beginning of the Nazi persecutions until the end of the war and after, there was a strong inclination either to deny the need to make any such connexion, or to say as little about it as possible. There were some who even managed to ignore it altogether. The Glasgow *Daily Record* succeeded in writing a leader headed 'Palestine Problem' without any reference to immigration whatever.[29] Not many papers went so far as this. But in 1933, the *Daily Telegraph* was already quoting with unreserved approval the statement of the British delegate to the Permanent Mandates Commission that 'quite definitely, the Palestinian Government's immigration policy was, and must be, wholly unaffected by the situation of the German Jews'.[30] In a generally sympathetic leader on the twenty-first anniversary of the Balfour Declaration, *The Times* maintained that the problem of Palestine had to be separated from the situation of the Jews in Europe,[31] while on the eve of the 1939 conference the *Telegraph* referred to that situation in the following terms:

On the one side stands the Zionist demand for the fulfilment of the Balfour Declaration and the League Mandate, the provision of a National Home for the Jews, where, in an increasingly inhospitable world, they may come and settle as of right . . . on the other . . . the policy which demands the permanent cessation of Jewish immigration and an independent Arab Palestine.[32]

A week after the events of the 'Crystal Night' had become known in detail, this attitude received its clearest expression in the editorial of *Great Britain and the East*:

Humanitarianism and the Jews

. . . the connection between persecution and Palestine, is sentimental and coincidental. . . . At the risk of being accused of lack of humanitarian

---

[29] *Daily Record*, 25 Jan. 1939.   [30] *Daily Telegraph*, 31 Oct. 1933.
[31] *The Times*, 3 Nov. 1938.   [32] *Daily Telegraph*, 7 Feb. 1939.

feeling, we say explicitly that British obligations in Palestine cannot forever or even temporarily be influenced by the malefactions of certain European States towards their Jews.[33]

In February 1939 the *Contemporary Review* had an article on Palestine by the *Daily Telegraph* special correspondent in the Middle East, declaring that

. . . the time has come to view the Palestine problem from the entirely practical aspect, to decide what is for the general good of Palestine as a whole without regard for sentiment or humanitarian ideas. . . .[34]

And what was this 'general good'? A substantial proportion of the Press believed it to be more or less identical with the Arab demand, that is the suspension or restriction of Jewish immigration, either immediately or in the near future. More important than this attitude itself is what was said in its support, and what was omitted. *The Times*, for example, in the course of a long survey of the White Paper, included only a very short comment on its provisions for immigration: 'A vehement cry' on the part of Jewry was unjustified. 'Five years' grace' had been granted, and future entry would depend 'on the form of the constitutional development the British Government now pledged itself to promote'.[35] There was no word about causes nearer than Palestine, which might conceivably provoke such a 'cry'. The *Daily Telegraph* gave its White Paper leader the title

FAIR MEASURE FOR JEW AND ARAB[36]

When the Paper was debated in the House, the *Telegraph* declared that the immigration proposals 'already exceeded the bounds of prudence', since, for climatic reasons, at least half of Palestine could never be settled at all.[37] The *Sunday Times*, less sure about the wisdom of the new Government policy, was prepared to give it a trial. It too made no mention, at least editorially, why the inception of this policy at that moment might be an exceptionally painful blow for European Jewry.[38] The *Observer* thought the

---

[33] *Great Britain and the East*, 17 Nov. 1938; cf. similar views expressed on 12 Jan. 1939.
[34] *Contemporary Review*, February 1939.
[35] *The Times*, 18 May 1939.   [36] *Daily Telegraph*, 18 May 1939.
[37] *Daily Telegraph*, 24 May 1939.   [38] *Sunday Times*, 21 May 1939.

White Paper solution was 'logical' and declared that hopes of its working 'must centre in the practice of toleration'. It did not discuss the 'logical conclusions' of a refugee whose chances of safety were thus being curtailed, nor the type of 'toleration' hitherto extended by the Arab to the Palestinian Jewish immigrant.[39] The *Daily Worker* proclaimed that the representatives of the Jewish Agency 'are open supporters of British imperialism'.[40] The *Daily Express* heartily welcomed the Government plan as a 'supremely wise act of statesmanship . . . which has been urged by this newspaper unceasingly for close on a quarter of a century'.[41] It also saw fit to pronounce on British Jewry's moral duty to support the plan. The *Daily Sketch* called the White Paper 'sound' without giving readers of its editorial any details.[42] The *Evening News* spoke with obvious satisfaction of 'the bitter pill' all this would be for 'international Jewry'.[43] Even the *New Statesman* was prepared to accept the Paper as a working basis. It dismissed out of hand what it called 'the appeal to mercy, so to speak'. The Government's final figure for immigrants might well be increased, perhaps even doubled, but the chief need in Palestine was the abandonment of 'intransigence'—by Jews as well as by Arabs.[44]

There was an almost complete absence of serious discussion on Palestine's actual or potential absorptive capacity, despite impressive evidence of Palestine's prosperity supplied by the British Press itself.[45] There was no reference whatever to the *specific* requests of the Jewish Agency, merely general statements that Palestine could only help the refugees 'fractionally' and thus could not 'solve' the refugee problem. Finally very few newspapers seemed to appreciate precisely why, in the spring of 1939, something like the White Paper would be such a deadly blow to refugee hopes.

The *News Chronicle*, however, pointed out that [46]

[39] *Observer*, 21 May 1939.   [40] *Daily Worker*, 10 Feb. 1939.

[41] *Daily Express*, 15 Mar. 1939; cf. 1 Mar. 1939; 11 Mar. 1939; 18 May 1939 (where it blandly remarked that every country in the world had immigration restrictions).

[42] *Daily Sketch*, 18 May 1939.   [43] *Evening News*, 18 May 1939.

[44] *New Statesman*, 20 May 1939.

[45] See, e.g., feature articles in *The Times*, 8 Jan. 1936; *Manchester Evening Chronicle*, 18 Jan. 1934; leader in *Daily Telegraph*, 2 May 1934; *British Trade Journal*, May 1934. Innumerable references in the *Manchester Guardian* are deliberately omitted. They might have been called 'Zionist' propaganda.

[46] *News Chronicle*, 18 May 1939.

A time when Jews are being hounded out of Central Europe in vast numbers is hardly the time to slam the door of what they have long regarded as their rightful home.

The *Daily Mirror*, too, commented with some degree of prophetic accuracy: 'It is therefore suggested that the Jews should give in and be grateful—like certain other people whom we have appeased by extinction.'[47] And, needless to say, the *Manchester Guardian* was explicit enough:

The Jews, on our invitation, with our pledge and by our action, have made Palestine—what it was not before—a living country with a splendid promise. Is it suggested that at the very moment when their need is bitterest we should repudiate one of the few generous, creative ideas that came out of the war and that has already nobly succeeded? It is unthinkable.[48]

But comment of this kind was very limited.[49]

Undoubtedly the Press shared in the Government's belief that Britain might 'risk having the whole of the Moslem population in the East and in India against it'.[50] In some quarters there was also genuine sympathy for the Arab case, and a vague feeling that Zionist propaganda had somehow managed to manoeuvre the Mandatory power into a false position. I have no intention of discussing the rights and wrongs of either attitude since neither is strictly relevant here. But all the hostility in the world towards Zionism, all the conceivable weight given to British guarantees for an Arab Palestine, all the anxiety about British strategic interests in the Middle East, while it might explain Press support for the White Paper, cannot justify a consistent refusal seriously to relate Palestine to the well-known, and often violently deplored, European situation of the Jews.

Perhaps judgement should be suspended until after consideration of Press attitudes later in the war and in the immediate post-war

[47] *Daily Mirror*, 18 May 1939.

[48] *Manchester Guardian*, 6 Mar. 1939.

[49] The *Daily Herald* attacked the White Paper and the occasional unfavourable comment may be found in various sections of the provincial Press. See, e.g., *Daily Herald*, 18 May 1939; *Derbyshire Advertiser*, 19 May 1939; we have also thought it undesirable to cite such journals as *Truth* and the *Weekly Review* in the present context as their virulence on the other side was equally unrepresentative.

[50] *Daily Mail*, 28 Oct. 1933; cf. *The Scotsman*, 21 July 1939.

period, when the implications of the White Paper were subjected to the test of events. The inclination to dissociate the problem of Palestine from that of the refugees, and later the 'displaced person', became more and more striking, as the problem itself became more and more desperate. The picture of Press opinion on Palestine between 1939 and, say, 1947, is indeed remarkable, if one relates it to what was happening to the Jews of Europe during those years. Two other factors should be taken into account. The first is that before the war, the Jewish Agency as well as the vast bulk of Jews all over the world believed that Palestine had a special and specific part to play in helping to save Jews under Nazi rule. During the war and after it was held as even more axiomatic that the natural place for any remnant managing to escape the massacre was, and had to be, the 'National Home'. Secondly, the White Paper was held to be not only morally and logically repugnant, but legally invalid. It had been rejected by the Mandates Commission, and the League Council had never met. Britain had therefore no authority to apply its provisions for the restriction of immigration, and thus every Jew who could manage to do so had the legal, as well as the moral, right to make his way to the promised land.

Both these arguments can be disputed, yet they did express the basic beliefs of a section which had some standing in the matter— the victims themselves. It is equally incontrovertible that the story of Palestine under the White Paper (that is from 1939 until 1947, when the matter was once again brought before an international tribunal) became the story of the struggle around the practical application of these two arguments: the struggle of the refugees to find shelter in Palestine, and the struggle of the British authorities to keep them out, at times altogether, at other times in anything but token quantities. It became, in short, the story of the illegal immigrants,[51] the story of those heroic little ships which tried to land their cargoes on the shores of the 'National Home'.[52]

The Press began by reporting the events of this first period with

[51] To avoid the unsightly necessity of perpetual quotation marks around 'illegal' or the perpetration of some such phrase as 'uncertificated immigrants', I have left the description as it was accepted both officially and by the Press as a whole. The Hebrew word *m'apil*—overcomer of obstacles—is probably best here, but there is no satisfactory English equivalent.

[52] The best and fullest account is in Hebrew: *Sefer ha-M'apilim*, ed. Moshe Basuk, Jerusalem, 1947. For an English version see Trevor, op. cit., pp. 1–36, 177–341. There were a total of 54 ships, according to Wischnitzer, op. cit., pp. 305–7, which brought 67,000 immigrants.

the minimum of comment, but with a gradually growing mixture of embarrassment and irritation. At the end of May 1939, for example, *The Times* printed a moderately sympathetic account of the discomfort and suffering that these voyages entailed, mingled with less sympathetic comment. It typified a widely held attitude:

Placing the illegals in concentration camps is no solution. It is only a method of delayed admission. It has been suggested that they might be admitted and a corresponding number deducted from the legal quota for the month, but the number of illegals probably exceeds the quota, and upsets the careful plans to secure admission of the right kind of immigrant.[53]

The *Daily Telegraph* agreed editorially, while its 'Special Correspondent in the Middle East', the same gentleman who had advised that the question of Palestine ought to be separated from all considerations of 'sentiment or humanity',[54] now claimed that the illegal immigration was often disapproved of by Palestine Jewry itself, 'because it brings in elements unwanted by any self-respecting community'.[55] The same idea had already been expressed, though more mildly, in a leading article in the *Birmingham Post*,[56] and the *News Chronicle*, while putting the matter more mildly still, said much the same:

The normal immigration quota is intended to apply to selected immigrants, and it is highly undesirable that their places should be taken by persons whose qualifications are unknown.[57]

The *Sunday Times*, indeed, went out of its way to explain that it was 'not entirely a matter of refugees' since, according to the Minister, about 40 per cent of the illegals came from Rumania and Poland.[58] Sixty per cent then, even according to this commendably calm analysis, had been 'selected' as victims of 'official' anti-Semitism. The rest had only to fear the Rumanian 'Iron Guard', and such incidents as those already mentioned in Warsaw University.[59]

This resembled the attitude which stressed Britain's readiness to admit only 'useful' or 'desirable' refugees—yet there was a

---

[53] *The Times*, 31 May 1939.
[54] *Daily Telegraph*, 21 July 1939, and see above, p. 184.
[55] *Daily Telegraph*, 18 Aug. 1939.   [56] *Birmingham Post*, 21 July 1939.
[57] *News Chronicle*, 14 July 1939.   [58] *Sunday Times*, 23 July 1939.
[59] See above, pp. 122–3.

fundamental difference. The Jewish Agency had offered repeated guarantees that not a penny would have to be paid for absorption purposes either by the Palestinian Government, or by any element of the non-Jewish population. It was prepared to shoulder any difficulties there might possibly be, and to set in train an orderly plan which would give a chance of saving many of the potential victims. There were no Press references setting forth the Agency's point of view. The *News Chronicle* said that the Jewish Agency ought 'in its own interests' to check illegal immigration.[60] The *New Statesman*, while feeling that there was 'something peculiarly revolting about the plight of refugees who wander about the Mediterranean', could only suggest, with frightening prophetic power, that the Government set up camps in Cyprus for their reception.[61] The Labour Press certainly attacked, with an energy which could hardly have been bettered, the Government's interpretation of the White Paper as 'incredibly mean'.[62] No one could have foretold Labour Party policy when, six years later, the chance came of applying a more generous interpretation.

Another point was often made. These attempts to get into Palestine could not be approved for a simple and, within its own terms, irrefutable reason: they were against the law of the land, which was the White Paper. 'It was an organised movement to break the immigration law and to smash the Government's policy.'[63] Britain stood for the rule of law everywhere, and the law must be defended.

It is instructive to compare this attitude with that manifested when the Permanent Mandates Commission declared that the White Paper itself was in conflict with the terms of a higher legal instrument—the British Mandate in Palestine. The *Daily Telegraph* called that decision 'by a majority of one'—. . . 'undoubtedly a present embarrassment'.[64] The *Scotsman* spoke about 'logic chopping'.[65] The *Daily Mail* called the whole thing 'sheer nonsense'.[66] The *Observer* and the *Yorkshire Post* both stressed that the Commission had ignored 'hard facts' and 'practical results',[67]

[60] *News Chronicle*, ibid., 14 July 1939.   [61] *New Statesman*, 19 Aug. 1939.
[62] See, e.g., *Daily Herald*, 14 July 1939; 20 July 1939; *New Statesman*, 5 Aug. 1939.
[63] *Sunday Times*, ibid., 23 July 1939.
[64] *Daily Telegraph*, 19 Aug. 1939.
[65] *Scotsman*, 18 Aug. 1939.   [66] *Daily Mail*, 18 Aug. 1939.
[67] *Yorkshire Post*, 18 Aug. 1939; *Observer*, 20 Aug. 1939.

while the *Birmingham Post* was clearest of all in its understanding of what such attitudes implied, when it roundly declared that policy mattered more than law.[68] *The Times* was almost alone in its belief that the legal issue merited serious discussion, and, incidentally, it was one of the very few newspapers to mention that 'the majority of one' had been only over the more extreme of two formulations.[69]

The *Manchester Guardian* stood in striking and consistent contrast. It was now, even more than at any other time, that the *Guardian* displayed its outstanding appreciation of an admittedly complex issue, as it immediately affected the people most deeply concerned: the Jews who stood on the edge of physical annihilation. It went straight to the heart of the matter: it was essential that emigration should go on. And it returned to that point again and again. For the *Guardian*, all else was a disgraceful irrelevancy.[70]

This was particularly noticeable in the affair of the *Struma*, a converted yacht which foundered off Istanbul with the loss of nearly all its passengers—when having been compelled to sail in an unseaworthy condition, after protracted efforts to give her a legal clearance for Haifa had failed. *The Times* actually said that 'the responsibility for this tragedy rests entirely on the Rumanian Government which drove away these unfortunates'.[71] The *Manchester Guardian* gave its account of the disaster a headline which, once again, stressed the fundamental point—'*Palestine Entry Barred*'. And it commented on one simple but awkward circumstance. The *Struma* passengers could have been admitted into Palestine as part of the White Paper's 'certificated' quota.[72]

These basic attitudes persisted after the war was over. But two new factors have to be taken into account. The first was that the problem of Jewish 'displaced persons' was not the same as the problem of Jewish refugees. The Jew was now not in actual danger —if such events as the Kielce pogrom of 1946 be excepted. A qualitative change had taken place: the 'Jewish question' no longer demanded a compulsory and immediate solution; there was at least some element of choice. The second new factor was the development of events in Palestine itself. On 18 June 1945, the

[68] *Birmingham Post*, 18 Aug. 1939.
[69] *The Times*, 18 Aug. 1939.
[70] *Manchester Guardian*, 18 Aug. 1939; cf. 28 Nov. 1940; 4 Dec. 1940.
[71] *The Times*, 27 Feb. 1942.
[72] *Manchester Guardian*, 26 Feb. 1942; cf. 9 Mar. 1942; 11 Mar. 1942.

Jewish Agency once more applied for 100,000 immigration certificates. The application was refused, just as it had been seven years
previously. From that date until the abandonment of the Mandate
the Government strove to implement this refusal by force (in the
end by means of five brigades with Air Force and Navy support);
it strove to do so under Labour leadership as well as under Conservative, and it continued to do so after it had accepted the
findings of an Anglo-American Committee of Inquiry—that the
100,000 immigrants could and should be admitted. On the other
hand the Jews, too, gradually began to answer violence with
violence until a situation was reached where only a programme of
systematic massacre could have beaten down Jewish resistance.

It would be absurd to judge British Press reactions as though
only a question of displaced persons or illegal immigrants was
involved. It may be argued that these two new factors, particularly
the last, militate against the validity of any questions drawn from
this period. But this is not so. In one essential the situation had not
changed. There was still only one true test of attitude: to what
extent Jewish suffering in Europe was given some weight; to what
extent the Press took note of what, rightly or wrongly, the struggle
was about.

During the autumn of 1945, when it was becoming obvious that
the new Government was not going to alter immigration policy,
the significance of the situation as it affected European Jewry was
expressed in the course of Press comment on Palestine; particularly
after 13 November when the Labour Foreign Minister, Ernest
Bevin, announced a purely token immigration, and that 'with the
consent of our Arab friends'—the announcement that included the
famous remark about Jews trying 'to push to the head of the
queue' (for rehabilitation). The *Daily Mirror* declared that the
problem of European Jewry could only be solved in Palestine and
published a striking cartoon.[73] But there were few references to
that side of the question. The White Paper continued to be accepted as the unalterable basis for all discussion, and the Conservative
Press united in praising the Labour Party's recognition of the fact.
The Labour Press itself was less happy, but even in its more left-
wing sections there was the odd impression that the Government

[73] *Daily Mirror*, 15 Nov. 1945; 17 Nov. 1945; cf. also *News Chronicle*,
6 Oct. 1945. After the *Manchester Guardian*, the *News Chronicle* is perhaps most
striking in this respect.

had decided on a compromise, because although the White Paper stood, there would be a Committee of Inquiry. An odder impression still was that the chief obstacle was not the 100,000 certificates, but 'the rigid Zionist insistence on "Palestine as a Jewish State" .'[74]

It is, of course, not surprising that, by the middle of 1946, when tension had considerably increased due to the Government's refusal to implement the Committee of Inquiry's recommendation, the overwhelming Press emphasis should have been on the maintenance of law and order. Journals such as *Truth* and the *Weekly Review* spoke with ill-concealed glee of 'war' and 'open battle' between Britain and the Zionists.[75] What does deserve mention is that in a total of fifty-two extracts of Press opinion on Palestine collected by the Wiener Library in July (including specific references to the 100,000), there is only one which mentions the issue behind all the violence: the rescue of those 100,000 people from a Europe which only a few months previously had seen the completion of the annihilation of six million Jews.[76] And the additional material available to the author does nothing to alter this proportion.

There were few indeed to echo the *News Chronicle*:

It is hard for non-Jews to realise the sense of bereavement or the passionate desire for asylum which the massacre of more than one in three of the world's Jewish population by the Nazis, must have created in Jewish minds. . . .[77]

[74] *Tribune*, 16 Nov. 1945; 23 Nov. 1945.
[75] *Truth*, 5 July 1945; *Weekly Review*, 4 July 1946.
[76] *News Chronicle*, 8 July 1946; cf. Jewish Central Information Office (The Wiener Library), *The British Press and its Reactions to Recent Events in Palestine*, London (1946). (In typescript.)
[77] *News Chronicle*, 8 June 1946.

VII

The Press and the Community

IN the course of this survey, we have repeatedly stressed one fundamental circumstance: from the beginning to the end, few facts of Nazi anti-Semitism were left unstated by the British Press. This was affected neither by a paper's own political allegiance nor by the obvious difference in general attitudes to Germany before and during the war. And the Press, with the few exceptions we have noted, was uniformly disgusted by those facts. All this is positive truth whose value is self-evident, both as part of the historical record and as a civilized reaction against Nazi barbarities.

But we have also noticed a frequent failure to appreciate the full significance for the Jews under Nazi rule of all that which was known and deplored. To a limited extent this failure can be connected with political or quasi-political attitudes. For example, the failure to appreciate the central character of anti-Semitism for the Nazis, the fact that from the beginning they were putting into practice, stage by stage, a deliberately worked-out plan, was understandable on the part of those who before the war advocated the 'understanding' of the new Germany, and were unwilling to accept that so unpleasant an element also had to be 'understood'. On the other hand, in the eyes of much Liberal and left-wing opinion, the Nazi system was so plainly outside the bounds of sensible analysis beyond the plain declaration of its wickedness, that there was a tendency to minimize the significance of particular stages. Thus even the *Manchester Guardian* did not immediately see what the Nuremberg Decrees meant for the German Jew,[1] while *The Times*, which had continually tried to differentiate between 'official' and 'extreme' Nazis,[2] was instantly sensitive to this formal abrogation of a basic principle: equality before the law. Again the tendency to place responsibility for the holocaust else-

[1] See above, p. 45. [2] See above, p. 45–6.

where than in Germany, and to express reservations on the discoveries in the camps, often arose from the suspicion that political use was being made of the situation. But this explanation does not cover the comparative failure to appreciate what the Jews were trying to do themselves, or the most striking contradiction of all: knowledge and loathing of what was happening on the one hand, and a somewhat passive approach to the refugee question on the other. It is true that this last issue cannot be taken in isolation. After all, unemployment caused genuine anxiety in the thirties, just as Palestine did in the forties. But it is difficult to explain why attempts at a detached discussion of the economic risks of a more generous refugee policy were ignored, or why the problem of Palestine was successfully separated from 'considerations of humanity'.[3]

One reason for this has already been suggested: the psychological commonplace that, with the best will in the world, it is hard to grasp the meaning of suffering wholly outside one's immediate experience and for which, moreover, there is very little historical precedent. But was the inadequate response to Jewish suffering in Europe also the result of widespread dislike for Jews in England; were denunciations of Hitler less unanimous than they sounded?

In this context, Press references derogatory to the Jew are not hard to find in our period, as may be illustrated by the two following examples. 'There is no doubt', affirmed a Northern provincial paper, 'that at least nine-tenths of the inhabitants of the British Isles think the worse of a man if they are told he is a Jew.'[4] A little later, the *East Anglian Daily Times* was less statistically sure but equally explicit:

The fact has to be recognised that Christians generally do not take kindly to the Jewish race. . . . Not a few Englishmen regard Jews with a vague unfriendly toleration not far removed from dislike . . . and share . . . the wonder expressed in the lines 'How Odd of God To Choose The Jews'.[5]

[3] See above, pp. 167, 184.

[4] *Daily Dispatch*, 17 Oct. 1932; that this is a little before our period is not important in the present context.

[5] *East Anglian Daily Times*, 2 Mar. 1934.   It is possible to find, outside the Fascist Press itself, plain abuse, without any pretence of a detached estimate as in these two examples; see, e.g., a headline, 'Blow the Sheenies!' in the *Hereford Bulletin*, 12 Sept. 1936; a straight anti-Semitic cartoon (with no explanatory text to balance it as in the *Reynolds* instance, above, p. 169) in *Everybody's Weekly*, 14 Oct. 1933.

Nor is it difficult to find passages where reasons for dislike, or at least for this something less than love, were given. There is nothing original about those reasons, which were usually no more than a polite rephrasing of standard accusations. Two examples will be enough since their source gives them added weight. The first is from an article in the *New Statesman* at the time of the Fascist outrages in the East End of London (then the main Jewish area), an article 'designed', as the editor put it, 'to sketch the background'. In the course of an intelligent, informative, and out-spoken attack on Fascism, the writer (a doctor) pointed out that whereas 'many Jews were the very salt of the earth', there was to be found among them 'a pushful and unsporting minority' and also those who were 'decent, law-abiding, but money-seeking-at-any-price-to-others'. It was not their fault in a way, since 'the average poorish Jew has a different glandular make-up from the average poorish Englishman'.[6] The second example is from the *Spectator*, from an unsigned article which must be taken to express editorial opinion. In the course of an appreciation of Jewish services to England, contrasted with Nazi stupidity in depriving Germany of some of her best talents, the following observation was made:

It is quite true (the Nazis are right there) that the Jewish mentality is a distinctive thing. Even those Englishmen who are most deeply attached to their Jewish friends must feel at times a profound sense of the generic, and not merely individual differences that mark them off. One would not wish England to be represented in the world solely or even mainly by Jewish minds; for in truth then she would cease to be England. But a great nation, sure of itself, will not harbour this fear.[7]

What is the significance of these four passages? They show that the belief existed that 'nine-tenths' of Englishmen, or at least 'not a few' of them, disliked the Jews because they were 'different'. This difference might be 'generic', it might be 'glandular', but of the fact itself there could be no doubt. And whether it was in the polite phraseology of the *Spectator* or in the less polite language of the survey 'designed' for the *New Statesman*, the implications of that difference were—inevitably—derogatory ones.

It would be entirely unjustifiable to assert on the basis of the evidence given here that any of these passages represent a majority

[6] *New Statesman*, 7 Nov. 1936.   [7] *Spectator*, 3 Jan. 1936.

Press attitude towards the Jews. Their real interest lies rather in the fact that they bear a close similarity to a common attitude noted in the last chapter—that towards the 'alien' who was in the overwhelming number of instances himself a Jew, and was known to be so. He, too, was 'different'. His methods, too, left much to be desired. In spite of his many acknowledged services in pre-war and wartime England, the alien could under no circumstances be 'accepted'—in the truly English meaning of the phrase. Whatever the representative character of the passages quoted, they are at least an indication that the 'anti-alien, anti-refugee' attitude in its most typical form was only the particular instance of a general phenomenon: a basic attitude to the Jew as such, no matter whether that attitude was widespread or no. The fact that opinions of this kind could be found in the ordinary British Press is of great significance, and closely related to our question—how to explain the negative attitudes of newspapers clearly and genuinely sympathetic to Jewish suffering.

Before carrying the argument further, it is necessary to ask what the British people actually thought about the Jews during the Hitler period. In other words, was the assertion that 'nine-tenths' disliked them at all justifiable?

Direct evidence on this point is not very easy to find. The most obvious, perhaps, is that which appears in the actual material of our inquiry—for example in 'Letters to the Editor'. The field here is an extremely wide one, and it would serve little purpose to attempt a comprehensive survey of references to Jews or Jewish topics. It is preferable to take some specific issue. In December 1933, for example, the Middlesbrough Motor Club decided to admit no more Jews to its membership. This action provoked copious correspondence in the local Press, and one or two references in papers of wider circulation such as the *Yorkshire Post*.[8] It was certainly a small enough affair, with little bearing on the position of the Jews in relation to the more serious events of the day, but it had the interest of any incident of this type in that it attracted comment about the Jews far removed from the original subject. Those participating in the correspondence who thought that the Club had acted correctly did not attack Jewish motorists as inconsiderate to other road users or as accident-prone, in the way that some insurance companies apparently did at the time;

---

[8] *Yorkshire Post*, 6 Jan. 1934.

they merely echoed the kind of criticisms just quoted. Thus there were references to Jewish 'arrogance', Jewish lack of professional standards, Jewish business and commercial shortcomings. Some of the writers expressed themselves in ways which would have been hard to find in editorial or semi-editorial sections, but the point made was much the same: the Jew was no Englishman and the difference was not to the Jew's advantage:

As an Englishman I have not yet descended, or ascended, if some think that way, to consider it a desirable distinction to be employed by a Jew, nor a valuable privilege to be allowed to mix socially with them on their terms.[9]

Outbursts of this kind were not uncommon both before and during the war. Letters almost identical in phraseology were to be found in a number of Scottish newspapers after a suggestion had been made about settling Jewish refugees in the underpopulated areas of the Highlands.[10] In February 1942, the *Spectator* thought it 'proper to raise' the question of anti-Semitism in England and, once again, all the old tales saw the light, this time with the peculiarly vicious twist we have already noted in certain war-time attitudes towards the alien.[11] It goes without saying that the existence of a Fascist movement in England, particularly during its most active period from 1934 to 1937, also called forth a wide newspaper correspondence on Jewish questions, and that very much the same opinions were expressed by Fascist sympathizers. But the evidential value of this is obviously qualified by its involvement with all sorts of extraneous matters: attitudes to the Spanish Civil War, to parliamentary government, to Communism, and so forth.

Side by side with letters attacking Jews there naturally appeared letters defending them—and those by no means all from Jews. But a very rough survey of the material available shows that the defenders tended to be in a minority. If this was so, and if it be assumed that it was a circumstance entirely uninfluenced by edi-

[9] *Northern Echo*, 9 Jan. 1934. The correspondence lasted from the middle of December to the middle of January chiefly in this paper and in the *North-Eastern Daily Gazette*.
[10] See, e.g., the protracted correspondence in the *Edinburgh Evening Dispatch*, in April and May 1933.
[11] Cf., e.g., *Spectator*, 6 Feb. 1942; 13 Feb. 1942.

torial bias in selection, it would constitute an argument *against* the assertion that anti-Semitic views were very widely held in Britain, since the correspondence columns of the Press are a forum where the most active participators are inevitably the holders of some minority attitude. It would for instance hardly be possible to find that a correspondence on the value of the monarchy as a British institution was initiated and largely conducted by its defenders. It is also true that the accusations made against the Jews in these letters and the phrases employed were often so remarkably similar, that it indicated a comparatively limited group inspired by ideas emanating from an identical source rather than a widely held view, indicating, that is, the existence of a number of organizations which had some form of anti-Semitism as part of their programme.[12] They point to a vocal anti-Semitic opinion. But they are insufficient evidence that the majority of the British people disliked the Jews.

The other main category of evidence is the public opinion poll. This has to be approached with considerable caution. In the first place, the accuracy of a poll on a relatively abstract issue, that is on something distinct from the popularity of a particular political candidate or a particular soap, cannot be submitted to the conclusive test—the test of results. It should also be remembered that an analysis of its implications has become a more and more specialized task. The application of the public opinion poll to work in sociology and similar fields has become highly complex. It is based upon the techniques of a new science, or, at least, the beginning of one—'the science of communication'—a methodical investigation into the methods and effects of mass information media in forming public opinion. Whatever may be its final merits, it is a science which has already produced a copious literature, including periodicals replete with all the apparatus of scholarship,[13] and a reasonable acquaintance with it is a prerequisite for any detailed analysis of the significance of the polls. With this warning in mind, it is nevertheless possible to attempt a sensible discussion— from the point of view of an acknowledged layman.

[12] See below, pp. 201–2.
[13] The oldest established periodical is the *Public Opinion Quarterly*, published from Princeton University. A useful collection of introductory essays is to be found in *The Communication of Ideas*, ed. L. Bryson, New York (1948). For a history of public opinion measurement, see W. Albig, *Modern Public Opinion*, New York (1956). In Britain, *The Press and Its Readers* (see above, *Introduction*) was one of a series of opinion measurement attempts begun in 1937.

In the summer of 1939 a poll was conducted on the refugee issue. The following question was asked:

Should refugees be allowed to enter Great Britain? If 'Yes', should they be allowed to enter freely or with restrictions designed to safeguard British workers and taxpayers?[14]

Seventy per cent of those questioned replied 'Yes' to the first part, but of them eight out of ten thought that entry ought to be governed by the restrictions suggested. The main factor in the attitude of those who opposed entry was precisely the fear that such restrictions implied: the fear that refugees would endanger British standards of living.

This result suggests two conclusions. First of all, here was a *prima facie* justification of a point made by the majority of the Press, when it explicitly claimed that it represented public opinion. There were very few who thought the refugee situation justified what might be thought of as a personal risk. Thus the Press, in discouraging really drastic emergency action, was only mirroring what was thought on the subject. The second conclusion is that such papers as the *Evening News* were quite unjustified in talking about 'waves of anti-Semitism' as a consequence of the refugee crisis. The overwhelming majority of the refugees were Jews and were known to be Jews; had there been a 'wave', it is inconceivable that no hint of it would have appeared in the replies to this poll. On the other hand, it is a reasonable inference that a small proportion of the 30 per cent who opposed entry were motivated by some form of anti-Semitism: that the Jews threatened standards in the trades and professions was, as we have seen, a common anti-Semitic argument.

A more striking illustration of the same point was provided by a poll held shortly after the 'Crystal Night'. The question then put was 'Do you think the persecution of the Jews in Germany is an obstacle to the good understanding between Britain and Germany?' A large majority answered 'Yes' to this question[15] and

[14] *News Chronicle*, 31 July 1939. This poll was conducted by the British Institute of Public Opinion. It was (and is) known as the Gallup Poll from the name of its American originator.

[15] *News Chronicle*, 28 Nov. 1938. The report spoke of 'more than four out of five of those who expressed an opinion' but gave no table of percentages on this occasion; H. Cantril, *Public Opinion 1935–1946*, Princeton (1951), p. 382, gives the figures as 'Yes'—73 per cent.; 'No'—15 per cent.; 'No opinion'—12 per cent.

there was no significant difference of opinion between Government and Opposition supporters (i.e. between the pro-appeasers and the anti-appeasers) on the Jewish aspect of appeasement—in contrast to the two trends of Press opinion on Munich in this context.[16] On the other hand, it is equally noteworthy that there was a small minority who answered 'No', and who undoubtedly included a core of active anti-Semites—a circumstance indicated by the comment in the poll report that 'the survey revealed little violent anti-semitism among those questioned'.[17] The only inference could be that *some* noticeable anti-Semitism was, in fact, revealed.

Finally, two interesting polls were held during the 'Displaced Persons' period. The first, in 1946, was part of the ordinary series of polls on various topics published from time to time by the *News Chronicle*. Those interviewed were asked if they had any ideas about solving the problem of the post-war homeless Jew. Eight per cent answered *either* that the problem was insoluble (as distinct from 47 per cent who said that they themselves could offer no solution), *or* that the Jews deserved little sympathy.[18] Here, again, some positive anti-Semitism can be inferred, though how much is not at all clear, except that it did not exceed 8 per cent. of the total.

The second poll gives a rather clearer picture. It was held in 1948 as part of a U.N.E.S.C.O. survey intended to elicit attitudes of one nation to another, against the background of the more obvious problems of the post-war world. Question No. 12 was: 'Which foreign people do you feel least friendly toward?' Three per cent. answered that they felt least friendly towards the Jews.[19] This answer was especially significant for two reasons. Firstly, the question was what is known as an 'open-end' one, i.e. no answer was suggested. The answers were therefore the result of a completely undirected choice. Moreover, the poll was held in eight other countries: Australia, France, Germany (twice, and in two

---

[16] See above, pp. 63–8.   [17] *News Chronicle*, 28 Nov. 1938
[18] *News Chronicle*, 14 Nov. 1946.
[19] W. Buchanan and H. Cantril, *How the Nations See Each Other*, University of Illinois (1953), p. 140. It is interesting that this answer, when divided according to various social and economic categories, showed the highest figure (5 per cent.) for those classified as 'Leftists' (those who thought the then Labour Government 'too Right-wing')—as against 2 per cent showed by the 'Rightists' (i.e. those who thought the Government 'too Left-wing'). The' wealthy' showed 1 per cent as against the 'very poor' who showed 5 per cent.

separate zones), Holland, Italy, Mexico, Norway, and the United States. In none of these countries did Question No. 12 elicit any reference whatever to the Jews. So it is permissible to conclude that, bearing in mind all our necessary reservations on public opinion surveys, there is here evidence of a real though limited anti-Semitism in Britain.

Two serious pieces of investigation carried out between 1947 and 1949 were based on the public poll technique, i.e. the personal interview, but were specifically directed towards a statistical conclusion about the extent of anti-Semitism in general. The first showed that within a typical middle-class group 4 per cent were 'extremely' anti-Semitic, while 43 per cent were 'capable of anti-Semitic statements'.[20] The second, conducted in a working-class area of London, showed 8·7 per cent as 'extremely' anti-Semitic and 42·7 per cent as 'capable of anti-Semitic statements when pressed'.[21] Both investigations, therefore, gave somewhat greater weight to post-war anti-Semitic attitudes than might be inferred from the polls. The first, indeed, went so far as to add that probably only 20–25 per cent of the population had 'no hostile, derogatory, or at least unfavourable view towards the Jews as a whole'. Both, however, more or less agreed with the polls in the percentage they allotted to the active anti-Semite.

There is of course also the normally accessible evidence on the existence of anti-Semitism in Britain. Its value is less, any serious statistical evaluation being impossible. But it can hardly go unmentioned. We have already spoken of the Fascist movement. Before the war there were several such groups of which the largest was probably the British Union of Fascists, led by Sir Oswald Mosley. All of them preached some degree of anti-Semitism. Then there were the various Anglo-German organizations which tried to spread the Nazi ideology, inevitably including its anti-Semitic element; such were the 'Link', the Anglo-German Friendship League, and various semi-official offshoots of German Governmental, diplomatic, and commercial bodies.[22] It is hard to say what influence any of these organizations actually had, since an

[20] H. J. Eysenck, 'The Psychology of Anti-Semitism', *The Nineteenth Century and After* CXLIV (1948), pp. 277–84.

[21] J. H. Robb, *Working Class Anti-Semite*, London (1964), pp. 69–72, 92.

[22] See a list (apparently very comprehensive but with no attempt at an evaluation of influence) in *Wiener Library Bulletin* IX (1955), p. 44, and of their post-war successors, ibid., VIII (1954), p. 35.

unbiased account, still less a serious estimate of membership, simply does not exist. Our opinion (based on personal recollection and on some years' residence close to the East End centre of the Mosley organization) is that, to the extent that there was popular support, it was for the anti-Communist rather than for the anti-Semitic aspect. As we have seen, the 'active' or 'professional' anti-Semite would identify the one with the other, but this was not so commonly done by the periphery of supporters. Nevertheless these organizations did exist and were additional evidence of an active anti-Semitic nucleus.

The existence of this nucleus has an important relation to Press attitudes. That is not to say that we are suggesting a direct influence: on the contrary. The only part of the Press of which this was strictly true was of course the Fascist Press itself, i.e. the organs of the various Fascist movements. Something similar might be asserted of *Truth*, which was once described in the House of Commons as an openly anti-Semitic journal,[23] or of the *Weekly Review* which, on its demise in 1947, proclaimed that part of its task had been 'a consistent struggle against a political clique of cosmopolitan Jewry'.[24]

But it would be absurd to suggest that the rest of the Press gave any weight to the basic presuppositions of the active anti-Semite. In fact, the Press paid little overt attention to the sort of evidence we have just summarized or, for that matter, to any anti-Semitic activity at all. This is particularly striking in connexion with the public opinion poll. There were two extraneous reasons why the Press should have been particularly aware of its work. Firstly, the *News Chronicle* held the exclusive rights of publishing the findings of the main British poll—a circumstance likely to provoke reactions from other papers. Secondly the circulation war had begun to make the Press sensitive to various possibilities of assessing public opinion, and attempts were beginning to be made, by means of much the same technique as the polls were using, to discover the reasons for the choice of a particular newspaper or the response to a particular type of advertising. And yet, as far as we know, no special notice was taken, for example, of the findings which we have quoted on reactions to German policy, or to the admission of refugees.

Again, none of the Fascist organizations was ever treated

---

[23] *Daily Telegraph*, 18 Oct. 1941.   [24] *Weekly Review*, 12 June 1947.

seriously, except when they succeeded in causing some spectacular breach of the peace, as Mosley did at Olympia in 1934, or in the East End of London (the famous 'Battle of Gardiner's Corner') in 1936.[25] Occasionally a particular Fascist group received some adventitious publicity. This was always the result of some entirely accidental circumstance: for example, one such group had the distinction of a leader called Serocold Skeels.[26] The various Anglo-German organizations got even less mention than did their British variety. The Press, in short, did not believe that active anti-Semitism in Britain had any importance. The Rothermere campaign for British Fascism in 1934 was called off for the declared reason that the anti-Semitism in Mosley's policies was out of consonance with the British character.[27]

Soon after the war, there were a number of attempts to make anti-Semitism illegal. They were all unsuccessful. There was very little support for the view that anti-Semitism constituted any real danger. A proposal to outlaw anti-Semitism was rejected by the Labour Party Conference in 1946, and a similar motion put in the House of Commons two years later failed to get past its first reading. The question is not whether it would have been good to pass such a law, but what the Press thought about the possibility. There is no doubt that the *News Chronicle* spoke for the vast majority when it denied the need for it on the ground that it could only affect 'the occasional political or religious fanatic'.[28] Later in 1948, a Government inquiry into the possibilities of framing laws against attacks on any racial or religious group reported that most of the evidence before it had, in fact, been of attacks upon Jews. It advised, however, that there were no special circumstances here which could not be covered by the existing laws on seditious libel.[29] *The Times* and the *Manchester Guardian* supported this conclusion.[30]

It is because the Press did not believe that active, organized anti-Semitism had any importance—still less, of course, that it merited any sort of encouragement—that the anti-Semitic statements and inferences we have noted become so significant. No

---

[25] For accounts of this latter episode, see the national Press for 5 Oct. 1936. It made a great impression.
[26] *Daily Herald*, 11 Jan. 1934; *Sheffield Independent*, 13 Jan. 1934.
[27] See above, p. 20.   [28] *News Chronicle*, 16 Jan. 1948.
[29] Report of the Porter Committee, HMSO, Cmd. 7536, London (1948).
[30] *The Times*, 21 Oct. 1948; *Manchester Guardian*, 21 Oct. 1948.

responsible editor really believed that 'nine-tenths of the British people disliked a man for being a Jew', or that if he printed one or even two letters asking for a modicum of civilized tolerance for every one containing a Streicher diatribe, he was really giving a fair picture of public opinion. The *Spectator* could not have thought in 1942, when it published the letters that it did, that these represented anything but their writers—or the pre-concocted propaganda of some 'professional' anti-Semitic body. The editor of the *New Statesman* could not really have believed that a working-class Jew was 'glandularly' different from a working-class non-Jew. But such material occasionally appeared, for several reasons. The very fact that the anti-Semitic nucleus was so small, so extremist, so much an element which the Press could with justice describe as un-British, gave it news-value. A Jewish community (or any other) living at peace with its environment is far less interesting than the possibilities of some violent clash. Although during our period as a whole markedly little attention was paid to organized anti-Semitism (and, perhaps, even because of this), every now and then the anti-Semitic nucleus made an impact out of all proportion to its direct influence, as almost any minority occasionally tends to do. But because it was a remarkably unpleasant minority, whose German counterpart had succeeded in gaining power and putting its ideas into practice, there may have been an additional feeling, we think, that it was commendably broad-minded, and slightly daring, to print this kind of thing at all.

Another point is that the anti-Semitic nucleus was there. It was small but it existed. Its influence was small but that existed too. The claim that 40 per cent or so of an average section of the population were capable of an anti-Semitic statement was, with every reservation about public opinion surveys, somewhere near the truth. And although real anti-Semitism was inconsiderable, potential anti-Semitism was not. Somehow, between 1933 and 1939, the atmosphere became slightly but noticeably infected. The well-known Nazi effort to export anti-Semitism had succeeded to some slight extent, and it is not surprising that the Press could not remain immune. There is one other interesting piece of evidence for this infection. In 1939 a certain M. G. Murchin, widely supposed to be the pseudonym of a leading working journalist, asserted in a book of definitely anti-Semitic slant that a high proportion of the news-gathering side of the Press was either actually in Jewish hands or in those of 'newspapermen with left-wing sympathies who tend to favour the inclusion, all being equal, of pro-Jewish rather than pro-Fascist news'.[31] The *Newspaper World*, giving a favourable review to the book, quoted these remarks without comment.[32] It is difficult to believe that this could have happened before, say, 1938; or for that matter in 1964.

We have noted a marked lack of interest in statistics. Clearly it was closer to the tradition of popular journalism to talk of waves of refugees bursting the frontiers of the Reich and flooding a world (especially a British world) ill-equipped to receive them, than to inquire into some easily accessible figures. But it was not only the popular Press which wrote thus. When the *Observer* announced that Britain now had more Jews than Germany had ever had, it too was allowing its sense of the dramatically appropriate to overcome its normal instinct for examining the known facts and reporting them as objectively as possible. And what are we to think of the language used by the *Evening News* and the *Sunday Dispatch* about refugee and alien? We have seen how an essentially similar attitude would appear in the most unexpected places. Through the medium of Britain's anti-Semitic nucleus, anti-Semitism somehow infiltrated far wider circles, different and distinct from it though they were. The Nazis managed not only to assist this general process but also, to a small but definite extent, to transfer to the non-Nazi world an attenuated version of their own image of the German Jew—the dishonest and dangerous parasite. Ambiguities and failures of the imagination on the part of the Press were often the fruit of ceaseless propaganda from Berlin; propaganda which proclaimed the real threat to European security, to European economic and cultural standards, to come from the virus carried by the refugees. There was unemployment in Britain, and thus fear of extra competition for the jobs which did exist. It was only an exaggeration of these circumstances which led to the pervasiveness of this propaganda. Nor must it be

---

[31] M. G. Murchin, *Britain's Jewish Problem*, London (1939), p. 73.

[32] *Newspaper World*, 20 May 1939. It is, of course, infinitely more significant that an organ of the profession should let this kind of thing pass, than that *Truth* should (e.g. 9 Feb. 1940) proclaim it. It is in this context of a possible 'infection' that we must also take the excerpts from the *Hereford Bulletin* and *Everybody's Weekly* cited on p. 194 above.

forgotten that there was more news value in prophesying disaster than in advocating an ordered absorption of what was, when all is said and done, a tiny percentage of the working population of Britain.

Finally, we have to repeat that negative attitudes to the refugee, as to any other aspect of the problem, were often the result of a simple inability to understand that there was anything negative about them—that to talk about 'a profound sense of generic difference' or of 'a different glandular make up' was to lay oneself open to misinterpretation at a time when the persecution of the Jews had its theoretical basis in identical beliefs. Negative attitudes, in short, sprang from a lack of imagination, which can probably only be explained by a long excursus into British history and geography.

The main consequence of negative Press attitudes towards Jews under Nazi rule was that they gave a distorted picture of British public opinion. In a sense that distortion was no different from that which exists in any Press report of the most trivial event, and for which automatic allowance is made. When we read that 'all London was shocked by such and such', or 'all England welcomed the arrival of so and so', we are quite capable of translating it into something nearer reality. It would not have been difficult to translate exaggerations about public reactions to a specific Jewish issue in a similar way. But how much did hatred of the Nazi crime against the Jews, as mirrored in the Press, really mean? Possibly it meant very little. From a reasonable selection of Press comment, the conclusion could be drawn that the British attitude was the product of an anti-Semitic substratum lightly covered over by a mixture of vague humanitarianism and fear of German conquest. This was, in fact, what Nazi propagandists proclaimed over and over again. Whenever they thought they saw in Britain even a pale reflection of their own anti-Semitism, they contemptuously insisted that the British would do anything for the German Jew except take him off German hands—and undoubtedly they drew some encouragement for this reading of British public opinion from the British Press. It was a distorted reading. We have tried to show that there is very little evidence for the kind of anti-Semitism that such an attitude would imply. But it was a possible reading, and one for which the Press could hardly escape responsibility.

The other consequence of a negative attitude was the loss of an opportunity. Potential anti-Semitism was undoubtedly fairly widespread in Britain. Negative attitudes served to perpetuate existing prejudices, if not to strengthen them. Apart from those few sections of the Press which conscientiously tried to do so, there was little attempt at destroying the basis of this vague anti-Semitic thinking—the British version of a Jewish stereotype. Much less vicious, of course, than the Nazi variety, it tended to portray the Jew as 'shrewd, mercenary, industrious, intelligent and loyal to his family'[33]; in other words, as a potential danger to the happy-go-lucky Briton. It was precisely during our period, when the Jewish population of the United Kingdom was noticeably increased,[34] when many a Gentile met a Jew for the first time in his life, that an opportunity presented itself of really showing that, in those respects which had apparently worried the Gentile, the Jew was much the same as he. In other words, the only good that might have come out of all this evil was a better understanding between differing cultures, a lessening of traditional British isolation.

Of course, this did not only apply to Jewish refugees on British soil. It applied equally to all the others who found asylum there— to a better understanding of the Frenchman, the Dutchman, or the Pole. But at any rate as far as the Jew was concerned, this opportunity was not taken.

Can we go further and assert that all shortcomings and ambiguities considered together had any more directly deleterious consequence? In introducing this inquiry, we reviewed the evidence for treating with great reserve any concept of the Press in our period which would make of it an institution powerful enough effectively to influence Government policy. There is no evidence at all that it succeeded in doing so on any aspect of the Jewish issue. Not a single refugee was prevented from landing in Britain because of anything written in the *Daily Mail*, the *Sunday Dispatch*, or the *Evening News* about unwanted aliens, any more than a single pound less was spent on European goods because of what was written in the *Daily Express*, the *Sunday Express*, or the *Evening Standard* about Empire Free Trade. The Government was no readier to forgive Hitler the Crystal Night and to continue

---

[33] Eysenck, op. cit., p. 277; cf. Robb, op. cit., pp. 25–29, for a slightly more hostile formulation.

[34] Probably by 21.7 per cent, cf. Tartakower, op. cit., p. 316.

its appeasement policy, no more set on enforcing the White Paper, because of what was written in *The Times* or the *Daily Telegraph*. Doubtless it derived comfort from this support, as it had done ever since the age of aggression had begun with the Japanese seizure of Manchukuo. But in 1938 as in 1931 Government policy was decided and pursued with scant reference as to whether it enjoyed a good or a bad Press.

Of course, policy had *some* relation to public opinion, of which Press attitudes certainly formed a part. In that sense, Press ambiguities on the Jewish issue were one of a number of not easily measurable factors which between them made up a climate of opinion wherein both continued appeasement and the White Paper were practical politics. But it would be wrong to insist on such a connexion. At most, these ambiguities meant, once again, an opportunity lost. A much wider and stronger expression of support for practical measures on behalf of the refugees might conceivably have given an extra push towards a less strict interpretation of regulations in Palestine, and a more generous interpretation of entry regulations at home. Here too, if negative attitudes have consequences, they were to be found in what was not done rather than what was.

The final impression of the attitudes of the Press must be a contradictory rather than a negative one. Side by side with all these ambiguities and hesitations, there was often a very genuine positive approach, as repeatedly quoted in the course of this survey. The horror at the crimes the Nazis were committing was a genuine horror, the sympathy for the victims was, within the limitations we have given it, a genuine sympathy. And the wish that the perpetrators of Buchenwald and Dachau should be punished was also positive and genuine. These positive aspects had some practical results. The support of *The Times* and of the *Manchester Guardian* helped to establish and maintain the Academic Assistance Council. Favourable publicity helped to raise money for various refugee schemes. The reaction to the discoveries in the concentration camps probably hindered, at least for a time, an open expression of post-war anti-Semitism. But, just as in our consideration of negative aspects, it is important not to exaggerate practical results. Sympathy and horror never succeeded in producing a genuine Press campaign, as it did, for example, over the general political issue of appeasement. A campaign on behalf of the refugees, that is an organized attempt on the part of a reasonably wide section of the Press to get something done, existed only in the minds of those least sympathetic to such attempts,[35] and, as we have seen, the vast bulk of the money raised by refugee organizations came from Jewish sources, whence it would probably have come without any Press publicity at all.

The importance of both positive and negative attitudes does not lie in their political or financial results but in their psychological meaning. Negative attitudes were partly caused by an anti-Semitic infection; partly by the less noble element in the profession of journalism; but mostly, perhaps, by an inveterate British inability to grasp imaginatively what could happen on the continent of Europe. Positive attitudes are the other side of the medal. They expressed the proper professional urge to discover and report every relevant fact, and they illuminated another British characteristic equally rooted in British history: a love of tolerance and of political moderation, a loathing of manifest injustice. But the true picture only emerges if both sides are remembered. A picture of understanding and lack of understanding, a picture of willingness to help and hesitation in actually doing so, a picture of sympathy and bewilderment in the face of the great cataclysm of our day.

---

[35] E.g. Murchin's (op. cit., p. 43) fantastic statement: 'In the whole history of the British Press there have been few more concentrated campaigns than that launched on behalf of refugees, most of them Jews.'

It is worth remarking that of four histories of important newspapers published recently, two make no reference whatever to Jews under Hitler (E. F. Lawson (Baron Burnham), *Peterborough Court: The Story of the Daily Telegraph*, London (1955); H. R. G. Whates, *The Birmingham Post 1857–1957*, Birmingham (1957)). M. A. Gibb and F. Beckwith, *The Yorkshire Post: Two Centuries*, Leeds (1954)), p. 87, have one reference in the context of the *Post*'s anti-appeasement stand, while S. Morison, *History of The Times*, Vol. IV, London (1952), pp. 178 and 769, has two very indirect references.

Register of Newspapers and Periodicals

THIS register is intended to provide some background information on the newspapers and periodicals referred to in the course of this survey. It is not intended as a definitive evaluation of any of them, still less as an original contribution to British Press history.

All remarks (unless otherwise indicated) apply to *both* of two key periods: (I) 1938–9; (II) 1944–5. Remarks applicable to either *one* of these periods are prefaced by the appropriate sign, i.e. (I) or (II). Bracketed words indicate a paper's *own* description of its political allegiance. In the present context, 'Unionist' and 'Conservative' may be treated as identical, even in the case of Northern Ireland. (No Comment) indicates that no such description is furnished.

Unless indicated by the name of a paper or otherwise stated, the place of publication is London. Weekly publication is designated by w, monthly by M, and quarterly by Q.

A Note on the Groups

An important development in period II was the acquisition of a number of well-known provincial newspapers by one or another of four newspaper combines or 'groups'. These were:

Name	Founded	Political Tendency[1]
Daily Mail Group	1928	Conservative
Kemsley Newspapers	1927	Conservative
Provincial Newspapers	1930	None emphasized
Westminster Press	1927	Liberal

It is worth noting that the *general* tendency of the provincial Press irrespective of all official and unofficial labels was, with a few obvious exceptions, likely to be right-wing rather than left.[2]

---

[1] The opinions in the last column are, of course, our own but they are supported by Berry, op. cit., pp. 15–20.

[2] Again a personal opinion, but see *The Press and its Readers*, pp. 74–77.

Name	Founded	Remarks
Aberdeen Evening Express	1879	(Independent); (II) acquired by Kemsley Newspapers
Aeroplane	W 1911	Oldest-established flying journal
Architects' Journal	W 1895	Second oldest architectural journal
Baptist Times	W 1885	Organ of the English Baptists
Birmingham Evening Despatch	1891	(Independent); (II) acquired by Westminster Press
Birmingham Gazette	1741	(Liberal); (II) acquired by Westminster Press
Birmingham Mail	1870	(Unionist)
Birmingham Post	1857	(Unionist)
Bolton Evening News	1867	(No Comment)
Bournemouth Daily Echo	1900	(Independent)
Bristol Evening World	1929	(Independent); (II) acquired by Daily Mail Group
British Medical Journal	W 1832	Journal of the British Medical Association
British Trade Journal	M 1863	*Not* a Board of Trade publication
British Weekly	W 1886	A Protestant journal
Brixton Free Press	W 1882	(Independent)
Catholic Herald	W 1894	Popular Roman Catholic journal
Catholic Times	W 1859	Oldest established Roman Catholic weekly in U.K.
Cavalcade	W 1936	Popular illustrated of the class of American *Time*
Christian World	W 1857	Evangelical and of Liberal religious views
Contemporary Review	M 1866	Literary review of Liberal tendencies
Coventry Standard	W 1741	(Conservative)
Daily Express	1900	(I) (Imperial and Democratic); (II) (Independent)
Daily Herald	1912	(Labour)
Daily Mail	1896	(Independent) Conservative; supported British Union of Fascists January–June 1934
Daily Mirror	1903	(I) (Independent) largely non-political picture paper; (II) left-wing trend, supported Labour in General Election
Daily Sketch	1909	(Independent) picture paper; (II) acquired by Kemsley Newspapers

Daily Telegraph	1855	(Unionist) acquired *Morning Post* in 1937
Daily Worker	1930	(Communist) official organ of the Communist Party of Great Britain.
Darlington Times	w 1847	(Independent)
Derby Evening Telegraph	1932	(Independent); (II) acquired by Daily Mail Group
Derbyshire Advertiser	w 1846	(Unionist)
Draper's Record	w 1887	Trade paper
Dundee Courier	1926	(I) (No Comment); (II) (Independent)
East Anglian Times	1874	Ipswich (Independent).
East London Observer	w 1856	(Independent)
Eastern Evening News	1882	Norwich. (I) (No Comment); (II) (Independent)
Eastern Daily Press	1870	Norwich. (I) (No Comment); (II) (Independent)
Economist	w 1843	(No Comment) moderately right-wing; usually serious and objective
Edinburgh Evening Dispatch	1886	(Conservative-Unionist) evening version of the *Scotsman*, q.v.
Edinburgh Evening News	1873	(Independent); (II) acquired by Provincial Newspapers
Empire News	w 1917	Manchester, Sundays. (I) (No Comment); (II) (Conservative), acquired by Kemsley Newspapers
Evening News	1881	Evening version of *Daily Mail*, q.v. (Independent)
Evening Standard	1827	(I) (Conservative); (II) (No Comment); evening version of *Daily Express*, q.v.
Everybody's Weekly	w 1927	(I) popular illustrated; (II) not published
Financial News	1884	(Independent)
Financial Times	1888	(No Comment); (II) amalgamated with above
Free Europe	1939	Fortnightly articles on German-occupied Europe from a rather Right-wing angle
Freethinker	w 1881	Organ of 'rationalist' i.e. anti-religious movements in Britain

Friend	w 1843	Organ of the 'Quakers' (Society of Friends)
G.K.'s Weekly	w 1925	Edited by G. K. Chesterton and amalgamated with *Weekly Review*, q.v.
Glasgow Bulletin	1915	(Independent)
Glasgow Daily Record	1847	(No Comment); (II) acquired by Kemsley Newspapers
Glasgow Evening News	1876	(Independent); (II) acquired by Kemsley Newspapers
Glasgow Evening Times	1876	(Independent) associated with *Glasgow Herald*
Glasgow Herald	1805	(Independent)
Glasgow Sunday Mail	1895	(No Comment); (II) acquired by Kemsley Newspapers
Great Britain & The East	1911	(No Comment) review of industry and commerce. (I) w; (II) m
Guardian	w 1846	A Church of England journal. Not to be confused with the *present* (1964) name of the *Manchester Guardian*
Hampstead & Highgate Express	w 1860	(Independent)
Headway	m 1920	Organ of the League of Nations Union
Hereford Bulletin	w 1934	(No Comment)
Hereford Times	1832	(No Comment); bi-weekly publication
Hibbert Journal	Q 1902	Theology and kindred subjects
Illustrated	w 1939	An Odhams Press popular publication
Illustrated London News	w 1842	The oldest established illustrated paper; Conservative in tendency
Inquirer & Christian Life	w 1842	Religiously liberal and socially progressive
John Bull	w 1906	(Independent) an Odhams Press popular illustrated magazine given to exposing miscellaneous scandals
John O'London's Weekly	w 1919	A semi-intellectual literary periodical
Lady	w 1885	Mainly items of feminine and domestic interest

Leader	W 1922	Hulton Press popular illustrated
Leeds Mercury	1718	(Conservative) (I) amalgamated with *Yorkshire Post*, q.v.
Lincolnshire Echo	1893	(Independent); (II) acquired by Daily Mail Group
Liverpool Echo	1879	(Independent)
Manchester Daily Dispatch	1900	(Independent); (II) acquired by Kemsley Newspapers
Manchester Evening Chronicle	1897	(No Comment); (II) acquired by Kemsley Newspapers
Manchester Evening News	1868	Associated with *Manchester Guardian*
Manchester Guardian	1821	(Liberal) foremost daily with Liberal views
Manchester Guardian Weekly	1919	Weekly edition of above
Manchester Sunday Chronicle	W 1885	(I) (No Comment); (II) acquired by Kemsley Newspapers
Midland Daily Telegraph	1891	(No Comment); (II) name changed to *Coventry Evening Telegraph* and associated with *Birmingham Post*, q.v.
Month	M 1864	Catholic literary review
Montrose Review	W 1811	(I) (Liberal); (II) (No Comment)
Morning Post	1772	(Independent) strongly Conservative; merged in *Daily Telegraph*, 1937
National Review	M 1883	Non-party Conservative review of current affairs
New Leader	W 1922	(No Comment) organ of the Independent Labour Party
New Statesman	W 1828	(Independent) pre-eminent organ of the Left-wing intelligentsia
Newcastle Daily Journal	1711	(I) (Conservative); (II) (No Comment) acquired by Kemsley Newspapers
Newcastle Evening Chronicle	1885	(No Comment); (II) acquired by Kemsley Newspapers
News Chronicle	1930	(Liberal) popular national daily with Liberal views
News of the World	W 1843	Sundays. (II) largest sale of any newspaper in the world
News Review	W 1936	Odhams Press. Similar to *Cavalcade*, q.v.

Newspaper World	W 1898	Trade paper
Nineteenth Century	M 1877	Literary review of Conservative trend
Northampton Echo	1931	(No Comment); (II) acquired by Provincial Newspapers
North-Eastern Gazette	1936	Middlesbrough. (No Comment) (II) name changed to *Evening Gazette* and acquired by Kemsley Newspapers
Northern Despatch	1914	Darlington. (Independent); (II) acquired by Westminster Group.
Northern Echo	1869	Darlington. (Liberal) (II) acquired by Westminster Group
Northern Whig	1824	Belfast. (Unionist)
Nottingham Evening News	1885	(Independent); (II) acquired by Westminster Group
Nottingham Guardian	1861	(Conservative)
Observer	W 1791	Sundays. Generally Liberal attitude
Oldham Evening Chronicle	1880	(Liberal)
Oxford Mail	1928	(Independent); (II) acquired by Westminster Group
Pearsons Weekly	W 1890	Popular picture paper
People	W 1881	(I) (Conservative); (II) (No Comment) popular Sunday paper from Odhams Press, supported Labour in General Election
Picture Post	W 1938	(Independent) most successful illustrated weekly with slight left trend
Punch	W 1841	(No Comment) satirical right-wing review
Quarterly Review	Q 1806	(Conservative) important literary review
Record	W 1828	Organ of the Methodists
Record	M 1921	Organ of the Transport and General Worker's Union
Review of Reviews	M 1890	Name changed to *World Review*, 1936. Semi-popular literary review owned by Hulton Press
Reynolds' Illustrated News	W 1847	(Democratic) Sundays. Organ of the Co-operative movement

Round Table	Q 1910	A review of Colonial affairs supporting a graduated grant of independence. Supposedly of great influence in Government circles
Saturday Review	w 1855	(I) (Conservative) extreme right, largely expressive of editor's personal views; (II) not published
Scarborough Evening News	1876	(Independent)
Scotsman	1817	Edinburgh. (Conservative-Unionist)
Sheffield Independent	1819	Up to 1938 (Liberal), then merged in *Sheffield Telegraph*; (II) acquired by Kemsley Newspapers
Sheffield Telegraph	1855	(Conservative); (II) acquired by Kemsley Newspapers
South London Press	1865	(Independent)
South Wales Argus	1892	Newport, Mon. (I) (Liberal); (II) (No Comment)
Southern Daily Echo	1888	Southampton. (Independent)
Spectator	w 1828	(Independent) literary review of broadly right-wing views
Sphere	w 1900	Society and fashion news illustrated
Staffordshire Sentinel	1873	Stoke-on-Trent. (Independent); (II) acquired by Daily Mail Group
Star	1888	(I) (Liberal); (II) (Independent-Progressive); evening version of *News Chronicle*
Statist	w 1878	(Independent); financial and industrial review
Streatham News	w 1868	(I) (Independent); (II) (No Comment)
Sunday Dispatch	w 1801	(Independent) associated with *Daily Mail*
Sunday Express	w 1918	(Independent) Sunday version of *Daily Express*
Sunday Referee	w 1877	(No Comment) merged in *Manchester Sunday Chronicle*, 1939
Sunday Times	w 1822	(Independent) marked right-wing trend; (II) acquired by Kemsley Newspapers
Sussex County Herald	1870	(Independent)
Tablet	w 1840	Roman Catholic literary review

Tatler	w 1901	Society and fashion illustrated
The Times	1788	The leading British newspaper. Fairly described as 'conservative'
Time & Tide	w 1920	(Independent) literary and political review originally feminist, then broadly Liberal
Times Literary Supplement	w 1902	Title self-explanatory
Tribune	w 1937	(I) (Labour); (II) (Socialist) organ of non-Communist Left-wing in Labour Party
Truth	w 1877	(No Comment) extreme Right for all except first few years of whole period covered by this survey
Universe	w 1860	Popular Catholic weekly
Week-End Review	w 1930	Merged in *New Statesman*, q.v., 1934
Weekly Review	w 1938	Catholic literary and political review advocating return to a medieval society
Weekly Scotsman	w 1817	Weekly edition of the *Scotsman*, q.v.
West Africa	w 1917	Non-official periodical of West African affairs
West London Observer	w 1855	(Independent)
Western Mail	1869	Cardiff. (Conservative); (II) acquired by Kemsley Newspapers
Western Morning News	1860	Plymouth. (Independent)
Wolverhampton Express	1874	(Independent)
Women's Wear News	1935	Trade paper
Yorkshire Evening News	1872	Leeds. (I) (Liberal); (II) (Independent) acquired by Provincial Newspapers
Yorkshire Evening Post	1890	Leeds. (I) (No Comment); (II) (Conservative) associated with *Yorkshire Post*, q.v.
Yorkshire Observer	1834	Bradford. (Liberal); (II) acquired by Westminster Group
Yorkshire Post	1754	Leeds. (Conservative); (II) incorporating *Leeds Mercury*. In many ways Conservative equivalent of *Manchester Guardian*

Bibliography

I. BIBLIOGRAPHIES

P. Friedman, *Bibliography of the Warsaw Ghetto* (Jewish Book Annual XI), New York, Jewish Book Council of America, 1952–3

J. Robinson and P. Friedman, *Guide to Jewish History under Nazi Impact*, New York, Yad va-Shem and Y.I.V.O., 1960

U.N.E.S.C.O., *Tentative International Bibliography of Works Dealing with Press Problems*, Paris, 1954

Wiener Library, *Books on Persecution and Resistance under the Nazis*, London, 1960

Yad va-Shem and Y.I.V.O., *Bibliography of Books in Hebrew on the Jewish Catastrophe and Heroism in Europe* (in Hebrew), Jerusalem, 1960

II. COMPILATIONS: DIRECTORIES

Keesings' Contemporary Archives, London and Bristol, from 1931

H. S. Lindfield, *Statistics of Jews 1931*, New York, American Jewish Committee, 1931

Newspaper Press Directory & Advertiser's Guide, London, from 1845

Wiener Library, *The British Press and its Reactions to Recent Events in Palestine* (unpublished)

III. GOVERNMENTAL AND INTER-GOVERNMENTAL SOURCES

GERMANY

An Official Nazi Report on the November Pogroms in Vienna (Text— Yad va-Shem Bulletin II, 1957)

Catalogue of Camps and Prisons in Germany and German-Occupied Territory September 1939—May 1945, Arolson, 2 vols. and supplement, International Tracing Service (Record Branch), 1949–51

GREAT BRITAIN

House of Commons

Buchenwald Camp: The Report of a Parliamentary Delegation, London, HMSO, Cmd. 6626, 1945 (reprinted in the same year by the *Daily Mail* in pamphlet form under the title *Lest We Forget*)

Report of the Porter Committee, London, HMSO, Cmd. 7536, 1948

Report of the Royal Commission on the Press, London, HMSO, Cmd. 7700, 1948–9

Foreign Office

Documents on British Foreign Policy 1919–1939 (edited by E. L. Woodward and R. Butler), Second Series, 6 vols., London, 1947–57

Documents on German Foreign Policy 1918–1945, Series D, 10 vols., London, 1949–57

Papers Concerning the Treatment of German Nationals in Germany 1938–9, London, HMSO, Cmd. 6120, 1939

Persecution of the Jews (Conditions in Occupied Territories No. 6), London, HMSO, Ministry of Information Pamphlet 70-421, 1942

Report of the Anglo-American Committee of Enquiry Regarding the Problem of European Jewry and Palestine, London, HMSO, Cmd. 6808, 1947

Military Tribunals

War Crimes Trials (edited by David Maxwell Fyfe), 9 vols., London, 1948–52

LEAGUE OF NATIONS

Report of the High Commissioner for Refugees for October 1939, A 18(a) 1939 (XII), London, 1939

REPUBLIC OF POLAND

Ministry of Foreign Affairs

The Mass Extermination of Jews in German-Occupied Poland, London, 1939

UNION OF SOVIET SOCIALIST REPUBLICS

Commission for the Ascertainment and Investigation of Crimes of the German-Fascist Invaders and their Associates

The Documents Accuse, 2 vols., Moscow, State Publishing House, 1943–5 (in Russian)

UNITED NATIONS

War Crimes Commission

Trial of the Major War Criminals before the International Military Tribunal Sitting at Nuremberg, Germany, 14 November 1945–1 October 1946, Nuremberg, 1947–9

UNITED STATES OF AMERICA

Documents on American Foreign Relations, Vol. IV (1943–4) (edited by L. M. Goodrich and M. J. Carroll), Boston, World Peace Foundation, 1945

Nazi Conspiracy and Aggression (Chief of Counsel, Prosecution of Axis Criminality), 9 vols., Washington, Government Printing Office, 1946–8

Trials of War Criminals before the Nuernberg Military Tribunal under Control Law No. 10, 15 vols., Washington, Government Printing Office, 1951–2

IV. OTHER PUBLICATIONS

H. G. Adler, *Theresienstadt 1941–1945*, Tübingen, J. C. B. Mohr, 1955

R. Aizenstein, 'The Enemy Within', *Wiener Library Bulletin* XIII, 1959

W. Albig, *Modern Public Opinion*, New York, McGraw-Hill, 1956

American Zionist Emergency Council, Press Book on *Palestine Jewry's Contribution to the War against the Axis*, New York (n.d.)

Anonymous, *The Yellow Spot*, London, Victor Gollancz, 1936

—— 'What Happened to the Nazi Leaders', *Wiener Library Bulletin* X, 1956

Association of Jewish Refugees in Great Britain, *Dispersion and Re-settlement: The Story of the Jews from Central Europe*, London, 1955

—— *Britain's New Citizens, 1941–1951*, London, 1952

M. Basuk (ed.), *The Book of the M'apilim*, Jerusalem, Zionist Federation, 1947 (in Hebrew)

M. Basuk and I. Zimmerman (eds.), *The Book of Ghetto Battles*, 3rd edition, Tel Aviv, Yad va-Shem, 1956 (in Hebrew)

C. Belfrage, *Let My People Go*, London, Victor Gollancz Ltd., 1942

N. Bentwich, *The Rescue and Achievement of Refugee Scholars*, The Hague, M. Nijhoff, 1953

M. Berg, *Warsaw Ghetto—A Diary*, New York, Fischer, 1945 (extracts also appeared in *Contemporary Jewish Record* VII, 1944, Nos. 5 and 6)

W. E. Berry, Viscount Camrose, *British Newspapers and their Con-trollers*, London, Cassell & Co. Ltd., 1947

Board of Deputies of British Jews, *The Jews in Germany—Persecution at a New Pitch* (reprints from *The Times* of 8 November, 21 November, and 30 December 1935), London, 1936

Board of Deputies and Anglo-Jewish Association Joint Foreign Committee, *The Persecution of the Jews in Germany*, 2 pamphlets, London, 1933

L. Bryson (ed.), *The Communication of Ideas*, New York, New York Institute for Religious and Social Studies, 1948

W. Buchanan and H. Cantril, *How Nations See Each Other: A Study in Public Opinion*, Urbana, University of Illinois (for U.N.E.S.C.O.), 1953

P. Calvocoressi, *Nuremberg: The Facts, the Law and the Consequences*, London, Chatto & Windus Ltd., 1947

H. Cantril and M. Stzunk, *Public Opinion 1935-1946*, Princeton, Princeton University Press, 1951

B. Caspar, *With the Jewish Brigade*, London, Edward Goldston, 1948

A. W. Cooper, *The Nuremberg Trial*, London, Penguin Books, 1947

R. H. S. Crossman, 'Palestine Regained', *Encounter* XV, 1960

H. Cudlipp, *Publish and Be Damned*, London, Dakers, 1953

H. J. Eysenck, 'The Psychology of Anti-Semitism', *Nineteenth Century and After* CXLIV, 1948

G. Feder, *Hitler's Official Programme* (trs. E. T. S. Dugdale), London, Allen & Unwin Ltd., 1934

P. Friedman (ed.), *Martyrs and Fighters: The Epic of the Warsaw Ghetto*, New York, F. A. Praeger, 1954

M. Gafen, H. Grossman and others (eds.), *The Jewish Partisans*, Jerusalem, Yad va-Shem, 1958 (in Hebrew)

G. Gallup, *A Guide to Public Opinion Polls*, London, Oxford University Press, 1948

M. A. Gibb and F. Beckwith, *The Yorkshire Post: Two Centuries*, Leeds, Conservative Newspaper Co., 1954

G. M. Gilbert, *Nuremberg Diary*, New York, Farrar, Straus, 1947

J. Gill, *The Jewish Brigade*, Tel-Aviv, Yavneh, 1950 (in Hebrew)

N. Glas, *The Jewish Question: A Problem of Mankind*, Sheffield, Educational Settlement, 1944

J. Goebbels, *Der Nazi-Sozi*, Munich, 1929

—— *The Goebbels Diaries* (edited and translated by L. P. Lochner), New York, Doubleday, 1948

B. Goldstein, *The Stars Bear Witness* (translated by L. Schatzkin), London, Victor Gollancz Ltd., 1950

K. R. Grossman, *The Jewish D.P. Problem: Its Origin, Scope and Liquidation*, New York, Institute of Jewish Affairs and World Jewish Congress, 1951

C. J. Hambro, *Newspaper Lords in British Politics*, London, Macdonald & Co. Ltd., 1958

W. R. Harris, *Tyranny on Trial*, Dallas, Southern Methodist University Press, 1954

H. Herd, *The March of Journalism: The Story of the British Press from 1622 to the Present Day*, London, Allen & Unwin Ltd., 1952

J. Hersey, *The Wall*, London, Hamish Hamilton, 1950

A. Hitler, *Mein Kampf* (12th edition), Munich, 1932

J. W. Hobson and H. Henry, *Hulton Readership Survey*, London, Hulton Press Ltd., 1947

Sir John Hope Simpson, *The Refugee Problem—Report of a Survey*, London, Oxford University Press, 1939

J. C. Hurewitz, *The Struggle for Palestine*, New York, Norton, 1950

Inter-American Jewish Conference, *Jews in Nazi Europe February 1933–November 1941*, Baltimore, 1941

H. Jaeger, 'Refugees' Internment in Britain 1939–1940', *Wiener Library Bulletin* IX, 1955

Jewish Black Book Committee, *The Black Book, the Nazi Crime against the Jewish People*, New York, 1946

—— *The Black Book of Hungarian Jewry* (ed. L. P. Davis), Zürich and Vienna, 1948

—— *The Black Book of Polish Jewry* (ed. J. Apenszlak), New York, 1943

G. Kirk, *The Middle East and the War* (Survey of International Affairs 1939–46), London, Oxford University for the Royal Institute of International Affairs, 1952

L. Kochan, *Pogrom 10 November 1938*, London, André Deutsch, 1957

A. Koestler, 'On Disbelieving Atrocities', *New York Times*, January 1944; reprinted in *The Yogi and the Commissar*, London, Jonathan Cape, 1945

M. Korzen, 'Problems Arising out of Research into the History of Jewish Refugees in the U.S.S.R. during the Second World War', *Yad va-Shem Studies* III, 1959

E. F. Lawson, Baron Burnham, *Peterborough Court: The Story of the Daily Telegraph*, London, Cassell, 1955

Z. Lederer, *Ghetto Theresienstadt* (translated by K. Weisskopf), London, Edward Goldston, 1953

M. Lowenthal, *The Jews of Germany*, Philadelphia, Jewish Publication Society of America, 1936

W. H. McNeill, *America, Britain and Russia 1941–1946* (Survey of International Affairs, 1939–45), London, Oxford University Press for the Royal Institute of International Affairs, 1953

C. Madge and T. Harrison, *Mass-Observation: The Press and its Readers*, London, Art & Technics Ltd., 1949

Market Research Society, *Readership Surveys—A Comparative Study*, London, 1949

F. H. Maugham, *U.N.O. and War Crimes*, London, John Murray, 1951

S. Morison, *History of The Times*, Vol. IV, London, Times Publishing Co., 1952

E. A. Mowrer, *Germany Puts the Clock Back*, London, Lane Publications, 1933

M. G. Murchin, *Britain's Jewish Problem*, London, Hurst & Blackett Ltd., 1939

C. Newman (ed.), *Gentile and Jew: A Symposium on the Future of the Jewish People*, London, The Alliance Press, 1945

W. J. B. Odhams, *The Business and I*, London, Martin Secker Ltd., 1935

A. Prinz, 'The Role of the Gestapo on Obstructing and Promoting Jewish Emigration', *Yad va-Shem Studies* III, 1959

G. Reitlinger, *The Final Solution*, London, Vallentine, Mitchell & Co. Ltd., 1953

—— *The S.S.: Alibi of a Nation 1922–1945*, London, William Heinemann Ltd., 1956

J. H. Robb, *Working-Class Anti-Semite*, London, Tavistock Publications Ltd., 1954

W. Rosenstock, 'Exodus 1933–1939: A Survey of Jewish Emigration from Germany', *Leo Baeck Yearbook I* (1956), Leo Baeck Institute

W. Schaeffer, *Konzentrationslager Oranienburg: der Antibraunbuch über das erste deutsche Konzentrationslager*, Berlin, Buch-u Tiefdruck Gesellschaft, 1934

J. Schechtman, *European Population Transfers 1939–1945*, New York, Cornell University Press and Oxford University Press, 1946

S. M. Schwartz, *The Jews in the Soviet Union*, Syracuse, Syracuse University Press, 1951

J. Sloan (ed.), *Notes from the Warsaw Ghetto*, New York, McGraw-Hill, 1958

K. Spiesman, 'In the Warsaw Ghetto', *Contemporary Jewish Record* VI, 1941

V. I. Stalin, *The Great Patriotic War of the Soviet Union*, Moscow, State Publishing House, 1944 (in Russian)

W. Stuckart, *Kommentare zur deutschen Passengesetzgebung*, Munich, C. H. Beck, 1936

M. Syrkin, *Blessed is the Match: The Story of Jewish Resistance*, London, Victor Gollancz, Ltd., 1948

A. Tartakower, 'The Jewish Refugee', *Jewish Social Studies* IV, 1942

—— *Jewish Migrations throughout the World*, Jerusalem, Institute for Zionist Education, 1947 (in Hebrew)

J. Tenenbaum, *Race and Reich*, New York, Twayne, 1956

—— 'The Crucial Year 1938', *Yad va-Shem Studies* II, 1958

—— *Underground*, New York, Philosophical Library, 1952

The Times, History Through The Times: A Collection of Leading Articles on Important Events, 1800–1937, London, Times Publishing Co., 1937

A. J. Toynbee (ed.), *The Realignment of Europe* (Survey of International Affairs 1939–46), London, Oxford University Press for the Royal Institute of International Affairs, 1955

A. J. Toynbee and V. Toynbee, *Hitler's Europe* (Survey of International Affairs 1939–46), London, Oxford University Press for the Royal Institute of International Affairs, 1954

A. J. Toynbee and V. Toynbee, *Survey of International Affairs 1938*, London, Oxford University Press for the Royal Institute of International Affairs, 1951

D. Trevor, *Under the White Paper: Some Aspects of British Administration in Palestine from 1939 to 1947*, Jerusalem, The Jerusalem Press, 1947

A. Weissberg, *Advocate for the Dead: The Story of Joel Brand* (translated by Constantine Fitzgibbon and Andrew Foster-Melliar), London, André Deutsch, 1958

H. R. G. Whates, *The Birmingham Post, 1857–1957*, Birmingham, Birmingham Post & Mail, 1957

F. Williams, *Dangerous Estate: The Anatomy of Newspapers*, London, Longmans, Green & Co. Ltd., 1957

M. L. Wischnitzer, *To Dwell in Safety*, Philadelphia, Jewish Publication Society of America, 1948

Index